leadership for school transformation

Also available from Bloomsbury

Transforming Schools, Miranda Jefferson and Michael Anderson

Transforming Education, Miranda Jefferson and Michael Anderson

Transforming Organizations, Michael Anderson & Miranda Jefferson

How Schools Transform, Michael Anderson and Miranda Jefferson (Eds)

leadership for school transformation

action, practices and context

Miranda Jefferson and Michael Anderson

BLOOMSBURY ACADEMIC
LONDON • NEW YORK • OXFORD • NEW DELHI • SYDNEY

BLOOMSBURY ACADEMIC
Bloomsbury Publishing Plc, 50 Bedford Square, London, WC1B 3DP, UK
Bloomsbury Publishing Inc, 1359 Broadway, New York, NY 10018, USA
Bloomsbury Publishing Ireland, 29 Earlsfort Terrace, Dublin 2, D02 AY28, Ireland

BLOOMSBURY, BLOOMSBURY ACADEMIC and the Diana logo are trademarks of Bloomsbury Publishing Plc

First published in Great Britain 2026

Cover design: Matt Thame @ Studio Auto

A catalogue record for this book is available from the British Library.

A catalog record for this book is available from the Library of Congress.

ISBN: HB: 978-1-3503-3144-0
PB: 978-1-3503-3143-3
ePDF: 978-1-3503-3145-7
eBook: 978-1-3503-3146-4

Typeset by RefineCatch Limited, Bungay, Suffolk
Printed and bound in Great Britain

For product safety related questions contact productsafety@bloomsbury.com.

This book is dedicated to all teachers, school leaders and others in education that work towards making transformation a reality.

Contents

Practices

Figures

Tables

Acknowledgements

We would like to acknowledge the following colleagues who contributed to the development of *Leadership for School Transformation.*

Carol Anderson
Naomi Crain
Christine Grice
Mark Hopkins
Jamie Gerlach
Anastatia Liolo
Kirsti McGeoch
Natalie Quinlivan

The following figures are the property of 4C Transformative Learning and are used here with their permission: Figures 1.2, 2.2, 2.3, 2.4, 2.5, 2.6, 2.7, 3.2, 4.4, 5.3, 6.2, 6.4, 6.5, 9.2, 9.3, 9.4, 9.5, 9.6, 9.8, 9.10,10.2

We acknowledge the Gadigal people of the Eora Nation, the Traditional Custodians of the unceded lands on which we wrote this book. We pay our respects to Elders past and present, and recognise the long traditions of teaching, learning, and knowledge-sharing that continue to shape these lands.

List of Abbreviations

4Cs	Creativity, Critical Reflection, Communication and Collaboration
AI	Artificial Intelligence
HR	Human Resources
OECD	Organisation for Economic Co-operation and Development
SDT	Self-Determination Theory.
The Dial	The Conditions for Learning Dial
UNESCO	United Nations Educational, Scientific and Cultural Organization
VUCA	Volatility, Uncertainty, Complexity and Ambiguity

Introduction

Leading for transformation

Educational leadership faces a persistent temptation: the promise of easy answers to complex problems. In an era defined by urgency and measurement, leaders are pressured to deliver immediate results, fuelling a fascination with seemingly effective approaches – be they learning sciences frameworks, 'teach to the test' mandates, or rigid models of direct instruction.[1] These solutions are often presented as efficient and measurable, providing an illusion of simplicity in the face of complexity. Yet, as research warns, such quick-fix solutions rarely achieve sustainable or equitable change.[2]

Transformative school leadership is far more complex and relational. Rather than enabling growth, overreliance on prescriptive or standardized approaches often leads to narrowed curriculum, compliance-driven cultures, and overlooked contextual needs.[3]

Who this book is for

We have written this book because we know how demanding, creative and hopeful the work of school leadership can be. We have seen, up close, the dexterity and care that leaders bring to their schools every day. We've also felt the tension: between the need to manage the present and the need to transform, between short-term pressures and long-term purpose.

This book is for all leaders living in that space. It is for anyone or aspires to lead within a school or educational setting. This book is for teachers, heads of department, heads of year, heads of wellbeing, principals etc. in any educational setting. It's for leaders who are tired of short-term fixes and want to create something more lasting and meaningful in their sphere of influence. It's for those trying to navigate change in schools while keeping the needs of learners at the centre of everything they do. And it's for educators who understand that leadership is not just about position or power, but also about values, relationships, culture and shared commitment to make learning richer and more engaging.

Over many years, we've worked in partnership with schools and systems across early childhood, primary, secondary and tertiary contexts.[4] This book brings together what we've learned from those experiences and reflects recent research. It offers a way of understanding leadership for transformation that is grounded in practice, responsive to context and guided by values.

What we mean by transformation

We use the word transformation deliberately. It's not a synonym for change. It signals a deeper shift – one that involves reimagining the values, structures and assumptions that shape our schools. It doesn't mean we ignore the day-to-day demands or the necessary work of beneficial change, but it does mean we make space for different questions: What could schools become? What kind of leadership will get us there?

Transformation, as we see it, isn't something delivered from the top down or necessarily driven by charismatic individuals. It happens through every day actions, small shifts, collective insights. Transformation is incremental and often patchy. It emerges when leadership becomes a shared cultural practice, and when schools create the conditions for creativity, collaboration, critical reflection and intentional communication. These four human capabilities, the 4Cs, are at the heart of this book.

One of the challenges of leading in complex systems is creating coherence. That's why this book employs several coherence makers or frameworks that bring clarity to ideas that might otherwise feel abstract or overwhelming. These coherence makers are not formulas. They're tools to help leaders think with intention, reflect deeply, and act wisely.

The most significant of these is the Leadership Lantern, which forms the foundation of the book. Like a lantern, it casts light in many directions – illuminating what's around us, but also helping us see where we might go. The Lantern frames the kind of leadership that supports transformation in schools: it's fuelled by the 4Cs, structured by values and context, and expressed through both individual and cultural leadership. We return to this Lantern throughout the book – it holds the structure for how leadership can work in real schools, with real people, facing real challenges.

What this book offers

This book is not a step-by-step manual. It doesn't pretend to offer easy solutions. Instead, it provides a collection of ideas and practices that can help leaders ask better questions, build stronger teams, and develop cultures where transformation becomes possible.

Each chapter focuses on a different aspect of leadership for transformation. Along the way, we provide practical frameworks – the Creativity Cascade, Collaboration

Circles, the Critical Reflection Crucible, the Communication Crystal and the Leadership Wheel that support professional thinking and action for transformational leadership. These are grounded in research, theory and our experience of what works in transforming schools. They're designed to be picked up and used by leadership teams, teacher groups and individuals committed to reflection and growth.

Most chapters include Practices that are structured activities that support reflection, dialogue and planning. These Practices are invitations to work differently, to slow down, to engage your team and to explore strategies and actions that will make transformation possible in your context.

If you've read our other books, *Transforming Schools*, *Transforming Education*, *Transforming Organisations* or *How Schools Transform*, you will see familiar themes. Those books explored transformation through curriculum, pedagogy, policy and culture. This book turns the spotlight onto leadership itself and how it's developed, enacted and shared.

In some ways, this is the most practical of the series. It builds directly on the 4Cs, but it also deepens our thinking about how leadership works in context. We wanted to write something that could sit on the desk of a school leader, not as an inflexible plan but as a partner in each leader's journey of transformation. Something that could be read in pieces or discussed in teams, and that could help you make sense of the work you're already doing and the plans you have for the future.

Throughout this book, you'll see us return again and again to the idea that leadership is not an individual act, it's a collaborative endeavour. While courageous individuals are essential, sustainable transformation happens when leadership becomes part of the culture. We explore this through the concept of leadership-as-practice: the everyday sayings, doings and relatings[5] that shape what leadership looks and feels like in a school.

We also reflect on courageous leadership that is the internal work of leading with purpose and clarity, even when the path is uncertain. Leadership for transformation is rarely comfortable, but it can be deeply fulfilling, especially when grounded in values, shaped by context, and fuelled by the 4Cs.

In these chapters, we invite you to step away from the noise of quick solutions and narrow metrics. Instead, we ask you to engage with what we see as a deeper, more sustaining conversation about what leadership in schools can be. The work of transformation is not linear, nor is it always visible in data sets or dashboards. It unfolds in relationships, strategies, decisions, wise actions and the culture we shape as leaders in our schools every day. This book is an invitation to take up that work with intention and to lead with curiosity rather than certainty, with courage rather than control. If educational leadership is to move beyond the limits of compliance and standardization, it must reconnect with its deeper purpose: to create learning where our young people can thrive, and where educators can lead with integrity, creativity and care.

Leadership for transformation

1

Figure 1.1 Malala Yousafzai – example of courageous and critically hopeful leadership

Our discussion about leadership and transformation begins in an improbable place – the Swat Valley in Pakistan, 9 October 2012 on a bus full of school children heading home after an exam. A Taliban gunman enters the bus and shoots three girls in an attempted assassination. Kainat Riaz, Shazia Ramzan and Malala Yousufzai are injured. Malala, who was targeted by the Taliban for her activism for girls' education, suffers life threatening injuries. She picks up the story when she woke from a coma several days later:

> The nurse told me that I had been shot on the school bus. She said two of my friends on the bus had also been shot, but I didn't recognise their names. She explained that the bullet had entered through the side of my left eye where there was a scar, travelled 18 inches down to my left shoulder and stopped there. It could have taken out my eye or gone into my brain. It was a miracle I was alive.[1]

Malala's story did not end there. She recovered and then worked tirelessly and courageously to create change in education and particularly education for women and girls. Considering Malala's age and her injuries you may have expected her to be silent. She wasn't silent, she bravely fought on, and on 10 December 2014 seventeen-year-old Malala delivered her Nobel Lecture as the youngest ever Laureate. She described a future she is now making possible through her advocacy and leadership:

> Let us become the first generation that decides to be the last that sees empty classrooms, lost childhoods and wasted potentials. Let this be the last time that a girl or a boy spends their childhood in a factory. Let this be the last time that a girl is forced into early child marriage. Let this be the last time that a child loses life in war. Let this be the last time that we see a child out of school. Let this end with us. Let's begin this ending . . . together . . . today . . . right here, right now. Let's begin this ending now.[2]

Malala continues to lead through her advocacy for educational change (particularly for women and girls) through her writing, speaking, and film and television production. She has led discussions all over the world with a focus on critical hope and action. It is not, however, these achievements nor her Nobel Peace Prize that we want to highlight. Rather it is her ability to be critically hopeful and courageous in the face of seemingly overwhelming challenges.

This opening chapter establishes the foundation for understanding how educational leaders can drive meaningful change in schools through the lens of critical hope and transformational leadership. We explore how critical hope serves not merely as optimism, but as a practical mindset that acknowledges challenges while maintaining focus on possibilities for beneficial change. The chapter addresses the urgent need for educational transformation in our rapidly evolving world, examining why traditional educational models, designed for a previous time, fall short in preparing students for today's complex social, economic and technological landscape. We argue that transformation is not optional but essential for addressing persistent inequities and preparing students for an uncertain future.

Central to this discussion is the introduction of the 4Cs framework – creativity, collaboration, communication and critical reflection – as the foundational capabilities that enable transformational change. We also present the Learning States Dial, a practical tool that helps leaders assess their school's readiness for transformation. Effective transformation depends on two key factors. It requires both individual leadership capabilities and a culture that supports collective action towards change. The chapter concludes by exploring myths of leadership in schools, and argues for critical hope, courage and the 4Cs as the essential foundations for transformational change. Let's begin with critical hope that motivates and sustains transformation.

Critical hope

Critical hope strives to transform structures, processes and practices while simultaneously understanding barriers, challenges and opportunities in each context. Educational thinker Paulo Freire argues: 'hope is something shared between teachers and students. The hope that we can learn together, teach together, be curiously impatient together, produce something together, and resist together the obstacles that prevent the flowering of our joy'.[3] Critical hope is not a form of mindless optimism. Rather, it allows us to understand that each context has its challenges, but it also has inherent opportunities and resources. In the schools we have worked with, we see it in the lives and work of students, teachers and leaders as they work to bring about equity, change and growth.

For Malala, even though the task may have seemed insurmountable, she applied hope and a realistic understanding of the challenges she faced to forge ahead. This was not only an individual achievement, but it also spread to those around her. In our view, critical hope is not necessarily a heroic or inspirational quality. It is a mindset all leaders of transformation require to make beneficial change happen. It is, however, pointless unless it leads to action through practice.

Critical hope as practice

Critical hope is not just an abstraction, it must infuse our practice as educators and leaders. As educational researcher, Kari Grain argues, critical hope is the practice of 'relentless incrementalism':

> Practice is firmly rooted in action, consistency, incremental, change, and a conscious choice to do the labour involved in change making . . . critical hope as a practice requires the understanding that change often involves 'relentless incrementalism' to occur over time, and with an eye to shifting, contexts and iteration . . . Critical hope, as a practice may ebb and flow and is strengthened through collective commitments by people who have the capacity to do the work.[4]

In a transforming school, critical hope allows leaders to deliberately and incrementally move towards beneficial change in values, curriculum, pedagogy and other elements of the school's operations. In Grain's description of the practice of critical hope, the 'work' and 'labour' is emphasized. Critical hope is values in action. It is sensing the need for change, understanding context and then working step-by-step over time to make slow but meaningful change.

Contrast this approach with the obsession some education systems have for 'roll outs' and 'quick fixes', and critical hope seems counter-cultural. By contrast, critical hope provides space for meaningful and enduring change that the 'silver-bullet' solutions cannot create.

Critical hope is a great starting point but those intent on transforming learning need clarity about the need for transformation. Before we go much further into the *how* of leading for transformation let's discuss *why* transformation is necessary for schools.

Why is transformation required in education?

Educators and schools are self-evidently in the transformation 'business'. Learning is a kind of transformation as we facilitate each student's development and aim for them to grow and mature – to transform. As schools see the changes in their students, they also need to transform to meet the needs of their students in a rapidly changing world. In the last decade, transformation has been a topic of great interest internationally. The 2022 UNESCO report 'Reimagining our futures together: A new social contract for education' argues educational transformation is the key to societal transformation:

> Education – the ways we organize teaching and learning throughout life – has long played a foundational role in the transformation of human societies. Education is how we organize the intergenerational cycle of knowledge transmission and co-creation. It connects us with the world and to others, exposes us to new possibilities, and strengthens our capacities for dialogue and action. But to shape the futures we want, education itself must be transformed.[5]

This is a vision of an education system that transforms itself while playing a central role in beneficially supporting community transformation. Given the threats and opportunities that we face globally, UNESCO's view is that change is required now.

Traditional educational models, designed for a bygone era, fall short in preparing students for today's rapidly evolving social, economic and technological landscape. Schools must transform to meet these contemporary challenges. Transforming education means fundamentally reimagining each school's foundational features: values, learning approaches, teaching methods, curriculum design, teacher preparation, and leadership. Educational transformation also addresses systemic inequities by seeking to redress inbuilt societal disadvantage and make quality, relevant learning a right for all students.

Given the gravity, immediacy and urgency of the need for transformation, you might assume that schools would be inclined to change. You might expect that evidence of societal shifts, community changes and complex global challenges would provide compelling motivation for educational transformation. The reality is transformation is hard and slow. If anything, the case for change has become more forceful than when we first argued for it in *Transforming Schools* in 2017. Despite a pandemic, an intensifying climate crisis, the rise of Artificial Intelligence, persistent inequalities and multiple wars, still many schools have either not transformed substantially or find transformation too difficult to achieve. If transformation is to be a reality in our schools, leaders will need to create beneficial change amidst the flux of a constantly changing world.

Why leadership is critical to transform schools

The next generation of educational leaders must re-imagine what education could be. The world continues to change, and our understanding of learning and teaching continues to evolve. These leaders face this transformational task whether they're ready or not. While the looming challenges and opportunities in education may seem to come from new places (technology, disengagement, increased mental illness etc) the same old problems remain unsolved. The issues that have blighted education for generations such as inequity and inequality. As the 2022 UNESCO report, referred to earlier asserts, maintaining the status quo will not meet the challenge that education faces. UNESCO argues, 'We urgently need to reimagine our futures together and take action to realize them. Knowledge and learning are the basis for renewal and transformation'.[6] For schools and leaders in education, this re-imagining may be daunting, but we have within our learning communities the 'raw materials' in people, know-how and motivation to make this a reality. The next tasks for leaders, convinced of the need for change and excited by the possibility of re-imagining schools, are what processes and strategies do they need to make this a reality?

Leaders are essential for educational transformation as they implement necessary changes at the school level and possess the 'next-level leadership' needed to reimagine education in a rapidly changing world. As educational leadership researcher Monica Mincu argues, leadership is fundamentally about 'organized agency and collective vision'[7] rather than just positional authority. Transformative change cannot happen through individual teachers alone – it requires school leadership to circulate and consolidate innovative practices into coherent collective action. Effective transformational leaders demonstrate the 4Cs: creativity, collaboration, communication and critical reflection. These capabilities directly determine their capacity to imagine, enable and enact change, especially during times of chaos and complexity.

Leaders play a vital role in shaping and sustaining transformative change. They create and communicate a clear vision, bringing people together across the school community to collaborate. This collaboration is grounded in critically reflective practices that ensure change remains aligned with shared values and benefits everyone involved. Strong leadership is guided by values, which act as a kind of 'lodestar' – a fixed point offering ethical direction and a sense of moral purpose or literally a star that guides the way.

These values are not merely abstractions; they are embedded in everyday decisions, relationships and actions. In complex contexts such as schools, values support leaders to navigate competing demands and make difficult choices with wisdom. By staying anchored in shared values, leaders build trust, maintain coherence and unite their teams around a common purpose.

Transformation also relies on leaders understanding and responding to their specific context. Transformation requires navigation of complex relationships between organizational structures, curriculum demands, governance frameworks, cultural influences and community needs to enable sustainable change. This requires more than technical expertise – it demands a commitment to both personal growth and collective capacity-building. Leaders must cultivate individual capabilities such as courage, empathy, critical thinking and adaptive judgement. At the same time, they foster a culture of leadership-as-practice, where leadership is distributed, relational and embedded in the daily life of the school. This dual focus supports a resilient and responsive environment in which uncertainty is embraced, and the balance between stability and meaningful change is thoughtfully maintained.

For leaders who take up this challenge and know 'why' transformation is urgent, the question is the 'how'. Where do we start with this seemingly overwhelming task? How do we understand and engage with all the tiny steps that leaders need to take on the road to transformation? What about the system? What about parents? What about the media? What about . . .?

School leaders can feel overwhelmed by the task before they even begin. That 'overwhelm' must be balanced by the gravity of the task. How we transform education in the twenty-first century has profound implications for peace, prosperity and democracy in a more uncertain and complex world. As Nelson Mandela said, 'Education is the most powerful weapon which you can use to change the world'.[8] Or, to slightly paraphrase, transforming education is the most powerful 'weapon' we have to respond to a changing world. This is the challenge this book takes on. UNESCO's view is the time is now and the people who can make this change already exist in our schools:

> We all have an obligation to current and future generations – to ensure that our world is one of abundance not scarcity, and that everyone enjoys human rights to the fullest. Despite the urgency of action, and in conditions of great uncertainty, we have reason to be full of hope. As a species, we are at the point in our collective history where we have the greatest access ever to knowledge and

to tools that enable us to collaborate. The potential for engaging humanity in creating futures together has never been greater.[9]

Moving beyond these critical but seemingly aspirational sentiments is the central question we return to throughout this book. The 'how'. How do we make transformation a reality through wise, strategic, contextual and agentic leadership that makes transformation in schools achievable?

The 'how'

This is not a general leadership book. There are libraries and bookshops full of those kinds of books already. The leadership training sector (those books have spawned) is a $366 billion industry.[10] This book isn't designed to be an all-purpose guide with silver bullet solutions. Those kinds of books offer what many leaders are tempted by: easy answers to complex problems. In a world obsessed with urgency and measurement, these books provide prescriptive, standardized approaches that are presented as 'one size fits all'. Rather than being a step-by-step manual or claiming there are easy solutions, we have attempted to embrace the complexities and opportunities of each educational context. This book recognizes that leadership is complex and relational. Real transformation happens through daily, shared practices and trusting relationships grounded in values and context, not formulas borrowed from business or anywhere else.

In this book we are addressing readers who are interested in driving transformative change in their school by developing a foundation in the 4Cs; creativity, collaboration, communication and critical reflection. These four interconnected capabilities are foundational for human thriving and transformation. They represent the essential skills and mindsets necessary for individuals and organizations to navigate complexity, foster innovation and achieve meaningful change. Creativity engages our imagination to enable new possibilities and approaches; critical reflection requires deep analysis and questioning of assumptions; communication enables clear articulation and shared understanding; and collaboration brings diverse perspectives together for collective action.

Like our other books this one is attempting to answer one central question, 'how'? How might we develop leadership for transformation as a personal quality and as a cultural capacity? To begin the answer to these questions we must first understand our context deeply to ensure we can deploy the 4Cs wisely. As we discuss throughout this book, the 4Cs are foundational for transformation, and the extent to which they are evident in a school will determine their readiness for transformation. Leadership can explore this in their school (or parts of their school through the Learning States Dial (The Dial) in figure 1.2.

Readiness for transformation

Figure 1.2 Learning States Dial

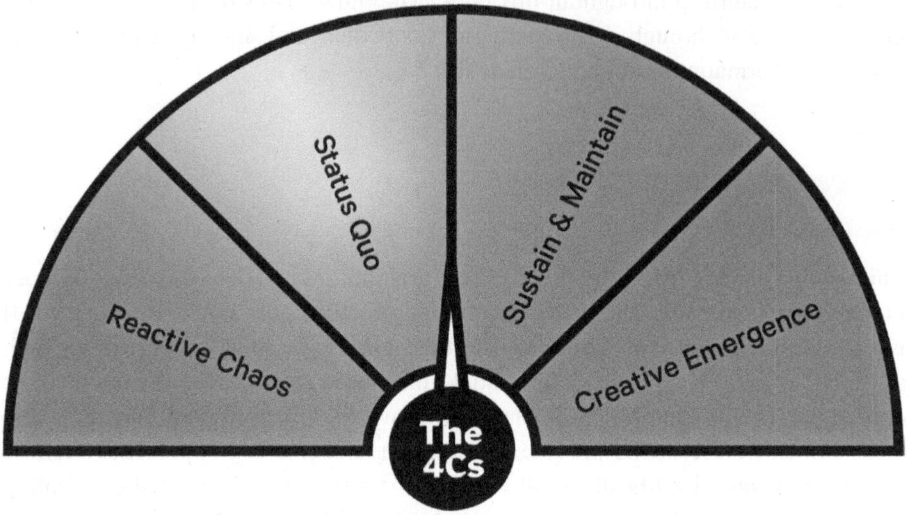

The Dial describes the conditions for change in a school or a classroom. We use the Dial to identify whether transformation is potential or evident in a school or any organization. As noted earlier, the 4Cs build and generate momentum for transformation and they are more apparent when schools are engaged in transformative change. Based on our experience working with schools there are four 'states' that schools might be experiencing. Let's explain the states in more detail.

Reactive chaos (emergency ward)

These schools or classrooms often present as busy places, but the activity is often around reacting to every new emergency that presents itself. These places are like an accident and emergency ward with a focus on reacting to the next incident rather than a focus on calm and systematic transformation. In reactive chaos, educators are often not able to contemplate transformation or meet their potential as the chaos constantly engulfs any productive work. This is often not the fault of the teachers or the school leadership as they often inherit or are presented with intractable problems.

In a recent study,[11] paediatrician David Ly and colleagues argue that schools in 'reactive chaos' often feature:

- High rates of risky behaviours
- Low engagement
- Negative social norms
- A low likelihood of following rules and behaving appropriately
- Disintegrating academic outcomes

To move from reactive chaos, schools need to establish and reinforce positive processes using the 4Cs to generate positive non-anxious action. We discuss how that might be possible with an understanding of context and values through the Leadership Lantern that we introduce in chapter 2.

Status quo (*Groundhog Day*)

The main theme of the film, *Groundhog Day*, is that everything from day to day is the same. In status quo there is no significant change. Michael Fullan argues that inertia is to blame for schools' tendency to stick to what they know.[12] Under stress, the brain does not like uncertainty; we 'flock' to what we know best, the old patterns of being'.[13] In status quo, there is a general calm but there is little creativity or critical reflection, although communication and collaboration may be present, albeit at somewhat perfunctory levels. Schools that are moving beyond the status quo often find themselves in the sustain and maintain 'state' that might also be called 'school improvement'.

Sustain and maintain (the constant gardener)

While these schools may not be in a process of transformation, there are often many beneficial processes at work. Typically, these schools are engaged in systematic professional learning that has a focus on students. There is often a collaborative approach evident amongst staff and students that provides a supportive environment. Creativity may also be present in the learning and teaching programs. Organizations often go through sustain and maintain phases, as being in transformation constantly can be exhausting.

Transformation can be delayed when these schools fail to transition into a state of creative emergence. At this point, schools still have the potential to stagnate or to embrace creative emergence. However, if schools stagnate, there's a risk of falling into and staying within the status quo. In situations requiring transformation, these institutions can concentrate on fostering and empowering 4C capabilities to facilitate a shift into a state of creative emergence (state of flow).

Creative emergence (state of flow)

In creative emergence, organizations are fulfilling their potential by drawing on the 4Cs to enable relevant and wise change. This creative emergence is the novel and sometimes unexpected creation that results from authentic collaboration. For instance, a school leadership team facing low teacher morale might authentically collaborate across the school community to understand the issue. Having understood the issues, they then co-design and implement a policy of self-directed professional learning design in areas of interest across the school. Unexpected innovations (creative emergence) from these groups could arise including, for example, interdisciplinary teaching teams and student-led assessments. At the heart of creative emergence are the 4Cs (we discuss the 4Cs in more detail in chapter 2) that fuel the process in the following ways:

Creativity involves imagining possibilities and new approaches that transcend the known. This process requires noticing, asking 'why, really why?', and playing with possibilities.

Critical reflection enables a thorough analysis that makes each individual's assumptions about knowledge and power transparent. Through enquiry and dialogue with others, critical reflection leads to an awareness of how to create transformation, and disrupts the 'taken for granted', which can lead to new insights.

Communication creates meaning, power and relationships. The clear articulation of ideas, in addition to supporting and challenging the voices of all in the school community, is essential.

Collaboration brings diverse perspectives together, which sparks new ideas and increases both motivation and the willingness to take chances. Through collaboration, people expand who they are and achieve their full potential by working toward a shared goal.

The 4Cs work together to generate new and unpredictable knowledge. These capabilities provide the core skills and knowledge for the 'heavy lifting' of transformation. They connect, extend and mobilize understanding to drive learning. When applied to organizational challenges, the 4Cs enable creative emergence. They represent a philosophy and mindset, rather than a program or procedure, which can transform an organization's culture.

In these schools, learners' needs are paramount, and their challenges shape the transformations taking place within the school. High levels of collaboration and creativity flourish, with a strong sense of agency emerging when creative flow occurs.

Flow, as described by psychologist Mihaly Csikszentmihalyi,[14] is a state of deep immersion and engagement. In this state, individuals experience effortless involvement, intrinsic motivation and a balance between challenge and skill when collaborating. Teachers and leaders work with heightened focus, embracing challenges with curiosity and adaptability. Flow supports creative emergence by allowing new ideas to surface organically. Individuals remain fully present in the process, open to discovery and engaged in meaningful work. When challenges arise, they respond calmly through critical reflection and wise action. Creative emergence is a dynamic process of continuous shaping and reshaping of leadership in response to each context's unique challenges and opportunities.

This capacity to respond with wisdom is not fixed but continually evolves. Through creative emergence, leaders adapt and reimagine their practice in real time, shaping leadership as both a response to and a catalyst for change.

What role does leadership play in transformation?

When we consider the how of transformation, leaders play a vital role in designing and supporting schools. Monica Mincu, suggests leadership is about organized agency and communal vision:

> . . . not managerialism, since it is an organizational quality, not merely a positionality attribute . . . if change is to be systemic and transformative, it cannot occur uniquely at the individual teacher's level. School organization is fundamental to circulating and consolidating new innovative actions, cognitive schemes, and behaviors in coherent collective practices.[15]

The responsibility and opportunity for leadership in whatever aspect or context in a school is to provide a coherent, understandable and contextually relevant series of processes and actions that will generate meaningful change. Leadership engages with the 4C capabilities to:

- Create a vision for sustainable change
- Communicate that vision with clarity
- Collaborate with all in the school community or context to make it happen
- Facilitate critically reflective practices along the way to ensure values driven transformation is taking place for the good of the whole school community or context

In Practice 1.1 we have provided an exercise that will assist in laying the groundwork for transformation.

Practice 1.1 Preparing for transformation: The dial and 4Cs readiness

Using the Dial (figure 1.2) and the descriptions of each 'state' in this chapter, develop a discussion about your school's or specific context's readiness for transformation. As far as possible discuss and describe where your school is now with a strengths-based approach. A strengths-based approach focuses on identifying and building on the existing strengths, skills and potential in your setting rather than only addressing deficits.

The 4Cs

As we have discussed, and the learning dial suggests, the 4Cs – creativity, collaboration, communication and critical reflection – are foundational to leading transformation. The following questions are designed to uncover to what extent they are evident and active in your context.

- *Creativity*: How are school leaders and staff fostering a culture of innovation and creative emergence in strategy and decision making?
- *Collaboration*: In what ways do leadership teams and staff enhance collaboration to drive school transformation and enhance student learning?
- *Communication*: How do we strengthen communication among staff, leadership and the wider school community to support a shared vision for change?
- *Critical reflection*: How does the whole school community engage in reflective practices to evaluate and refine teaching, leadership strategies, and school transformation efforts?

Transformation readiness

What do you notice about the attitudes and behaviours of students, staff and leadership in your school?

- Is there evidence of chaotic and destructive attitudes and behaviours?
- Do the attitudes and behaviours tend to reinforce the status quo?
- Are there behaviours and attitudes that are looking to support and improve the generally satisfactory operations of the school?
- Is there evidence of behaviours and attitudes that contribute to innovation and beneficial change that responds to the challenges and opportunities that emerge in the school?

The Dial

In a focus group of students, teachers and school leadership look at the Dial and identify where you are now. Consider the actions required to 'move the dial' and put them on a timeline. Be realistic and anticipate slow but steady progress. This kind of change in schools is the opposite of 'move fast and break things', rather it is 'move slow and create things'.

Combine the focus group findings and create a set of actions for transformation.

Understanding and mapping each school's or context's state of readiness for transformation is crucial. It is also necessary to establish approaches and ways of thinking that allow for flexibility and learning to enable transformation. Doing this creates a path for transformation by opening communication and encouraging realistic yet transparent communication. It encourages a playing with possibility approach.

One way to enable transformative mindsets is to avoid the lazy thinking that sometimes passes for educational discussion. One of the laziest in our view is the tendency to falsely dichotomize leadership. Dichotomous mindsets can delay or derail effective change.

False dichotomies in leadership discussions

False dichotomies abound in education such as assessment versus learning, group versus individual learning or embodied versus cognitive learning. They often reduce an argument to 'this versus that' and exclude the possibility of a more useful and nuanced discussion. As psychologist and researcher Vlad Glăveanu[16] points out, the human mind is drawn to dichotomies.[17] This 'on the one hand, on the other hand' thinking while sometimes useful can also lead us into false divisions.

Education is riddled with these dichotomies that we have discussed in previous books,[18] including assessment versus learning, cognitive versus sociocultural approaches and mind-body dualisms. In leadership discussions, there are several of these false and ultimately unproductive dichotomies that are particularly damaging when a more complex and nuanced understanding is required. Before we discuss how leadership for transformation might be constituted, we thought we might identify three of these dichotomies and why we think they are potentially damaging and false.

Individual factors versus cultural factors

The obsession with the hero leader who apparently single-handedly brings transformation has been evident in practice and popular culture for decades. Ethics and organizational researcher Annabel Beerel[19] explains that these stories are 'individualist and frequently decontextualized accounts that privilege individuals', for example, the hero leader who turns around a 'failing' educational organization. This hero approach is a damaging mythology. It relies in part on the 'strongman' approach to leadership that suggests all you need is a firm hand and discipline and any situation can be turned around singlehandedly.

The alternative approach argues that all you need is a good system and you can rollout change no matter what the context or situation.[20] Any transformation requires a combination of individual capacities for leadership and a culture of leadership. We refer to these interdependent forms of leadership throughout this book as courageous leadership and leadership-as-practice. They are described briefly below.

Courageous leadership refers to the capacities and capabilities required to take the courageous actions required to transform schools.

Leadership-as-practice is a way of understanding leadership by looking to the culture or cultural practices in an organization. As organizational development researcher Joseph Raelin argues '... leadership emerges and unfolds through day-to-day experience ... the people who are effecting leadership at any given time do not reside outside of leadership but are very much embedded within it. To find leadership, then, we must look to the practice within which it is occurring'[21] In other words, leadership is embedded and evident in the practices of an organization and the everyday leadership-as-practice of individuals. As we discuss throughout this book, leadership is not just a role, but a dynamic, collective process embedded in the everyday practices of each member of the school community.

For instance, faculty leaders demonstrate it by fostering collaboration, mentoring colleagues, and driving curriculum innovation. Students enact leadership through peer mentoring, active participation in decision-making, and leading initiatives that enhance school culture. The school executive models leadership-as-practice by shaping vision, facilitating inclusive dialogue, and empowering staff and students to take ownership of change. Rather than being tied to formal roles, leadership emerges dynamically through interactions, problem-solving and shared responsibility for school transformation.

Any transformation requires an effective combination of individual capacities (courageous leadership), and cultural leadership practices embedded in the activities of the organization (leadership-as-practice). These interdependent forms of leadership will enable an organization to transform within the constraints and opportunities of their unique context. This kind of transformative change requires both effective management and leadership, which leads to another false dichotomy.

Management versus leadership

Leadership and management are sometimes considered distinct from each other. In many discussions (including our own), leadership is associated with strategy, vision, inspiration and courage in whatever context. By contrast, management is associated with efficiency, processes and control. Anyone who has worked in leadership in a school knows that management and leadership are interdependent. Effective leaders of transformation need to be courageous and strategic. They must, for instance, manage the resources, engage with HR issues and ensure student learning and assessment are effective. In many ways the management lays the foundation for the opportunities for creative emergence. Schools undergoing transformation still need to ensure classes are taught and sports carnivals are organized while also being able to reshape curriculum or pedagogy. As Bereel argues:

> The confusion or spurious division between leadership and management can be eliminated if we see management and leadership as being roles rather than

being fixed positions with no fluidity allowed for one person assuming both roles. Managers can, and indeed must, exercise leadership, and leaders can and most often do take on the role of managing.[22]

In schools, leadership and management should be interdependent activities that ensure that the core business is taking place; students are safe and learning is effective. Simultaneously, leadership is about always noticing the context of the school or the area of responsibility and the needs of the students to imagine and then to make transformation happen.

Leaders and followers

Leadership and followership are often seen as a false dichotomy, with leadership being associated with power, authority and action, and followership being associated with passivity, obedience and submission.[23] While there are abundant discussions that promote followership and the qualities of followers,[24] it seems an odd fit for schools. It seems to us that many students, all teachers and all leaders in a school are engaged in leadership. Students are encouraged and given opportunities to lead their own learning, sometimes the learning of their peers and provide leadership around beneficial change in schools. Teachers are always leading learning in their classroom by curating engaging and productive learning experiences[25] and leaders are self-evidently leading (or should be).

We understand that the term 'followership' need not be docile and passive. However, in this book we are foregrounding the possibility that we are developing leadership in everyone in a school. The leadership capabilities (including the 4Cs) that we discuss are desirable for all. For that reason, we will be exploring how leadership might become a matter of personal growth and cultural transformation through the development of courageous leadership and leadership-as-practice.

Concluding reflections

Critical hope, courage and the 4Cs are the foundations of transformational change in schools. These qualities set schools up for success and unleash the potential for beneficial change that is inherent in every school. Transformation is not mystical in our view. It is a process like so many others that requires inherent human capacities such as the 4Cs, and a recognition that outmoded and irrelevant structures can and must shift to meet the needs of our learners. Now we have set the scene let's dive into explaining the 'how' of transformation in chapter 2 with the introduction of our coherence maker that enables leadership for transformation: The Leadership Lantern.

Key actions

1. Foster critical hope and courage. School leaders can actively cultivate critical hope and courage among staff, students and the broader school community. Encourage a mindset that acknowledges challenges but remains hopeful about the potential for transformation. Provide support and inspiration for individuals to tackle obstacles with resilience and determination.
2. Understand the transformation readiness of your school. Assess the school's readiness for transformation using frameworks like the Learning States Dial (figure 1.2). Identify strengths and areas for development in terms of organizational culture, leadership practices and engagement with the 4Cs. Use this assessment to guide strategic planning and resource allocation.
3. Integrate the 4Cs into all facets of school life. Emphasize the centrality of the 4Cs – creativity, collaboration, communication and critical reflection in driving transformational change. Encourage educators to integrate the 4Cs into teaching practices, curriculum development and professional interactions. Provide resources and professional development opportunities to support the integration of the 4Cs.
4. Address false dichotomies and reductive mindsets. Challenge and overcome false dichotomies in leadership discussions, such as individual factors versus cultural factors, management versus leadership, and leaders versus followers. Encourage a holistic approach that recognizes the interconnectedness of different aspects of leadership and management and promotes collaboration and inclusivity.
5. Develop and implement actionable strategies for transformation based on identified priorities and areas of need. Engage stakeholders in collaborative decision-making and empower them to take ownership of initiatives. Foster a culture of continuous improvement and adaptability to navigate challenges and seize opportunities effectively.

Leadership: Lighting for the path of transformation

2

Figure 2.1 Ernst Oppler's painting, 'Evening on the Baltic Sea' depicts the Lantern Walk held in Germany and France on St Martin's Day

Laternelaufen or Lantern Walk is a tradition that takes place annually around St Martin's Day, on 11 November in Germany and France. The walk celebrates St Martin, a Roman soldier who served and died in Gaul in 397 CE. He was best known for dividing his cloak and giving a portion to a poor man dressed in only rags in the freezing winter. This made him a beacon of hope for the poor. On St Martin's Day, young children walk the streets with lanterns, often singing traditional songs telling stories of the hope and light that St Martin brought into the world.

We begin our discussion of the 'how' of leadership with this action and symbol of hope and direction. Like Malala, St Martin's act of compassion is an example of practical leadership that shines down through the ages. Secondly, the lantern walk is a collaborative endeavour not an individual act. In the parade, the community walks together to mark St Martin's leadership.

In this chapter we will take you on a lantern walk of sorts. To unpack our conception of the 'how' of leadership for transformation we have developed a coherence maker (or framework) called the Leadership Lantern. The Lantern is designed to 'light the way' metaphorically so schools may collaboratively engage with transformation to walk together. The chapter explores how transformation occurs when the 4Cs fuel both courageous leadership and leadership-as-practice[1] framed by values and their context. Let's explore the Lantern in some more detail.

The Leadership Lantern

The Lantern we introduce in this chapter is more than a metaphor; it is the foundation of our exploration of leadership for transformation throughout this book. The Leadership Lantern serves as the central framework that illuminates how collaboration, creativity, communication and critical reflection (the 4Cs) intersect with values and context to enable transformative change in schools and learning communities. Throughout the chapters to follow, the Lantern will guide our discussions, shaping our approach to each aspect of leadership we discuss.

In the same way a lantern lights the way for walkers along a track or in a lantern walk, the Leadership Lantern illuminates the transformation journey of a school or other learning community. Leadership, like the lantern, has the potential to radiate light around everyone, in contrast with the necessarily solid beam of a torch or flashlight.

In this framework we are imagining a fuel lamp that uses a flame that can be variously illuminating, risky and warm depending on its context and the way it is used. Before we get too carried away with our own metaphor, let's break down the elements of the Leadership Lantern and how they interact with each other as a way of introducing some of the key themes that will emerge throughout the remainder of the book.

Figure 2.2 A lantern sheds light to make the path clear

Figure 2.3 The Leadership Lantern

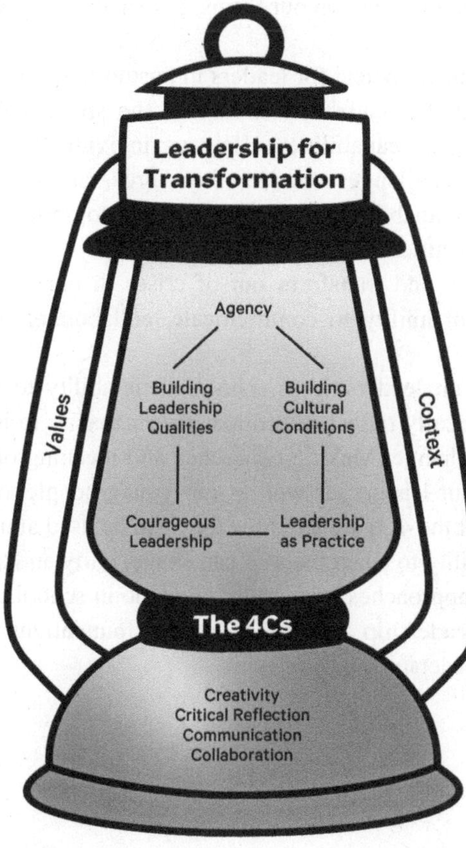

The elements of leadership for transformation

In the remainder of this chapter, we will discuss all the elements of this coherence maker for leadership, beginning with the fuel for transformation, the 4Cs.

The 4Cs

In the Leadership Lantern (figure 2.3), the 4Cs are the fuel that enables the lantern to glow and shed light. The 4Cs is shorthand for creativity, critical reflection, communication and collaboration that generates a foundation for everything we do in education. We argue throughout this book that leadership for transformation is only possible when the 4Cs are understood and enacted in individuals (building leadership qualities) and in schools (building cultural capabilities). As we argue in *Transforming Schools*, *Transforming Organizations* and *Transforming Education* the 4Cs are foundational to learning, pedagogy, curriculum and all other processes in schools.

The 4Cs are paradoxical. They are inherent in each of us, yet we need to develop and engage with them in our context to ensure we grow in our ability to apply them. In leadership for transformation, the 4Cs make action possible but only if we keep developing them in ourselves and in our teams. Like a muscle, the 4Cs need exercise to strengthen.

The 4Cs are even more critical for leaders in postnormal times[2] of chaos, contradiction and complexity.[3] A capability is having the space and skills to perform particular actions.[4] These capabilities allow us individually and collectively to respond with agility as challenges arise. In other words, rather than narrow skills, the 4Cs provide the core capabilities that allow leaders to anticipate and respond to challenges and opportunities as they emerge.

How we respond to and transform out of crises in our organizations and our world will rely on our ability to communicate, collaborate, create and critically reflect.

When we work with leadership in schools their ability to collaborate, create, communicate and critically reflect determines their capacity to imagine, enable and enact transformative change. Making coherence and meaning of these processes is vital, yet we expect our leaders, as well as our young people, our schools and our teachers to know what the 4Cs are and how they can be used almost by accident. An understanding and ability to enact the 4Cs can shape, unify and transform education through re-imagined approaches to everything we do in schools. Before we discuss the other features of leadership, let's begin with the foundations that metaphorically fuel transformative leadership.

Fuelling leadership through the 4Cs

We believe human achievement requires an ability to understand and enact the 4Cs.[5] Leadership for transformation, which we believe is a particularly challenging form of human achievement, relies on developing a sophisticated and flexible command of the 4Cs: creativity, collaboration, communication and critical reflection.

The 4Cs are not discrete capabilities, they interact dynamically in effective leadership to build a platform, vision, strategy and action for wise change. We use coherence makers to support understanding of critical concepts in learning (such as the 4Cs). Coherence makers are frameworks designed to bring meaning and structure to frequently discussed ideas in education. They organize knowledge and support reflection. They are designed to make intangible concepts understandable and actionable, and illuminate a structural meaning for ideas that are sometimes elusive. They offer a scaffold to support school leaders in navigating the complexity of aligning vision with practice. By breaking down complex ideas, they provide both clarity and strategies that generate action. Let's do a quick overview of what we mean by the 4Cs through the 4C coherence makers and explain further how they are relevant to leadership. We explore these in more detail later in this book.

Creativity

We are not the first to say schools are complex places. Add to that the dynamism and tension that transformation generates, and you begin to understand the need for creative approaches to transformation. Creativity is not necessarily loud or bombastic, it is more likely to be commonplace in leadership. Creative leadership might look like responding, resolving and problem solving small and large tasks. If you have been involved in leadership, you probably exercise creativity regularly sometimes without knowing it. Educator and researcher Anna Craft called this 'everyday creativity'.[6] In a tribute to Anna after her death in 2014, fellow educator Robin Alexander said, 'Anna saw creativity as an everyday and lifelong imperative, a problem-finding, problem-solving capability with possibility thinking – the transformation from what is to what might be – at its heart'.[7]

In this every day and unglamorous way, creativity is to imagine and problem-solve with possibilities by exploring the unusual and unexpected. Creativity engages our imagination to iteratively design and enact new approaches and processes in response to complex challenges. It is to not to fear failure, but rather to learn from trial and error and to know there is a creative response to each challenge, small or large.

To foster creativity, educational leaders must become meta-aware of the structural possibilities it opens up. Transformative change depends on the creative reimagining of processes, strategies and school cultures. Creativity enables leaders to move from shared vision to realized change. For instance, when faced with the challenge of transforming a school, creativity and its inherent steps of noticing, asking 'why,

Figure 2.4 The Creativity Cascade

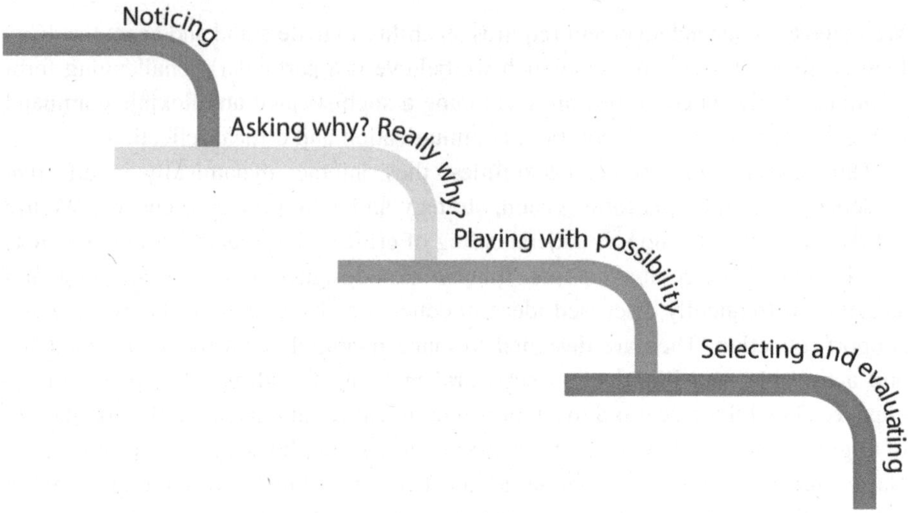

really why' and playing with possibility provide a pathway for designing and implementing structural change in schools. The Creativity Cascade coherence maker provides a schema for this approach (see figure 2.4).

The next component of the fuel for our Lantern is critical reflection.

Critical reflection

Some leaders believe mistakenly that critical reflection like creativity is a kind of soft, vague and unproductive process – a kind of navel gazing self-indulgence. Education researcher, Carol Rodgers disagrees,

> Once reflection can be talked about with precision by both teachers, [leaders] and researchers as well as students, it cannot be so easily dismissed as 'soft', nor lost in the flurry of vaguely defined movements. How to think reflectively, after all, is not a bandwagon issue. It is not a fad whose time has come and gone but perhaps the most essential piece of what makes us human, of what makes us learners.[8]

In our experience not only is critical reflection rigorous and demanding, it is perhaps the most powerful and difficult work to do in leadership as an individual and as a collaborative cultural practice but the most essential. It demands focus, honesty and trust, and an unflinching commitment to understanding and then acting wisely on that understanding. We see this in the work we do in schools through the processes of mentoring, coaching and reflective supervision (sometimes called professional supervision) that can change radically what's possible in leadership and ultimately in a school.

Figure 2.5 The Critical Reflection Crucible

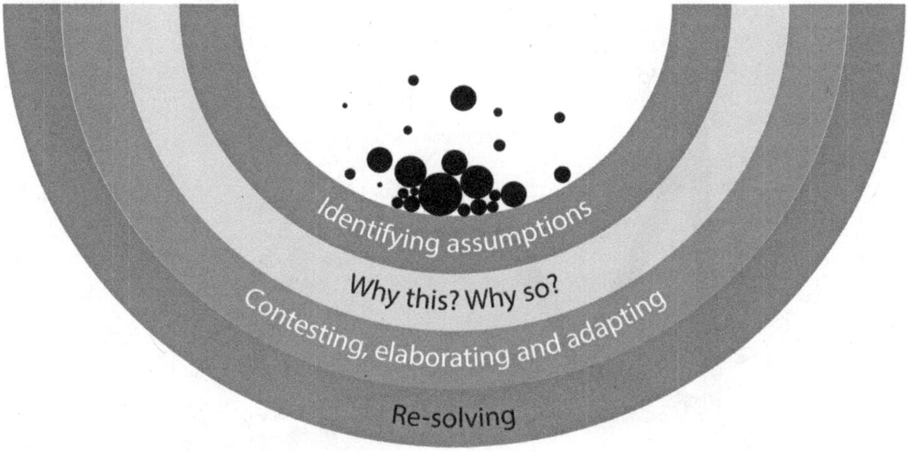

Critical reflection is to question, elaborate, analyse and explain. It is to develop thinking processes beyond asking 'what?' to asking 'why, how and what if?' To reflect critically is to first notice and then reflect on and re-solve problems through wise action. Critical reflection asks educators to question their assumptions, reform and reframe ideas and then collaboratively reconfigure and re-solve them, leading to transformative action. For instance, applying the critical reflection coherence maker leads to an honest reassessment of how the timetable is currently structured and how that might change to better meet student needs. The Critical Reflection Crucible coherence maker provides a schema for this capacity (see figure 2.5).

For reflections to have impact within an organization, they must be shared effectively. This is where communication becomes essential, as it is the next element in the 4Cs and a vital fuel for the Leadership Lantern.

Communication

A good proportion of leadership is communication. For instance, the way a leader or a leadership team constructs and conveys values happens in all kinds of verbal and non-verbal forms of communication. When pursuing transformative leadership, how you communicate is just as crucial as what you communicate. In other words, an inclusive and authentic interaction about issues arising in a school is likely to 'bring people along' rather than a curt email. Perhaps most critically, communication is about being alert to the messages (listening) to a diversity of voices in our schools before we craft our own messages as leaders.

Communication is to empower and respect all voices as authentic. Communication is about conveying messages and receiving them. Effective communication is critical in transformation as it allows educators to develop values, strategies and plans collaboratively and then convey that to the school community. For

Figure 2.6 The Communication Crystal

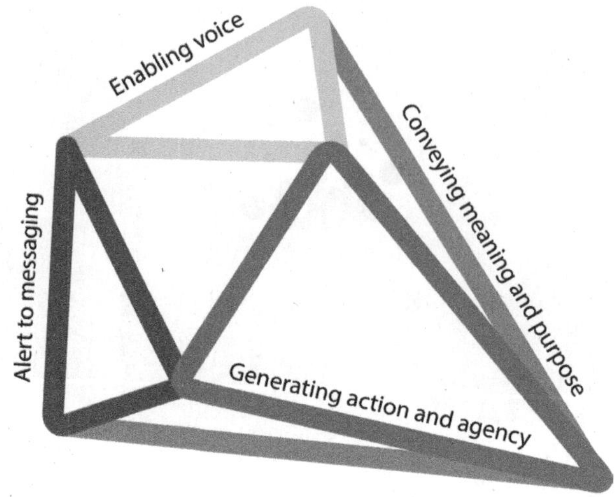

example, communication is critical when encouraging changes in pedagogy. Without clear communication that considers the anxieties, objections and concerns of members of the school community even the most critical and thoughtful pedagogical transformation can faulter. The Communication Crystal Coherence maker provides a schema for this capacity (see figure 2.6).

As we have already discussed, the individualistic hero leader is an often-damaging myth. As leaders work together across the school community they magnify their potential. As such collaboration is a critical ingredient in our fuel for the Leadership Lantern.

Collaboration

At the centre of building courageous leaders and leadership-as-practice in schools is collaboration. As we consider leadership for transformation we move away from the simplistic notion of the individual as leadership change-maker (the hero leader myth) and engage with the more complex ideas of leadership as a shared endeavour. Collaboration is at the centre of this relationship and is critical in building a culture of leadership within complex organizations such as schools. As Joseph Raelin argues:

> Leadership has been nearly universally associated with a single individual, but as a collaborative agentic practice, we would need to extract it from any single identified purveyor; otherwise, it becomes preselected as a rite or endowment available only to particular privileged people . . . Wouldn't we be better off letting those affected within the community decide how to proceed? . . . Is it not time to trust the process and trust the people?[9]

At face value this seems like common sense. Why wouldn't those affected by decisions have some role in leading those decisions? However, in a complex organization such as a school the 'how' of this approach is often elusive.

Collaboration requires trust and openness to challenging and being challenged by others. Educators require collaboration to build and sustain relationships that drive re-imagined processes in learning, pedagogy and curriculum. For instance, when the school is considering how a new syllabus might be introduced into the curriculum, collaboration can ensure teachers across year groups and key learning areas contribute to implementation that understands the impact and opportunities of the change across the school. The Collaboration Circles Coherence maker provides a schema for this collaboration (see figure 2.7).

Figure 2.7 Collaboration Circles

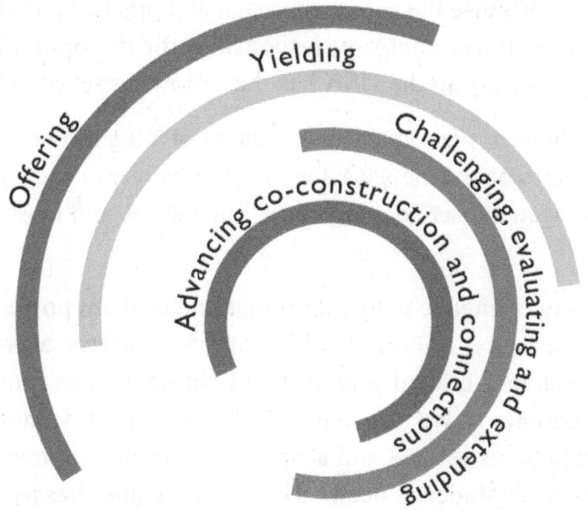

The 4Cs are the foundational capacities and capabilities that fuel transformation. For those leading transformation they need to be developed in relationship with other factors such as values and context to ensure transformation is beneficial and relevant to each school's individual needs.

An understanding of values provides an anchor and a guide to ensure our leadership is ethical and has a deep moral purpose. As you can see in figure 2.3 in the Leadership Lantern, values are a key structural feature giving the lantern its shape and strength.

Let's now move beyond the fuel and consider values and context. These are the structural elements that will differ depending on your school and its specific features. Let's start with the much-discussed concept of values.

Values

John McCain was a US Republican senator, Second World War hero and nominee for the US Presidential race in 2008 against Barack Obama. In 2018 at his funeral, former US Secretary of State Henry Kissinger said, 'Honor was John's lodestar. It is an intangible quality. It is not obligatory. It has no written code. It reflects an inward compulsion free of self-interest. It fulfils a cause, not a personal ambition. It represents what a society lives for beyond the necessities of the moment. Law makes life possible. Honor and nobility for John it was a way of life.' This short tribute illustrates how values can be made real in individuals. In this tribute Kissinger identifies McCain's honour as the value that drove him forward and showed him the way. McCain's honour according to Kissinger was not artifice, it was the very thing the charted the way for McCain to achieve what he did through his extraordinary life. Unfortunately, values do not always act as lodestars.

Recently, values have become a buzzword that people throw around without real meaning. Every organization has them in one form or another, but they rarely have the force of a lodestar shaping practice and driving transformation. In the worst cases, they can even disguise the actual approach and practices of organizations. For instance, the pharmaceutical company responsible for the opioid crisis that led to addiction, death and misery in the USA has the following set of values:

> We believe that Respect is grounded in our Values of Integrity and Courage, underpinned by Innovation, and always in Collaboration with each other.
> Together we make an impact on our growth, our culture, and most importantly, patients.[10]

There is another way to engage with values that makes them powerful and useful in transformation. In essence, values should shape and inform everything we do in schools, and they can be a critical way to shed light on the need and the impetus for transforming education. If we can harness the power of values, we can shape ourselves into courageous leaders and shape our learning cultures to be transformative and relevant to our student's needs. This is why values has a critical role on the operation of the Leadership Lantern.

In *Transforming Education,* we identified several values that we think drive transformational change in schools. We offer them now as an example. Any set of values are only meaningful if leaders and everyone else in the organization have a hand in shaping and implementing them. The values that we consider transformational lodestars are:

- Critical hope
- Wisdom
- Imagination
- Unlearning
- Deep and explicit learning
- Re-imagined pedagogy
- Connected and coherent learning
- Collaborative partnerships
- Praxis[11]

We have chosen values as a structural component of our lantern as they are crucial to supporting transformative change. In many senses they create a strong and robust set of aspirations to enable schools to design and act on making the changes required. Much like a lodestar (sometimes called a guiding star), when the tangle of transformation[12] becomes challenging, they create a way for leaders to look up from the minutiae and be reminded of what matters. However, values are meaningless without understanding the context in which the transformation is taking place. The other structural element we have identified for the Leadership Lantern is context.

Context

Context is an often-overlooked element in the rush to create silver bullet solutions for leaders. We see this in policies that are 'rolled out' in many areas of education such as literacy, technology, student behaviour and the like. We are not arguing that these areas do not deserve attention. Unfortunately, silver bullet solutions that ignore context often do more harm than good. In these 'one size fits all' approaches, the nuances and details of each context are ignored, forcing the square peg into round hole every time. In a wide-ranging survey of leadership theories, author Annabel Beerel argues:

> . . . many leadership theories that underpin some of the trainings are woefully weak when it comes to context, application, and understanding culture and group dynamics. While most of these theories in some way sit on the shoulders of the organizational theorists of the past, here too, a rigorous grounding in well-tested theory is often dismissed in favor of providing quick and easy techniques . . . Many [leadership development programs] ignore context and emphasize content when it is really context that matters most.[13]

Beerel argues here that the context not only matters, but it is also a crucial structural element for leadership. The specific context for school leaders varies significantly depending on both the school community they serve and their position within the school structure. A faculty leader in a high socioeconomic urban school faces different contextual challenges than an executive leader in a rural, low socioeconomic community. Similarly, a deputy principal's context differs significantly from that of a curriculum coordinator or wellbeing leader.

In our work with schools, we begin with context. Context is a structural element in the Leadership Lantern to signify that leading transformation must always be shaped and reshaped around context. While many of the same processes may be employed, their timing, sequence and approach must be designed and enacted perceptively to ensure transformation occurs effectively and sustainably in a particular context. For instance, if a school is considering a change to curriculum, time needs to be taken to allow for consultation and discussion before a proposal is 'socialized' with staff, students and parents for their response.

Transformative school leaders must also account for and understand that context encompasses multiple interconnected structures that shape a school's functioning and identity. Effective leaders navigate organizational structures including reporting lines, team compositions and decision-making frameworks that define how authority flows through their school and system. They simultaneously pay attention to curricular and pedagogical structures which determine how teaching and learning are organized and delivered. Operational and administrative structures determining resource allocation, scheduling and facility management require equal consideration, as do governance and compliance structures.

Perhaps most critically, transformative leaders must understand and engage with cultural and community structures that connect the school to its broader ecosystem of families, neighbourhoods and cultural traditions. The wise alignment of these varied structures with the school's context can support the work of transformation. In Practice 2.1 is a deep noticing into your context to surface some of the key opportunities and issues it presents.

Practice 2.1 Noticing your school's context

Using a modified citizen jury approach* randomly select members of the:

- Leadership team (2)
- Staff (4)
- Students (2 from each year grade) to work on the question

'What do you notice about the school?'

'What is distinctive about your school?'

'What is special about your school?'

Categories of noticing might include:

- Student factors (e.g. socioeconomic status, cultural background, English language learner status, special education status).
- Teacher factors (e.g. experience, education level, turnover rate).
- Community factors (e.g. economic equality, employment etc.).

The noticings can be presented in a non-written form such as a series of pictures, photographs or a podcast or a short video (if more time and resources are available) that involves all the citizen jury in the design and delivery process.

These questions can be used to analyse and/or discuss the results:

- Does what we have noticed align with our school's values?
- What could our school do to better meet the needs of its students?
- What are the challenges and opportunities in the school that could assist us achieve transformation?

- How might we embed noticing processes about our school and our context into the life of the school on a regular basis?

* A citizen jury chooses a representative sample of participants in an organization to consider and respond to an issue. Participants are selected randomly but contribute voluntarily. This approach is used by some governments to devise responses to difficult social issues and can be less adversarial than parliamentary decision making.

Let's turn now to how we build leadership for transformation in a school setting.

Courageous leadership and leadership-as-practice

Having considered the fuel (the 4Cs) and the structural elements (values and context) of the Lantern we turn to describing the light that the Lantern creates. The quality of this light makes transformation possible in a school. The light the lantern creates is made up of courageous leadership and leadership-as-practice.

The distinction you sometimes see between the individual as a leader and the development of collaborative leadership within an organization is often framed as an 'either-or' choice. Transformative leadership is not solely about the actions of a single, charismatic figure, nor is it merely the result of collaboration; it emerges from the dynamic interplay between individual agency and contextual factors and collaborative effort. Individual and cultural factors are interacting constantly. We have identified courageous leadership as the process leaders need to build in themselves and leadership-as-practice as the processes that we can develop to create a culture of effective transformational leadership in schools. To ensure that a school can transform we need to attend to both simultaneously. In the Leadership Lantern we have separated individual and cultural factors but indicated that they are critically interdependent. Let's consider the individual or personal qualities first.

Developing personal qualities – courageous leadership

Many of the top selling leadership books focus on what leaders can do to become more effective and efficient. Brené Brown and Simon Sinek's popular books speak directly to the ways individual leaders can be better and more effective at what they do. This is legitimate and worthwhile, and we have also written with a view to developing leaders' personal qualities. The coherence maker we use to explore personal qualities and leadership-as-practice is the Leadership Wheel discussed later in this book. The Leadership Wheel is a framework that describes the capacities required to lead transformation based on the psychological needs identified in Self-Determination Theory.[14] The wheel has three interrelated domains: autonomy, relatedness and competence. Courageous leaders who also employ leadership-as-practice in their teams create the conditions and environment for developing other people's autonomy, relatedness and competence.

The development of courageous leadership in individuals contributes to tackling challenges and making wise decisions. This must be coupled with developing cultural conditions by developing leadership-as-practice.

Developing cultural conditions

The culture in an organization is the 'way we do things around here'.[15] Organizational theorist Edgar H. Schein defines culture as 'a pattern of shared basic assumptions that was learned by a group as it solved its problems of external adaptation and internal integration, that has worked well enough to be considered valid, and, therefore, to be taught to new members as the correct way to perceive, think, and feel in relation to those problems'.[16] Culture is not necessarily positive and often the assumptions that are learned and integrated can be detrimental. For example, a school culture that prioritizes high academic performance at the expense of student well-being may generate stress and burnout among students and staff. Similarly, if there is a cultural assumption within a school that innovation is too risky, leaders may struggle to change entrenched and perhaps ineffective teaching practices.

As we develop a leadership for transformation culture, the focus shifts to building a collaborative, creative, communicative and critically reflective environment to enable transformation.

Schools which build the 4Cs as capabilities into their leadership culture can generate transformation through:

- Imagining, innovating and preparing for the future (creativity)
- Valuing others in a multi-way exchange (communication)
- Reflecting on assumptions and established practices (critical reflection)
- Employing and enabling the genius of the collective (collaboration)

The 4Cs are inherently agile strategies that create school cultures that do not stand still as the world whizzes by. The 4Cs make the complexity of transformation cohere, enabling transformative action. These schools can re-imagine the possible but can also learn deeply from their own experience. These agile, transformative qualities create the conditions where agency can flourish. In the Leadership Lantern, agency is a non-negotiable part of the light that makes transformation possible.

Agency

Deci and Ryan argue in Self Determination Theory[17] that there are three critical factors for thriving as a person – competence, relatedness and autonomy. All these influence the way agency is understood and expressed. Deci and Ryan's concept is closely aligned to the Organization for Economic Co-operation and Development's (OECD) definition of agency. The OECD defines agency as 'a sense of responsibility to participate in the world, and, in so doing, to influence people, events, and circumstances for the better'.[18] For leaders, there are a few key touchpoints in this definition. Key to this definition are the concepts of responsibility and influence for the better. We see those qualities evident in inspirational leaders such as Malala or Nelson Mandela. Critically in this definition, these leaders are not just doing what they want. Through their agency they are enabling the agency of others. In Malala's case, her agency (e.g. through her international advocacy) provides space for women and girls to engage more agentically in their contexts. As Vlad Glăveanu explains, agency is always understood in an interaction between the individual and the group:

> . . . person and society are not two completely separate entities. People exist within society and society exists within the person. The agency and creativity of the person have their origin precisely in this relational space defined by individuals and the world they inhabit. Neither of them are 'entities' or 'qualities' possessed by the person in isolation, but markers of the encounter between people, objects, and social institutions.[19]

As we consider how we might transform our schools, building agency is an opportunity to shift culture from a 'what is being done to us' to a 'what can we do together'? To enable those changes, we also need to build courage into everyone's capacity for joy and motivation that will support the growth of agency.

Joy and motivation for agency

Joy and motivation are fundamental for developing agency in schools, and can sustain transformative action when challenges arise. Joy enhances well-being and energizes people by connecting to their sense of purpose. When people feel joyful, they are more likely to engage in new behaviours. Joy fosters resilience and the ability to take on challenges. Leadership requires joy to encourage people to take the necessary steps to achieve challenging goals. Joy can be cultivated by school leaders who are not burnt out and stressed, enabling them to better motivate, support and learn from others. Motivation, particularly autonomous motivation, is a driving force behind commitment, effort, and engagement.[20] Autonomous motivation occurs when people take initiative because their actions align with their internal values. Autonomous motivation fosters a sense of ownership and dedication to a shared moral purpose, encouraging a willingness to act.

The development of agency begins with engaging deeply with the 4Cs within ourselves as leaders. This is expressed through courageous leadership and supported by how we enable others through leadership-as-practice.

The 4Cs – creativity, critical reflection, communication and collaboration are foundational to developing agency in an individual and in others. The 4Cs provide the skills and understandings that empower individuals to act and influence their lives and the world around them with agency. For instance:

Creativity enables the imagining of new possibilities and approaches, fostering the generation of novel ideas and solutions.

Critical reflection empowers the analysis of experiences and contexts, question assumptions, and understand power dynamics, which is critical for making informed choices and taking purposeful action.

Communication conveys meaning, expressing one's voice, and connecting with others and enabling shared perspectives.

Collaboration as a process of shared vision and mutual engagement, allows for the expansion of individual capabilities through shared work and learning, developing the capacity for collective action.

Together, the 4Cs enable individuals and teams to move from passive recipients to active agents in their own lives and communities. Agency is also key in generating the next component of the light for transformation in the Lantern, courageous leadership.

Courageous leadership

Even a passing glance at the demands and challenges of transformation will convince most leaders that it is hard. Many decide that transformation is too difficult and remain in the relative tranquillity of the status quo. Leading that exists in status quo is difficult enough but it takes skill, determination and particularly courage to engage with processes of transformation. If we return to the story of Malala Yousafzai, we see the qualities of courageous leadership. She demonstrates the qualities in the perseverance, influence and communication (that we discuss in the Leadership Wheel in chapter 9). She stands up courageously to unjust power and fights for her values.

Organizational researcher Bill George claims that: 'Courage is the quality that distinguishes great leaders from excellent managers'.[21] This is quality we see in effective leaders of transformation. Courageous leadership is not merely an abstract concept but a practical necessity for meaningful transformation in schools. Transformative leaders embrace uncertainty and question conventions, wisely balancing the demanded for stability and calm in schools with the imperative for meaningful change. A few individuals with these qualities cannot transform a school. As well as individual leaders acting with courage we need to build leadership practices into the fabric of the school. In tandem with courageous leadership, schools need to shift culture and develop leadership as practice.

Leadership-as-practice

In part, leadership-as-practice is a recognition that courageous leadership is not enough to effect sustainable transformation. Transformation is not situated in one person but rather it is collaborative work that looks beyond an individual's ability to lead for transformation. Educational leadership researcher and academic Jane Wilkinson argues that by 'understanding the practices and arrangements that hold particular kinds of educational practices in place, we are then better able to understand possibilities for educational change and transformation'.[22] The leadership-as-practice approach is influenced by Educational Researcher, Steven Kemmis's Theory of Practice Architectures that argues '. . . practices are composed of sayings, doings, and relatings that hang together in the project (purpose) of the practice. In turn, these sayings, doings, and relatings are enabled and constrained (and made possible) by cultural-discursive, material-economic, and social-political arrangements found in or brought to the site where the practice occurs'. These are defined and explained further in table 2.1, Sayings Doings and Relatings.

The things that are said, done and our relationships make up the culture of a school and to achieve change we need to shift these practices. Practice architectures

Table 2.1 Definitions of sayings, doings and relatings and how they become evident

Practices	Definition[23]	School-based examples
Sayings	The things practitioners (teachers/leaders etc.) say to each other about and during practice. Sayings are influenced by cultural and language factors, as well as how practitioners interact with each other.	• The discussions around the implementation of new syllabuses. • Comments about a new approach to teaching. • Executive discussions about student behaviour. • Teacher staffroom chat about parents.
Doings	The actions practitioners take individually and collaboratively. Doings are influenced by the materials and resources available, the work they do, and the physical space where the practice takes place.	• Trialling approaches to interdisciplinary learning in a particular year group. • The coaching of the soccer team. • Student/teacher meetings. • End of year assemblies.
Relatings	The connections practitioners form during practice. Relatings are influenced by social and political factors, like mutual support and the power dynamics evident in interactions.	• The relationship between the executive and the teaching staff. • Collaboration in learning between students and teachers. • Connections in networks of school leaders.

also recognize that these practices are impacted by resourcing, policy and other cultural factors. In other words, the realities of the context in terms of politics, resourcing, staffing, student demographics will have an influence on each school's sayings, doings and relatings, and their capacity for transformation.

Leadership-as-practice requires explicit mapping (see Practice 2.2) of strategy, processes and structures to grow leadership in the practices and culture of the school.

Practice 2.2 The cultural work of leadership-as-practice

Leadership-as-practice requires cultural work. As a starting point consider the sayings doings and relatings that currently exist in your school.

1. To develop a comprehensive picture, ask students, teachers and parents to develop their own tables to discuss practices as they currently exist in your context. The following table contains some examples, but you could explore any aspect of school practices that are most relevant in your context.

Practices	Teaching	Curriculum	Agency	Leadership
Sayings				
Doings				
Relatings				

2. As a way of encouraging new ideas to flourish, invite participants to fill out the same table with the sayings, doings and relatings they would like to work towards as part of the school's transformation.
3. Collate these as a series of 'findings' for the school community in two categories:
   - Sayings, doings and relatings as they are now
   - Sayings, doings and relatings that we would like to work towards

This approach provides a framework for schools to analyse their current leadership practice (sayings, doings and relatings) and can provide a starting point for change. But as Wilkinson argues, that is one part of the transformation puzzle. Structural processes also need transformation. As Jane Wilkinson maintains that changing practices is just one part of the transformation journey, 'it is not sufficient to change practices alone (such as the practice knowledge of teachers or leaders). Instead, the arrangements that hold these practices in place need to be revealed and interrogated and new arrangements or practice architectures need to be created'.[24]

For example, consider a primary school that sends teachers to a 'culturally responsive and inclusive classrooms' professional learning session. Despite learning strategies for incorporating Indigenous perspectives and adapting lessons for diverse learners, teachers revert to traditional practices because the underlying arrangements remain unchanged, including rigid curriculum expectations, an overreliance on standardized assessments that prioritize uniform testing, predominantly Anglo-centric classroom resources, fragmented timetabling, and deficit-based reporting systems. To create lasting change, the school would need to reveal and interrogate these constraining arrangements rather than simply focusing on individual teacher knowledge, which might involve:

- Restructuring curriculum delivery for engaging a diversity of learners
- Diversifying assessment methods
- Sourcing culturally diverse materials
- Developing strengths-based reporting frameworks

This example demonstrates that individual knowledge and skills exist within systems, and unless you change the system's architecture, even well-intentioned educators will be pulled back into the status quo by the very structures they work within.

In our view, transformation is achievable in schools through the agency generated by courageous leadership and leadership-as-practice. This is fuelled by the 4Cs and framed by values and context. We will interrogate this complex yet rich interchange between courageous leadership and leadership-as-practice as we explore leadership for transformation throughout this book.

Concluding reflections

The Leadership Lantern is a metaphorical way to explain the complexities of leading a transforming school. As schools transform, they engage agentically with their context to develop courageous individual leadership qualities and conditions for a transformative leadership culture within a school.

In our experience of transforming schools, when these features of the Lantern are enacted and align, schools begin to realize their potential. They achieve this transformation through re-invigorated agency leading to heightened motivation and joy that we discuss in later chapters.

The Lantern Walk is slow, methodical, collaborative and artful. It illuminates the way for others to also tread the path. This ritual commemorating the compassionate and courageous leadership of St Martin provides a metaphor for the way transformative change is made possible. Transformation like the lantern parade needs to be deliberate, creative and meaningful. The Leadership Lantern is one way we can make sense of all the moving parts of that process. The next chapters explore the fuel for the Leadership Lantern, the 4Cs, beginning with critical reflection.

Key actions

1. Have another look at the Leadership Lantern in the opening pages of this chapter. Where do you think your areas of strength and opportunity are? For instance, are there opportunities in your context for transformative leadership? Is there a leadership-as-practice culture already evident?
2. Consider the discussion of the 4Cs in this chapter. What are the areas which your school does well? What are the areas that could be supported with professional learning? For instance, is there a good understanding of critical reflection? If so, how is it evident in leadership practice?
3. What is distinctive about your school context? You might consider the approach of your students, staff, socio-demography of your area, relationship with parents and other stakeholders to learning and/or teaching. Do the values of your school help or hinder you to lead with contextual awareness or are they simply ignored?
4. Re-read the sections on courageous leadership and leadership-as-practice. Is there evidence of either in your school? Consider some initial steps to develop these practices and begin discussions with your school community about what these might look like in your community.
5. What are the most prominent sayings, doings and relatings in your school? Do they support the qualities identified in the Leadership Lantern? Are there ways that you could build transformative sayings, doings and relatings in your school? What would the first steps be?

Leading through critical reflection

3

Figure 3.1 Critical reflection is like a crucible[1]

The crucible of critical reflection

What image does the term reflection summon up for you? Perhaps it is a soothing rainforest or a tranquil stream? Rather than that picture, we would like to propose a more active and dramatic metaphor for critical reflection-the crucible (see figure 3.1).

In a crucible, raw materials are exposed to intense pressure and searing temperatures. The ore within the crucible undergoes a refinement and transformation process that retains the useful and removes the worthless to create something that is paradoxically the same but new – stronger, better, and fundamentally transformed.

Critical reflection operates in much the same way. It is not passive, but an active, often uncomfortable, engagement with experiences and knowledge. When leaders critically reflect, assumptions are tested, perspectives are challenged, and the familiar is questioned and often reshaped, producing new understandings that have the potential to generate action.

For educational leaders, engaging with critical reflection often means confronting the limitations of their current practices and recognizing the possibilities for growth. Just as heat and pressure reshape metal, the process of critical reflection can transform schools by enabling more effective responses to the complicated and complex challenges they face.

For example, a school leadership team who are grappling with persistent discipline issues may initially believe that stricter behaviour policies are the solution. However, through the process of critical reflection, they may reflect on the assumptions they have about behaviour management, explore why this is occurring, work with options for change and then act. This critical reflection reveals the potential for an engagement focused approach to managing behaviour that emphasizes student wellbeing, engaging pedagogical approaches and restorative practices.

To use the crucible analogy, this process is likely to be hot and will likely burn away less useful approaches and unevidenced assumptions. In other words, critical reflection requires effort and processes of (potentially painful) refinement but it can also provide sustainable responses to complex issues and opportunities in schools. Critical reflection provides the energy (along with the other 4Cs) that power the Leadership Lantern.

In this chapter, we discuss the definitions and evidence for critical reflection and argue that it is an active, transformative process where assumptions are challenged, and new understandings emerge that can lead to transformative action. We discuss how the Critical Reflection Crucible supports school leaders to enact deep and sustainable action and be the best version of themselves as leaders and bring out the best in others. Let's now turn to the 'what' by defining and describing critical reflection.

What is critical reflection?

In *Transforming Organizations*,[2] we define critical reflection as 'the capacity to understand power and how it is exercised. It provides an appreciation of how to navigate and have and enable agency in complex systems rather than creating organisations for passive individuals or, worse, victims'.[3] In the context of critical reflection power can be understood as the capacity or ability of individuals or groups to influence, shape or control the behaviour, beliefs and actions of others within a system or context.[4] This definition of critical reflection has two interrelated but relevant features for school leaders: critical reflection allows for the *analysis of power* and *navigating toward wise decisions and action.* Let's consider these features of critical reflection.

Analysis of power

Critical reflection allows for analysis of power relationships and helps school leaders understand how decisions are made in schools and in the education ecosystem more broadly. Understanding and analysing power is not simply about identifying who holds authority; it's about recognizing the subtle and often invisible ways that power operates within systems and structures. Practice 3.1 is designed to illustrate and explore these dynamics.

School leaders who grasp the dynamics of power in schools develop awareness of both their own agency and that of others, recognizing how these forces shape their leadership, impact different members of the school and potentially lead to transformation. Leaders who clearly understand organizational power structures and their place within them, navigate complexity with greater skill and drive meaningful change more effectively. For instance, perhaps the leadership team notices that during staff meetings, input emerges mainly from a few senior teachers, while newer or less outspoken staff rarely have a chance to contribute. Reflecting on this, the leadership team realizes this pattern may unintentionally create a power imbalance, where some voices dominate decision-making while others go unheard.

To address this, the group trials a rotating feedback system, where each meeting highlights perspectives from different staff members. They also propose smaller discussion groups to encourage participation from everyone before ideas are shared with the whole group. Over time, these practices allow for a wider range of perspectives, fostering a more inclusive decision-making process. This approach ensures influence and power is more evenly and representatively distributed amongst the teaching team at the school.

Practice 3.1 The power switch

This scenario is designed to help leaders and leadership teams understand how power is exercised in hidden, implicit and explicit ways. Feel free to devise your own scenarios to more closely meet the context of your school.

Scenario: A student has proposed starting a 'LGBTQ+ safe space' for students. The school executive supports it, but several teachers have concerns including the budget.

1. Everyone is assigned a role they don't normally play:
    - New student from a disadvantaged background
    - Parent council president
    - First-year teacher
    - Experienced department head
    - Student wellbeing coordinator
2. After a few minutes for preparation each person takes one minute to present an argument for why they support it or not:
    - Do you support the idea why/why not?
    - Explain your reasons
    - Explain the evidence you have for your decision
3. Discussion and reflection
    - What power do different individuals have in this situation?
    - Is the power related to influence, status, personal experience or something else?
    - Who is most persuasive and why?
4. Application

In your school discuss:

- Who really makes decisions?
- What unwritten rules are operating?
- How could power be shared differently?
- What assumptions need challenging?

Navigating towards wise decisions and action

Critical reflection enables leaders to question their knowledge assumptions and can facilitate more thoughtful decision-making and strategic action. This process helps leaders recognize that knowledge is not static but rather dynamic and shaped by individual preconceptions.

Consider a school leadership team with many members who believe teacher-centred instruction is the only effective approach, based on their collective past classroom experiences. Through critical reflection including co-teaching or Collaborative Classroom Visits,[5] they begin to question these assumptions after observing high levels of student engagement. Reflecting on experiences can become critical in transformational change.

When leaders engage deeply with their experiences through reflection, they move beyond simply cataloguing what happened, to understanding the deeper patterns and principles at work. This transformation of experience into insight requires both systematic analysis and openness to new interpretations as social work researcher Jan Fook explains:

> . . . learning from experience simply involves re-examining past personally experienced events to make new meaning of them in the light of other (subsequent or current) experiences and contexts. The 'learning' should involve turning the thinking involved from that early event into a broader principle or guideline (by perceiving patterns or commonalities with other experiences or events). The learning, however, should enable more expansive and flexible ways of thinking and acting, rather than more rigid or restrictive thinking.[6]

Fook emphasizes that experiences gain value through reflection; or as we often say in our work with leaders, 'if an experience is not reflected on it didn't happen'. In other words, leadership is strengthened by ongoing consideration of not just what happened but why.

When school leaders critically reflect, they can gain valuable insights by analysing experiences rather than simply accumulating them. For example, consider a leadership team that has experienced an unsuccessful curriculum implementation. Just acknowledging the issues has limited value. When leaders deeply examine specific challenges through reflection, they create insights that can shape their future actions. Maybe teachers were resistant to the implementation. Perhaps some communication strategies were rushed or imprecise. Perhaps teachers implemented strategies they hadn't reflected on and learnt from.

Educational pioneer John Dewey chimes with Fook's learning from experience definition. He explains reflection is '. . . turning a topic over in various aspects and in various lights so that nothing significant about it shall be overlooked – almost as one might turn a stone over to see what its hidden side is like or what is covered by it'.[7] That is, turning over the stone allows us to look deeply into an issue from different angles, in different lights to see the issue from many perspectives. The focus here is on learning from experience, not just the experience itself.

This may seem obvious, but in a busy school with multiple competing demands, reflection on experience may seem like a luxury that leaders and leadership teams can do without. A good way to begin this discussion is to look with the whole leadership team in your context at the Conditions for Learning Dial (see figure 1.2 in chapter 1). As we discussed in chapter 1, the dial can generate discussion about where a school, year group or program is tracking so that perspectives and assumptions are clear before the discussion begins. The goal is to embed critical reflection in leadership practice. Practice 3.2, Critical Reflection Time Capsule, can also support leadership teams to stop and reflect on experience. Before we explore the 'how' much further let's explore the 'why'. What are the benefits of critical reflection?

Practice 3.2 Critical reflection time capsule

This exercise explores how critical reflection can become an essential practice for school leaders by examining what critical reflection means, why it matters, and how it can be woven into daily practice.

1. Past self letter
   Choose a significant school decision or initiative from three years ago. Write a letter to your 'future self' (you now) explaining:
   - What you thought would happen
   - Why you made those choices
   - How you felt at the time

Write these individually, pretending you don't know the outcomes.

2. Checking in on reality
   Now write a response letter from your 'present self' addressing:
   - What happened
   - What assumptions you held then that in hindsight were wrong or misguided
   - What power dynamics you didn't notice at the time
   - How your emotions influenced decisions
3. Exploring patterns
   In pairs or small groups, share your letters and explore the patterns
   - What common assumptions did you hold?
   - What surprising patterns emerge about how your team makes decisions?
   - What 'that's how we've always done it/status quo' thinking can you spot?
4. Leadership time capsule
   Create a 'leadership wisdom time capsule' for your future selves to open in one year, including your predictions about a current initiative. Set a calendar reminder to open it.

The benefits of critical reflection

As school leaders navigate the challenges and opportunities of transformation, critical reflection can be a potent tool for refining thinking, becoming courageous and developing leadership-as-practice in the culture of schools. As we discussed in the opening of this chapter, the crucible metaphor signifies the refining power of critical reflection.

Critical reflection is more than a 'nice to have'. A review of the evaluative evidence by Jan Fook and colleagues[8] reveals substantial benefits for both individuals and communities across different professions. She argues critical reflection provides for individuals:[9]

1. A broader and more complex sense of their professional selves and, at the same time, a more affirmed, reflexive and empowered sense of themselves to act.
2. A way to reframe ideas about power that allowed them to feel more powerful and act in empowered ways.
3. A sense of being able to create new choices.
4. A better sense of themselves as responsible players with the agency to act in their context.

These benefits provide several potential opportunities. If school leaders can reframe their understanding of power – seeing it as collaborative rather than hierarchical – they discover new avenues for influence. This perspective shift recognizes that power isn't simply about authority but about building relationships, engaging with expertise and facilitating collaborative action. Rather than feeling constrained by organizational structures, they can identify opportunities within those structures where their leadership can make a difference.

The ability to create new options represents another crucial benefit of critical reflection. As leadership teams develop more complex understandings of a school's context, they begin to recognize choices previously invisible to them. This expanded perception allows them to move beyond false dichotomies or silver bullet solutions and develop innovative approaches to persistent challenges. When facing difficult situations, they no longer feel limited to habitual responses but can craft responsive strategies tailored to their specific situation. Having considered what critical reflection is and its benefits let's explore how it might be embedded in school leadership through the Critical Reflection Crucible.

Leading through the Critical Reflection Crucible

The Critical Reflection Crucible is used widely in schools to support teachers in understanding and teaching critical reflection in classrooms. However, it has other applications for professional and leadership learning. It is a coherence maker that defines and explains the enactment of critical reflection and describes a process for implementation in different contexts. This is not the only way to implement critical reflection. However, it does have the benefit of several years of application, iteration and innovation with leaders and leadership teams,[10] and has been useful in diverse school contexts. The first stage of the Crucible is identifying assumptions.

Figure 3.2 The Critical Reflection Crucible

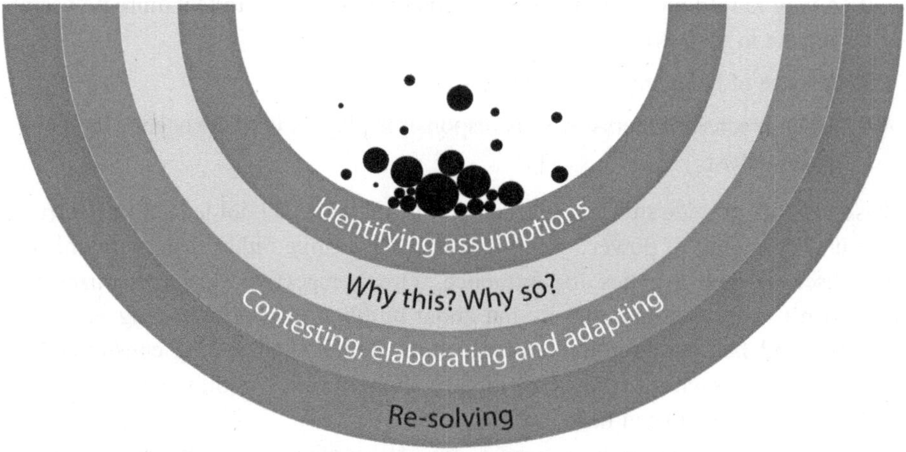

Identifying assumptions

The famous satirist and writer Douglas Adams said, 'The most misleading assumptions are the ones you don't even know you're making'.[11] Leadership assumptions can be particularly troublesome because they are often based on an impression that is fleeting or, in some other way, not fully formed or even unjust. For instance, the colleague you presumed is lazy who you later discover is struggling with an illness or a bereavement or both. This is not to say assumptions in themselves are necessarily wrong, they just need to be identified and examined. As critical reflection pioneer Stephen Brookfield says, 'Sometimes these assumptions are justified and accurate, sometimes they need reframing to fit particular situations, and sometimes they're just plain wrong'.[12] School leaders process enormous amounts of information daily, and assumptions can serve as mental shortcuts that help manage this cognitive workload. While efficient, these cognitive shortcuts can sometimes lead to oversimplified problem framing in complex educational contexts. Assumptions come from a need for cognitive efficiency.[13] Psychologist Daniel Kahneman explained in *Thinking, Fast and Slow*[14] that System 1 thinking – fast, intuitive and automatic – relies on assumptions to navigate complex situations. In school leadership, these assumptions often shape decision-making without leaders fully realizing their influence. Because System 1 operates effortlessly, it helps school leaders make quick judgements, but it can also lead to systematic errors when unchecked. Leaders often feel they 'just know' what is happening in their school without gathering evidence, an effect reinforced when others in the school shared the same unevidenced assumptions. This can generate an echo chamber where intuitive assumptions go unchallenged, and if these assumptions shape expectations about students or teachers, they can result in unintended biases.[15] These decisions are often guided by three distinct types of assumptions that Brookfield has identified as:

- Paradigmatic or *how* assumptions
- Prescriptive or *normative*
- Causal or *this leads to that*

Understanding the type of assumption assists in identifying the underlying beliefs driving decisions. By recognizing whether an assumption is paradigmatic (how things work), prescriptive (what is normal/normative) or causal (this leads to that), leaders can better analyse the impact of assumptions. Let's have a deeper look into each category of assumption.

Paradigmatic (how) assumptions are our fundamental beliefs about how education works. These deeply held convictions often operate invisibly yet powerfully shape our worldview. For instance, a leader might hold the following paradigmatic assumptions 'Every student can learn and succeed'. This could influence approaches to student support, resource allocation and expectations of teachers. Often examples might include:

'Teaching is primarily about knowledge transmission.' This assumption might limit exploration of other approaches like inquiry-based or experiential learning.

'Academic achievement is the primary purpose of schooling.' This assumption could undervalue social-emotional development, creativity or practical skills.

'Expert teachers are born, not made.' This could influence professional development and teacher selection.

The next kind of assumptions are about how we think schools should be. Prescriptive (normative) assumptions guide what we believe ought to happen in schools. These kinds of assumptions spring from habitual ways of doing things in schools established or accepted by 'common practice'. They are often the 'shoulds' and 'musts' that guide our expectations and decisions. They often feel like moral imperatives rather than choices. For instance, a leader might hold the following prescriptive assumptions:

> 'Staff meetings ought to focus on administrative matters rather than professional learning because they always have.' This could limit opportunities for teacher development and collaboration.
>
> 'Parent communication ought to be formal and structured because that's the only way I know.' This might restrict more flexible and responsive ways of engaging with families.
>
> 'Every teacher should use the same teaching methods.' This assumption about consistency might limit innovation and student-centred approaches to learning.

The next category of assumptions is causal.

Causal assumptions are our beliefs about what leads to specific outcomes in education. These drive day-to-day decisions about programs and practices. Causal assumptions are beliefs about how one action or condition leads to specific situations – essentially, they reveal our implicit theories about how things happen in education and often assumptions drive many day-to-day decisions in schools. They often influence how leaders attempt to create change or solve problems. Examples of causal assumptions might include:

> 'Student performance improves when teachers use more technology in the classroom.' This could lead to an over reliance on technology when there are other more effective responses.
>
> 'A strict discipline policy reduces student disengagement.' Leaders might believe that enforcing zero-tolerance policies or stricter rules will automatically lead to greater student engagement in learning.
>
> 'More homework leads to better academic achievement.' This may not hold true for all students and all tasks.

Understanding and identifying assumptions is not just an intellectual exercise it has real world effects. Assumptions can influence decision-making, policy development, and interpersonal interactions and as such need to be understood. When school leaders fail to critically examine their assumptions, they risk reinforcing biases, making ineffective decisions, and overlooking alternative perspectives that could lead to more equitable and transformative outcomes. Assumptions, when left unexamined, can limit a leader's ability to make sound, evidence-based decisions in dynamic school environments with diverse students, staff, and communities. If unchecked, these assumptions may result in policies or practices that fail to align with the realities of their school context.

Understanding these different types of assumptions transforms school leadership in crucial ways. It helps leaders recognize when they're operating on automatic pilot or accepting traditional practices without question. By examining their paradigmatic beliefs about education, their prescriptive views about what should happen, and their causal beliefs about what works, leaders can make more deliberate and contextual decisions.

This critical reflection process enables leaders to move beyond reactive decision-making to thoughtful leadership that creates meaningful change. It also helps them understand how their assumptions might affect different members of their school community, making power dynamics more visible and decisions more inclusive. Practice 3.3 is designed to explore the different kinds of assumptions we make whether they be paradigmatic, prescriptive or causal. Sometimes assumptions can be driven by unseen or even unconscious biases that can be understood through close attention to them.

Practice 3.3 The assumption maze

This exercise invites school leaders to explore paradigmatic, prescriptive and causal assumptions in an engaging and reflective way through movement and discussion. It is intended to help school leaders identify and reflect on different types of assumptions that could influence leadership practices, using embodied and collaborative processes.

1. Set up the maze
   - Use masking tape or string to create a large maze-like path on the floor. Along the maze, place 'assumption cards' at key decision points.
   - Each card should have an assumption (e.g. 'Technology always makes learning easier' or 'To improve performance, staff need regular positive feedback').
2. Walking the maze
   Participants walk through the maze individually or in pairs. When they encounter an assumption card, they pause and discuss or reflect silently on:
   - What type of assumption it might be
     - Paradigmatic or *how* assumptions
     - Prescriptive or *normative*
     - Causal or *this leads to that*
   - Whether they personally agree or disagree with it.
   - How this assumption might impact decision-making in their school context.
3. Sorting assumptions
   - After completing the maze, participants place their cards in the corresponding 'Paradigmatic', 'Prescriptive' or 'Causal' zones.
   - Practice leaders can prompt participants to explain why they categorized each assumption as they did.
4. Reflective walk
   - Participants take a second walk through the maze, this time reflecting on their own assumptions.
   - At designated stops (marked with guiding questions such as 'What assumptions guide your leadership style?' or 'What assumptions about student behaviour influence your decisions?'), participants write down one of their own assumptions and decide which category it fits.

5. Group discussion
Gather in a circle and discuss:

- Which assumptions were easiest to identify?
- Which were most challenging?
- How might unexamined assumptions impact leadership decisions?

Highlight the importance of questioning 'taken-for-granted' beliefs and share strategies for incorporating assumption-checking into daily practices.

Assumptions are driven by implicit bias

Assumptions may seem reasonably benign to many of us. They may be variously described as intuition or 'gut' responses. Problems arise when our assumptions are built on something more insidious. One of the critical roles of identifying assumptions is to unearth implicit bias in our individual and cultural assumptions. Implicit assumptions are described by educational researchers Floyd Beachum and Gina Gullo as '. . . the attitudes and associations made subconsciously that often do not reflect "actual or explicit, beliefs"'. In other words, leaders could believe that all students deserve to be treated fairly but still have unconscious biases based on race, sexual preference, class etc. They warn that implicit bias '. . . may result in reflex decisions that tend to favour certain populations despite explicit beliefs such as disadvantaged groups continue to receive less support than they should'.[16]

Unchecked bias can reinforce existing power structures and limit the agency of individuals in groups most likely to be affected by these biases. To address these kinds of implicit biases they need to be identified in the first place. Part of the identifying assumptions process is to recognize implicit bias exists and then explore strategies for individuals and the school to explore how they may be entrenching disadvantage.

The challenge for school leaders is to understand implicit bias that is driving assumptions and then generate consistent approaches and strategies to remove it from decision making.

The following strategies can be useful:

- Providing structured critical reflection workshops and implementing team teaching opportunities where colleagues provide constructive feedback on potential biases in teaching and interactions.
- Systematically seeking student feedback (through focus groups, surveys etc) to identify and address differences in student experiences. This would be followed up by programs to support students requiring support.

To support an understanding of each phase of the Crucible we will pose four questions for reflection (that can be considered individually or as a group). For the assumptions phase of the Crucible:

1. What core beliefs guide how I think education should be structured?
2. Are there assumptions influencing how we interpret staff or student behaviour?
3. Could any of my assumptions about what makes a 'good teacher' or 'good student' reinforce stereotypes?
4. What practical strategies can I use to uncover and rethink assumptions in decisions about staffing, discipline, or curriculum design?

The next stage of the Critical Reflection Crucible deepens and focuses reflection by asking Why this? Why so? In this phase of the Crucible we dig deeper beyond assumptions to ask deep questions about why something is happening.

Why this? Why so?

The Why this? Why so? phase of the Critical Reflection Crucible encourages school leaders to question assumptions and examine the knowledge, context and values influencing their decisions. This phase requires identifying the underlying beliefs and practices that shape school environments and questioning how power is being exercised.

For example, why has a row erupted about the best way to teach reading and writing? In other words, why this debate and why is it being held in the way it is? For instance, is there a political point being pushed or does someone stand to gain financially? In this way, Why this? Why so? can describe and disrupt assumptions. Practice 3.4 helps leadership teams explore Why this? Why so? in more depth.

Practice 3.4 Why this? Why so? in action

1. Analyse headlines
   Distribute a selection of articles, memos or reports on an educational leadership issue, such as fostering teacher collaboration or professional learning in schools. In small groups, analyse the headlines to identify:
   - The underlying assumptions or values
   - The Why this? Why so?
   - What is the 'Why this?' – the situation, priority or problem driving these headlines?
   - What is the 'Why so?' – the rationale, belief system or context shaping these perspectives?

   For example, in a conversation about teacher collaboration, the assumption might be that collaborative teams improve student outcomes, with the 'Why this?' focused on addressing achievement gaps, and the 'Why so?' tied to the belief that collective efficacy enhances teaching practices.

2. Create a storybook version of the headlines
   Using a flip chart or sheets of A3 paper, create a storybook version of the issue. This process helps to analyse and understand an educational issue by constructing a story from it. The story should simplify and clarify the story of the educational issue.

   Your story should include:

   - A title (e.g. 'The Quest for Collaborative Classrooms').
   - Characters, including key stakeholders such as school leaders, teachers, students, and possibly parents or the wider community.
   - Plot points that explore the underlying assumptions and the Why this? Why so? driving the issue.
   - A dramatic ending, such as an innovative solution, a challenge left unresolved, or a pivotal discovery.

3. Storytelling
   Each group presents their story as a dramatic reading.

   Follow the reading with a group discussion to reflect on:

   - Assumptions: What assumptions about leadership and the issue were revealed during the process?
   - Understanding: What insights about the Why this? Why so? emerged from exploring the story?
   - Actionable change: How might the discoveries about the headline and its assumptions lead to practical changes in leadership practices at the school?

Why this? Why so? as a describer and disruptor

As a describer, this phase enables a description of the issues or challenges in schools. Before we answer why *this*? We need to describe what *this* is. For example, if a school is facing challenges with teacher workload, defining and describing the challenge ensures that leadership has consensus on the scope, scale and nature of the issue before digging deeper into why. By clearly describing what *this* is, school leaders can identify the sources of workload stress before moving to questions like, 'Why are we prioritizing certain types of work?' or 'Why is the administration load being prioritized over teaching?' A clear understanding of *this* allows leaders to then consider how the issue might be disrupted.

As a disruptor, Why this? Why so? enables a deeper interrogation of assumptions. 'Why this?' challenges leaders to examine their focus: Why are we prioritizing this issue over others? Why are these stakeholders involved? Why do these priorities persist? Similarly, Why so? challenges methods and approaches: Why are we addressing issues in this way? Why do these structures exist? Why do certain voices consistently lead while others remain silent?

Why this? uncovers underlying patterns and recurring themes across situations, revealing where resources and attention flow. Why so? can reveal systemic structures, illuminating how power dynamics shape responses and which voices typically dominate discussions. This disruption and description help leaders to understand not just what is happening, but the complex web of relationships and influences that make it happen.

Why this? Why so? uncovers tensions (or 'stones' as Dewey puts it) as issues that, when examined, lead to a deeper understanding of systemic challenges. For instance, the debate over literacy and the use of synthetic phonics versus natural language learning is persistently contentions. Through critical reflection, leaders might ask why this dichotomy persists and why it is framed as a false choice rather than an integrated approach. This line of questioning includes asking, 'Why do I hold these views on literacy?' and 'Who benefits from framing the issue in this way?' These questions challenge the underlying power dynamics and assumptions that often go unnoticed in educational discussions.

By examining these assumptions and asking, Why this? Why so? leaders can move beyond superficial understandings of educational challenges. They are better equipped to make decisions that reflect a more complex understanding of knowledge, power and context. This process encourages school leaders to engage in deeper reflection, which not only disrupts entrenched and status quo thinking but can lead to creative and transformative action.

Here are some focusing questions for leaders and leadership teams to interrogate Why this? Why so? in school contexts:

1. In what ways might the power dynamics within our school, faculty, year group influence what or who we pay attention to?
2. Who benefits from narratives about what we do in our school, and how might these narratives serve to reinforce or challenge existing power dynamics?
3. How can we create a space for open dialogue among staff and the broader school community that encourages questioning of assumptions and deeper examination of the complexities surrounding educational practices?
4. What strategies can we employ to systematically review our focus?

The next phase of the Crucible refines and tests our reflections through contesting, elaborating and adapting them. In this phase the questions that emerge for Why this? Why so? are transformed into draft actions that can be contested, elaborated and adapted to the context and values of each school.

Contesting, elaborating and adapting

Figure 3.3 Brackish water found in mangrove forests generates life[17]

In his book *Sand Talk*, Tyson Yunkaporta discusses organizations that thrive on diverse and differing perspectives and not adversarial position taking. In *Sand Talk*, this is understood through an Indigenous perspective on mangrove forests as a place where knowledge and understanding come together. He uses brackish water as a metaphor to explain the mixing of different ideas. In a mangrove, brackish water is a mix of saline (salt) and fresh water that is a critical breeding ground for fish and reptiles and forms a barrier against extreme winds and seas. Tyson Yunkaporta says:

> I yarn about what I call *ngak lokath*, the brackish water found in the wet season when the freshwater floods down the rivers into the saltwater along the coast, an action that the Yolgnu[18] call *Ganma*, a phenomenon of dynamic interaction occurring when opposite forces meet in an act of new creation. It is a principle that guides the interactions of different groups and interest in society, a reflection of the natural processes of self-organizing systems.[19]

In the contesting, elaborating and adapting phase new ideas are formed sometimes as ideas come together from different places. The process of contesting, elaborating and adapting might seem messy, unattractive or 'brackish', but it is in the intermingling of perspectives that innovation can emerge for transformation. Metaphorically, the mixing of salt and fresh water gives life to possibility through the blending process, which is a process of contesting, elaborating and adapting.

The contesting, elaborating and adapting phase involves three key processes that overlap and interact:

Contesting existing understandings and 'taken for granted' assumptions allow ideas and responses to be tested. Often, schools operate under long-held beliefs that are seldom questioned, even when new evidence suggests they may no longer be effective. Standardized testing, for instance, is widely seen as the primary measure of student achievement. However, a school leader who contests this assumption might explore alternative assessment methods that provide a more comprehensive picture of student learning. A challenge could involve suggesting alternatives to standardized assessments such as portfolios, project-based assessments and teacher observations that can offer deeper insights into student progress. By fostering a culture where staff collaboratively examine traditional practices, systematically analyse evidence, and engage with diverse perspectives, leaders can develop more informed and balanced approaches to decision-making. School leaders could use the following approaches in the contesting phase:

- Encourage critical dialogue – facilitate discussions where staff and students question entrenched beliefs.
- Consider alternative approaches – trial alternative approaches that may be quite different to those that already exist.
- Engage with external perspectives – invite outside experts, consultants, or critical friends to review practices and provide fresh perspectives.

Having contested existing assumptions, the next step is to elaborate on the ideas that emerge through elaborating.

Elaborating enables school leaders to contest existing knowledge, as they begin to elaborate, refine and expand their understanding of the issues at hand. In elaborating, leaders move from challenges to building and enhancing ideas often by applying the values and context of the school to the proposition being considered. Leaders draw on the insights gained from the identifying assumptions and Why this? Why so? phases to develop more sophisticated perspectives and actions. For example, instead of choosing a false dichotomy between phonics and natural language literacy learning, leaders might take an evidence based and context sensitive approach to literacy learning across the school. School leaders could use the following approaches in the elaborating phase:

- Encourage student engagement – involve students in refining ideas, ensuring their voices and experiences are integrated.
- Promote inter-disciplinary dialogue – support conversations between different faculties or grade levels to explore diverse perspectives.
- Once ideas have been contested and elaborated they need to be adapted to the context and the values of the school.

Adapting allows school leaders to recognize that knowledge is not static nor universally applicable. Research-based strategies, policies and best practices must be thoughtfully adapted to suit the unique needs in each school. This process requires flexibility, creativity and a willingness to experiment with different approaches. For example, a leader responsible for student wellbeing may be developing a new wellbeing framework designed to promote grit. While the framework may be based on sound research, they realize that it must also account for the context. For example, in a particular context students may be facing high levels of academic pressure, social anxiety or personal challenges that require a more tailored approach. In this case, a leader could adapt the framework by collaborating with staff, students, and school counsellors to ensure that the strategies are relevant and accessible. In the adapting phase leaders can:

- Apply contextual relevance – encourage leaders to adapt and refine concepts based on the unique values, needs, and context of the school.
- Emphasize flexibility – encourage leaders to remain open-minded, recognizing that flexibility assists in changing circumstances.
- Monitor and adjust – continuously evaluate the effectiveness of adapted strategies, adjusting those strategies based on ongoing feedback.

The strategies we have discussed in contesting, elaborating and adapting can encourage growth, trust and psychological safety in school culture. They are processes that generate a culture of leadership-as-practice. By weaving these practices into the fabric of the school, leaders enable their teams to navigate uncertainty through deep reflection and creative action.

Practice 3.5 provides a hands-on exploration of this process. Contesting, elaborating and adapting necessitates a move away from a search for simple solutions and recognizes that transformation is an ongoing, rigorous and iterative process. By working together, school leaders can generate transformative action by challenging thinking, generating new ideas and developing more effective strategies for change.

In practical terms, the following approaches can enable the contesting, elaborating, and adapting phase in a school:

- Engaging in collaborative dialogue with staff, students and the wider school community to gather diverse perspectives and challenge existing assumptions.
- Conducting research to gather evidence that supports or challenges current practices.
- Visiting other schools to observe different approaches and learn from their experiences.

Practice 3.5 Contesting, elaborating and adapting (Brackish Water)

This practice is designed to engage school leaders in a structured process of contesting, elaborating, and adapting their context, inspired by Tyson Yunkaporta's brackish water metaphor. The metaphor is introduced to frame the expectations of collaborative and respectful creativity in this exercise.

Part 1. Identifying current practices

1. Divide participants into groups of three or four.
2. Ask each group to identify a current educational practice in their school that they believe could benefit from examination and potential adaptation.
3. In a group participants write on a large sheet of paper a description of a practice in schools (e.g. co-curricular programs) and its current implementation (e.g. after and before school).

Part 2. Contesting and elaborating
Using the metaphor of brackish water we featured earlier, explore how you might be able to enhance your idea.

1. Join with another group.
2. Present the chosen practice to the larger group.
3. For each practice, the group members that have just joined:
    - Stir the water (contesting): contest aspects of the practice by asking critical questions or highlighting potential issues.
    - Adding to the stream (elaborating): elaborate on the practice by suggesting refinements or enhancements based on their own experiences or knowledge.
    - Changing the stream (adapting): suggest ways to change the idea/practice based on the challenges and elaborations.

Part 3. Reflection to action
In the large group, facilitate a reflective discussion using these questions:

- How did framing this Practice through brackish water guide or change your approach to this Practice?
- What was most challenging about contesting and elaborating on your colleagues' practices?
- How was the process of adapting in response to similar or different to your usual approach?
- How might you incorporate this process of contesting, elaborating and adapting into your regular leadership practices?

Here are some questions for school leaders to use as a group or individually when exploring the contesting, elaborating and adapting phase of the Crucible:

1. Through the contesting process have we explored diverse perspectives to expand understandings of issues and opportunities?
2. Through the elaborating process what specific insights or views have we gained from the perspectives of staff and students that have helped us refine our understandings and strategies?
3. In what ways have we adapted our current practices to better fit the unique context of our school, and how have we ensured this adaptation is informed by evidence?
4. What processes have we embedded to make the contesting, elaborating and adapting phase of the crucible part of our practices?

Once our reflections have been refined through contesting, elaborating and adapting it is time to move to action in the re-solving phase of the Crucible.

Re-solving

Re-solving is the stage of the Crucible where all the contesting, elaborating and adapting produces tangible and sustainable action. The re-solving phase is like a spiral: as a spiral continuously ascends while circling a focused point, the process of re-solving enables a systematic progression of reflection, action and evaluation, always circling back to the issue or challenge while simultaneously iterating towards deeper understanding and more effective re-solutions.

In the re-solving process, leadership teams collaborate to plan and engage in transformative action. Re-solving is not a simple process. This phase of the Crucible is where school leaders translate insights gained from identifying assumptions, Why this? Why so? and contesting, elaborating and adapting into actions and strategies. Re-solving is not about quick fixes or silver bullets. Rather, at this phase, leaders use the insights from the previous phases to build sustainable strategies and actions that can flexibly respond to each school's context.

For instance, consider a school leadership team grappling with the challenge of a curriculum that is not relevant or engaging for students. This could lead to action such as reorganizing the curriculum and timetable. The aim would be to meet the needs of students identified during the identifying assumptions phase. Evidence gathered in this phase might indicate that students had a strong interest in vocational education. The timetable could then be changed to accommodate access to expanded vocational educational offerings.

In the re-solving stage, there are some critical guides for practice.

Re-solving is about action: this phase is not merely another reflective phase it must be a call to action (large or small). This moves the Crucible and critical reflection process in general from a navel-gazing exercise to an effective strategy for transformation. The actions that emerge could include restructuring leadership, creating spaces for more diverse decision making, reforming the curriculum to better suit student needs, developing more engaging reporting processes etc.

Collaboration is crucial: shared decision-making and the inclusion of diverse perspectives in the re-solving phase will ensure that transformative change does not emerge as a surprise but is understood and there is a sense of ownership of the decisions and strategy by all. This is not to say that there will be unanimous agreement but rather there is an understanding of the reasoning and evidence (inherent in the Crucible process) behind the decisions and strategies.

Reflection is ongoing: as we mentioned, the re-solving phase is like a spiral. Re-solving like the Crucible itself is not a 'one and done' solution. If reflection is to be integral time and energy needs to be invested to embed it in the culture. Practice 3.6 Crucible test drive can support the 'how' of critical reflection in schools.

Practice 3.6 Crucible test drive

This Practice is designed to apply the Critical Reflection Crucible and particularly the re-solving phase to challenges and opportunities that arise in schools. The Practice provides an opportunity for collaborative problem-solving, encouraging participants to use the Critical Reflection Crucible to implement transformative change in their schools through creative action.

1. Form teams of three or four.
2. Each team picks randomly from cards in two 'hats'. In the first 'hat' is the 'what' (e.g. curriculum, pedagogy or leadership). The first hat has the following cards:
   i. Curriculum (e.g. How might we design a more engaging and holistic curriculum?)
   ii. Pedagogy (e.g. How might we increase student engagement and motivation?)
   iii. Leadership (e.g. How might we develop a more distributed leadership model?)
   iv. Communication (e.g. How might we create a more transparent and trusting school culture?)
   v. School culture (e.g. How might we foster more respect amongst students?)
   vi. Wildcard: Teams can choose their own challenge based on a pressing issue within their school.

3. Use the second 'hat' to determine the process they will use.
   The cards in the second hat are:
   i. Identifying assumptions: What are the underlying assumptions about this challenge? What beliefs and values are shaping our current practices and policies?
   ii. 'Why this? Why so?': Question assumptions. Are they valid? Are they serving us well? What are the consequences of holding onto these assumptions? How might we generate evidence to test assumptions?
   iii. Contesting, elaborating and adapting: Explore alternative perspectives and responses. What are some different ways of thinking about this challenge? What are some promising practices from other schools or contexts outside education?
   iv. Re-solving: Teams work on resolving an issue.
      - Actionable: Strategies should be specific, measurable, achievable, relevant, and time bound.
      - Collaborative: Solutions should involve the collective wisdom and expertise of the school community.
      - Sustainable: Strategies should be designed to have a lasting impact and not simply be a quick fix.

   Whole group discussion about the following questions:
   - How did this Practice help you understand the different phases of the Critical Reflection Crucible?
   - What were some of the challenges you faced in the process you used?
   - How can you apply the skills and processes from this exercise to real-world challenges you face in leadership in your school?

Here are some questions for school leaders to use as a group or individually when exploring the re-solving phase of the Crucible.

1. In what ways are our actions and strategies grounded in the insights gained from previous phases of the Crucible, and how do we ensure that these insights translate into sustainable changes in the re-solving phase?
2. How can we evaluate the effectiveness of our actions during the re-solving phase, and what mechanisms do we have in place for ongoing evaluation and adaptation of our strategies?
3. What specific challenges have we identified that require immediate action, and how are we generating strategies to navigate them?
4. What steps can we take to avoid silver bullet solutions in our re-solving process, ensuring that the strategies we implement align with our context and values?

Concluding reflections

Critical reflection is described by social work researcher Sheila Ryan as 'interrupting practice'.[20] In many ways, critical reflection is more than an interruption it is a 'refining fire'. As we discussed in the opening of this chapter, the power of critical reflection is to provide refining heat so that leaders can expose ideas and strategies to diverse, wise and robust consideration. Once we move beyond the clichés of critical reflection, as a self-indulgence we can glimpse its power to help school leaders unearth assumptions, navigate issues, challenges and opportunities and drive transformative change.

Paradoxically, this is achieved by interrupting action and assessing why we do what we do in schools ('Why this? Why so?') and then contesting, elaborating and adapting until we have re-solved outdated practices into transformative action. The Critical Reflection Crucible provides leaders with a way to think through the complex and sometimes seemingly insoluble problems they face daily.

In these ways, critical reflection is a kind of learning for leaders. As educator Jack Mezirow argues, critical reflection is in essence learning: 'Emancipatory education is an organized effort to help the learner challenge presuppositions, explore alternative perspectives, transform old ways of understanding, and act on new perspectives'.[21]

We learn to lead through these processes inherent in critical reflection. When leaders understand the processes that underpin critical reflection, they have access to many of the tools for transformation. Here are some key actions that can embed critical reflection in schools.

In the next chapter we discuss collaboration that interacts with the other 4Cs to make transformation achievable.

Key actions

1. Develop a shared understanding of the school's direction and values through critical reflection sessions with leadership teams and staff.
2. Create regular opportunities for both individual and collaborative reflection among staff.
3. Trial the Critical Reflection Crucible process (identifying assumptions, asking 'Why this, Why so?', contesting/elaborating/adapting, and re-solving) to address key issues and opportunities in your school.
4. Use critical reflection to build coherence between the school's stated values and its day-to-day operations and decision-making.
5. Foster a culture of trust within leadership teams and staff groups to enable honest and productive critical reflection.

Leading through collaboration

4

Figure 4.1 Google's Project Aristotle provides insights into leading through collaboration

Project Aristotle

Can we create an algorithm for a perfect team? Google believed they could and instigated a research project to find the magic formula for who were the best people to make the perfect team. Google knows that teams collaborating deeply on projects are a key ingredient to their organizational success, so they spent two years studying 180 teams to find the algorithm. In the end, however, Google did not discover a formula for finding the right people. What they did find was that *how* the team worked together mattered much more than *who* was on the team. This is the first insight we need to make about leading through collaboration – *how* to collaborate is more significant than *who* is collaborating.

This chapter is about *how* to lead through collaboration, and *how* collaboration is profoundly different to people co-operating or working together. Collaboration is a process where everyone in a team is acutely invested in a shared goal or endeavour. What often passes as collaboration is not collaboration. True collaboration has the power to change people through the process of working towards and achieving something new together. Courageous leaders who want transformation in schools need to know the 'how' of true collaboration.

Another insight that emerges from Google's research was the name given to their investigation. The project was code named Project Aristotle named after the Ancient Greek thinker and the famous quote attributed to him: 'the whole is greater than the sum of its parts'. Research and history certainly support the contention that collaboration is a greater or more powerful process than working alone.[1] However, the quote is a slight misinterpretation of what Aristotle actually said.

In 350 BCE, Aristotle wrote in *Metaphysics*, 'In the case of all things which have several parts and in which the totality is not, as it were, a mere heap, but the whole is something beside the parts, there is a cause.'[2] In other words, in relation to people, individuals (as the 'parts') become a new entity (and not a 'mere heap' or collection of individuals) when they have a 'cause'. To collaborate means to have a common cause (or shared goal) that unifies people to achieve something new by working together. This matters when understanding what collaboration *really* is and *why* it is so powerful for leaders who want to transform schools.

A courageous leader wants to make a difference in their context. They can use the 4C capabilities to 'fuel' their own capacities and the conditions of the people around them to make that difference (see the Leadership Lantern in chapter 2). As one of the 4Cs, collaboration is a process that courageous leaders can introduce and develop as leadership-as-practice. Leaders who understand what collaboration is and galvanize its power, can transform people and school cultures. Knowing the skills of *how* to collaborate shapes a leader's and a team's success in achieving transformation.

Our coherence maker Collaboration Circles is a schema that explicitly describes the process and skills of *how* to collaborate. It describes how individual leaders (courageous leadership) can lead through the processes of collaboration and develop collaborative practice with their teams (leadership-as-practice). Too often collaboration is misunderstood or unproductive or viewed as too difficult. If done effectively, leading through collaboration turbocharges productivity, efficiency and innovation in schools.

Before discussing the 'how' of leading through collaboration, we consider the broader view of why collaboration is integral to transformation and building a culture of leadership and agency in schools. We use complexity theory to explain the 'big picture' strategy of how collaborations across a school can affect change. Leaders must understand their immediate context, but also be aware of the role that collaboration can have on the larger patterns and dynamics at play in schools.[3]

School leaders, regardless of their role or setting, need to balance a broad strategic vision with a clear understanding of daily realities. Strategy only becomes meaningful when they are connected to what is happening in practice in their context. Complexity theory can help leaders to connect collaboration on the ground with big picture strategies.

Complexity theory: how collaboration works towards change in schools

Complexity science explains how many parts, or 'agents' that become connected can give rise to evolutionary processes and often surprising emergent behaviours. The theory explains how change in a complex system is not created by a simple, linear cause-and-effect but instead by multiple effects and speeds that cause change. For instance, complex systems are evident in the human body, a living cell, global climate, eco-systems, financial markets, colonies of ants, transportation systems and school classrooms.

Complexity theory has been used in education to better understand why change such as reforms, improvements, innovations and transformation has or hasn't worked. To understand how change can happen in schools is to understand how evolution in a complex system works. The core components of understanding change in a complex social system are:

- Behavioural change is not defined by the nature of individual people, but by what emerges from the interaction and connections between people.
- Change is non-linear and relies on feedback loops between people to effect and shape evolutionary change.
- Many things can happen at once on multiple time scales and levels within a context.[4]

What collaboration does in a complex, social system is allow people to interact and connect and generate an internal feedback loop (communication) between its participants. Complexity theory explains how change can happen when different collaborative groups are externally connected in a non-linear way by feedback loops (see figure 4.2). Positive feedback loops are connections and relationships between people that feature communication that is transparent, inclusive and shared towards

Figure 4.2 Through complexity theory, we can understand how collaborations interact and connect and generate feedback loops to evolve change.

positive action. For example, when interested groups share expertise and learnings with each other. A negative feedback loop is communication that suppresses change and preserves the status quo. For example, when disinterested groups believe they have nothing to learn from each other.

Put simply, collaborations across a school connected by effective communication channels can have a positive ripple affect across the school affecting and transforming culture and practice. Collaborations across a school environment are instrumental to leading sustainable change. This is as long as the collaborations are purposeful, allow for iterations, learnings and emergence (see chapter 6 on creativity) and are connected by positive feedback loops (see chapter 5 on communication).

An OECD Education Working paper, 'The Simple, the Complicated, and the Complex: Educational Reform Through the Lens of Complexity Theory'[5] argues collaboration is integral to sustainable change in schools. It argues that to operationalize collaboration and a complexity approach to change in schools requires leaders to:

- Foster a collaborative working environment with opportunities (time and structures) for people to work together.
- Support ongoing collaborations and allow groups to experiment and then iterate what they are doing so they can evaluate and learn from their endeavours.
- Engage and energize team members through collaborative research and mentoring.

- Adopt a non-deficit and positive approach to change.
- Identify and address the most pressing issues (you can't do everything at once), and allow collaborating groups to address them with vigour and focus.
- Communicate the learnings of collaborating groups through interconnecting feedback loops and consider how they serve a shared goal or vision.

This is the big picture view of how leading through collaboration can allow for structures and opportunities across different groups to create and connect a wider vision for transformative practices and culture within a school. In the breakout box, Practice 4.1, the Electrical Mapping Strategy, is described for leaders to identify, explore and evaluate the collaborative opportunities and connections in their context.

Practice 4.1 The electrical mapping strategy

Figure 4.3 Electrical map[6]

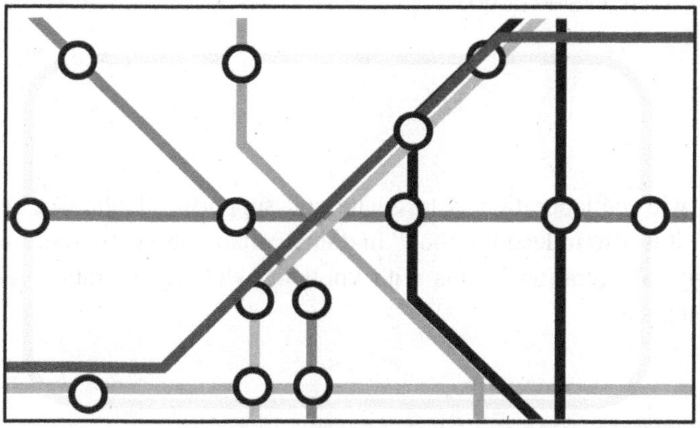

This Practice can be a group exercise for a team of leaders or undertaken by individual leaders to evaluate the collaborative structures in their context.

The 'how' of the Practice

This exercise is about mapping collaborations in a particular school or across a school, and identifying where the collaborations are and how they are networked to each other. The map is like an electrical diagram where collaborative groups are recognized and labelled, then networked by connecting lines if there are connections between those collaborations. The strength of the collaborations and the networks can be indicated as producing varying amounts of 'light or heat' according to the impact and productivity of those collaborations and the connections between them.

The 'why' of the Practice

- Evaluates how many and what type of collaborations are evident in a particular context.
- Identifies the productive impact of those collaborations and how they are networked (connected) to other collaborations in the school.
- Analyses the opportunities for collaborative structures, and whether they influence and impact each other through connections.

The 'where to next' with this Practice

Consider:

- Where and how opportunities for collaboration could be enhanced.
- How the lines (connections) between collaborations might be thickened or strengthened.
- How collaborations might be better connected by positive feedback loops (see chapter 5).
- Whether the collaborations across the school link to a shared, co-constructed vision or goal.

Leading with collaboration is to create and support collaborative structures in schools, but it is also to lead the 'how' in doing collaboration. To understand *how* to lead through collaboration begins with knowing what collaboration *really* is and what its benefits are.

What really is collaboration?

Collaboration is not simply people co-operating, sharing ideas and working together. Co-operating, sharing ideas and working together are good workplace practices, but they are not collaboration. Collaboration involves people having a shared vision, co-constructing something together and showing leadership and agency to achieve their common goal. When creativity and psychology researchers Seana Moran and Vera John-Steiner describe collaboration, we get more of an idea of what it is and why collaboration has the capacity to change people:

> Collaboration is an 'affair of the mind'. It is fundamentally different kind of interaction from the simple exchanges that occur among work acquaintances.

> Social interaction involves two or more people talking or in exchange, cooperation adds the constraint of shared purpose, and working together often provides coordination of effort. But collaboration involves an intricate blending of skills, temperaments, effort and sometimes personalities to realise a shared vision of something new and useful.[7]

Collaboration thrives on the diversity of people's individual differences because those differences bring different perspectives, expertise, resources, needs and talents together. Diversity increases team productivity as well as the quality of its outcomes. Diversity includes gender, ethnicity, career stage, personality, socioeconomic background, life experience, viewpoints, skills and how people view and solve problems.[8]

Commonalities and dissimilarities in collaboration allow for a 'representational' space for new understandings and possibilities. Research psychologist Vlad Glăveanu explains how collaboration is a fusion of individual thinking with the 'common representational space'[9] of the group's thinking. 'It is this common representational space where the group's creative dynamics take place and it is here where different thinking styles collide and by this spark the creative process.'[10]

If everyone in a collaboration communicates openly and intends to share and participate in the construction of a 'common representational space', the joint endeavour becomes a 'shared affair of the mind'. Collaboration is where team members can learn from and be influenced by each other, and this is how collaboration can change us. But that only happens when we collaborate properly or know *how* to collaborate.

For collaboration to work, everyone in the group must have agency to lead and take on the responsibility of co-constructing something together. That co-construction can be a group creating a new learning program together, experimenting with new teaching methods, implementing new work practices or re-structuring executive leadership roles etc. Leadership and learning expert Joe Raelin describes everyone truly collaborating in a group as 'leaderful practice'. He explains it this way:

> . . . think of a time when a team was humming along almost like a single unit. Working together was a joy. Each team member had a specific functional role but seemed able to implicitly to support each other when warranted. Any one of the team members could speak for the entire team. How would one characterize such a community? A common reference is that it is leader*less*, that there is no need for a leader. But it is hardly leaderless because it is not devoid of leadership, it is full of leadership; in other words, leader*ful*. Everyone is participating in the leadership of the entity both collectively and concurrently; in other words, not sequentially, but all together and at the same time.[11]

In the team Raelin describes, everyone is leading and contributing because they know how to collaborate, and they realize the benefits of leading through collaboration.

The benefits of leading through collaboration

To lead through collaboration is to know its benefits when undertaking decisions, activities, tasks or projects. The benefits for leading through collaboration are that they generate:

- *Innovation and better problem solving.* The diversity of thinking in a group allows for more ideas and better ideas. There is more 'genius' in a group to problem solve or create. Collaboration and creativity researcher Keith Sawyer explains that 'When we collaborate, creativity unfolds across people; the sparks fly faster . . . Collaboration drives creativity because innovation always emerges from a series of sparks – never a single flash of insight.'[12]
- *Personal growth through learning and development.* Sharing expertise and experience in a group expands our potential and capacities to take on further challenges. Vera John-Steiner claims, 'Through collaboration we can transcend the constraints of biology, of time, of habit, and achieve a fuller self, beyond the limitations and the talents of the isolated self'.[13]
- *Connections between 'siloes' of understanding and expertise.* Dealing with complex and multiple problems can be better problem solved by making deep connections across siloes or boundaries of discipline expertise. Management research finds that collaboration across areas of specialization has given organizations greater success with strategy, sustainability, innovation and efficiency.[14]
- *Trust, vulnerability and a sense of belonging.* These qualities are needed for collaboration to work, but the experience of collaborating (if done correctly) is the very thing that builds these dynamics in a team or school culture. In Project Aristotle, Google refers to this climate of high trust and vulnerability in collaboration as the dynamic of 'psychological safety'.[15]
- *Motivation, risk-taking and confidence.* Connecting with others towards a mutual goal multiplies energy, resources and efficacy. Spreading the risk through collaboration encourages groups to take more chances and have greater success when navigating uncertainty, ambiguity and challenge.[16]
- *Flexibility, reflection and adaptability.* These are needed for collaboration to work, but when people experience and reflect on the process of collaboration (metacognition) they can develop flexibility towards other people's needs, talents and ideas, and adapt to change.[17]

Leading through collaboration can be hugely beneficial but collaboration can be dysfunctional and unproductive. Here are some common complaints about collaboration when it is not working:

- People feel they are doing all the work because others don't contribute enough.

- Some team members do all the work without letting others participate.
- People can't say what they really think because they are thinking differently to the rest of the group.
- Team members believe they won't be listened to, or what they say will be blocked or even used against them.
- People don't feel fully committed to what the group is doing.[18]

What Google found from Project Aristotle was that productive and successful collaborations had the following characteristics:

- Psychological safety: team members feel safe to take risks and be vulnerable in front of each other.
- Dependability: team members get things done on time and meet a high bar of excellence.
- Structure and clarity: team members have clear roles, plans and goals.
- Meaning: work is personally important to team members.
- Impact: team members think their work matters and creates change.[19]

We also argue that collaboration is productive when there is clarity in 'what' and 'why' people are solving or creating together. For instance, in a school context, if an executive leadership team is leading initiatives in teaching and learning, everyone's role and goal in that initiative must be clear, the initiative must matter to them, and they must believe they can make an impact (see chapters 7 and 8 on motivation and agency). The 'why' is clear to everyone in the collaboration and there must be shared commitment, trust and high expectations towards a goal. We argue these dynamics are developed and built by learning about and experiencing the 'how' of collaboration.

How to collaborate

Collaboration is where everyone participates and leads in co-constructing something. However that is no easy thing and this is why we use schemas (coherence makers) and explicit processes to assist people in becoming more confident in the purpose, practices and skills of collaboration. Courageous leaders who lead through empowerment can use our schema Collaboration Circles (see figure 4.4) to learn and guide others to learn about how to collaborate effectively.

In our work with schools, we use Collaboration Circles to support leaders in the process of how to collaborate effectively. The coherence maker is a synthesis of what we know (in practice and research) about successful collaborations.[20] We use the metaphor of 'circles' to describe collaboration, as circles suggest connectedness, inclusion and equality. The circles of the coherence maker in figure 4.4 also suggest overlapping, recursive and iterative stages in the process of collaborating.

Figure 4.4 The coherence maker Collaboration Circles is a schema to understand the process of collaboration

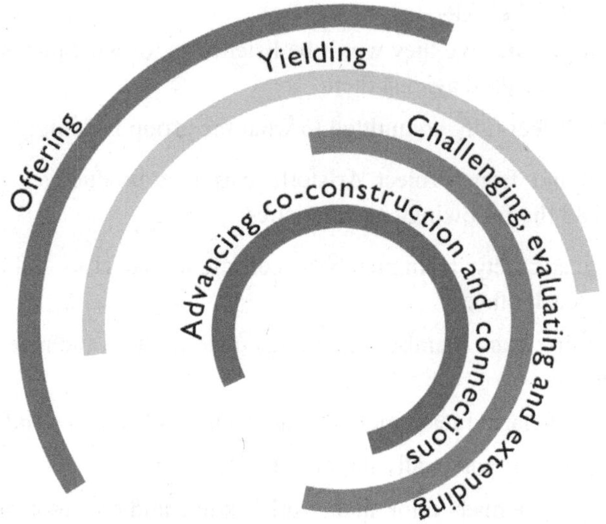

Collaboration Circles is a learning and leading tool that offers structure, intention and metacognition in the processes of how we collaborate. Collaboration Circles is a schema that can be used explicitly when leading and developing skills in collaboration, but the aspiration is that when these skills are embedded into everyday practice, they become tacit and effortless in a group's collaborative culture.

The schema for Collaboration Circles is:

- Offering
- Yielding
- Challenging, evaluating and extending
- Advancing co-constructions and connections

We discuss each part of the process in Collaboration Circles and what that means for collaborative leadership. We provide Practices to explore and learn about the processes in the coherence maker and offer reflective questions for leaders to consider about their collaborative leadership practice. We begin with the idea of 'offering' where leaders make 'space' for others to initiate ideas and actions in a team's collaboration.

Offering

Leading through collaboration means allowing all offers to be made and accepted. Leaders encourage others to offer ideas, and this may begin with an offer of how the group will organize itself, what the shared goal will be, or the first suggestion in solving a problem or generating ideas. Explicit processes can be used to focus, limit and encourage everyone to make an offer. This breaks habits of dominating team members who do all the talking and those who do little talking because they are deferential, unassertive or lack confidence.

There are a multitude of ways the process of offering can be done, such as giving everyone in a group a card or token with which they 'play' to make their offers, or everyone writing their offers on sticky notes. Everyone must make an offer, and all offers are 'on the table', but individuals are also limited to the number of offers they can firstly make. This simple process makes it clear that everyone must make an offer and in doing so, creates the beginning of shared ownership in the ideas and actions of the group.

The process of offering recognizes that everyone's ideas are worth considering, and it focuses, engages and encourages everyone in the group to initiate ideas. However, it also limits others who may habitually dominate a group with their ideas. Offering also encourages flexible and possibility thinking, that is, it reinforces that many ideas are more productive than a few (see chapter 6 on creativity). The process of offering contributes to the dynamics of collaboration by recognizing that everyone's ideas in a collaboration are equal to anyone else's. These are the first steps towards building trust in a group.

Trust, vulnerability and risk-taking are essential dynamics of an effective team. 'Offering' requires risk-taking because people are putting their ideas 'out there'. There is vulnerability in offering if people perceive negative judgement to their ideas from others. However, because everyone's ideas are equal in the offering process, offering begins to build confidence and trust in the group and taking risks with each other. Trust is contingent on people being empathic and vulnerable with each other. Without trust in collaboration, it is difficult to achieve a goal shared by everyone, and without a shared goal, trust is hard to build.

Offering is essential for establishing shared goals in collaboration (see Practice Creating a Shared Team Goal in chapter 9 for example). Leaders can develop skills to draw out and encourage offers from the group. Leading through collaboration is to support and encourage everyone to be open to making offers and being explicit about the process. Naming the process of 'offering' helps people to be self-aware of their habitual behaviours and metacognitive about how they play their role in the process of collaboration.

We describe a Practice we use for people to experience the process of offering and realizing the trust, risk-taking and vulnerability required to make collaboration effective for everyone. Practice 4.2 is an improvisatory exercise that involves giving someone a gift, and it also involves the next stage in the collaboration process, 'yielding'.

Reflection questions about offering for leaders:

- How often do habitually make the first or only offer with others?
- What do you observe from your team when you elicit offers from them?
- What happens when you use a card or token to limit the number of offers people can make?

Practice 4.2 The gift of offering and yielding

This is a group Practice but everyone simultaneously works in pairs.

Each pair will do a simple thirty-second to a minute improvisation where Person A imagines a gift for Person B but doesn't tell B what it is.

Person A mimes the imagined gift (in A's imagination it could be a candle, rhinoceros, car tyre or jazz orchestra, whatever they want it to be) and gives it to Person B by saying only, 'I have a present for you, I hope you like it'. B graciously receives the gift by saying, 'Thank you, I love it, I've always wanted a . . .' and B names whatever they imagine the gift to be, based on what they think A's non-verbal offer was. It is not a guessing game, it is about accepting and yielding positively so the improvisation can continue.

A responds to whatever B says the gift is even though it may be completely different to what they previously imagined when they offered the gift at the beginning. The dialogue between A and B continues as long as the pair can continue to improvise by offering and yielding.

Then B has a turn to begin an improvisation by offering A a gift of their imagining.

After the pairs improvise, all the participants should reflect as a group about what happens in the offering and yielding process of 'gift giving'.

The 'why' of the Practice

- Heightens awareness of not blocking offers, and the risks and vulnerability of making offers, yields and further offers and yields
- Creates an understanding of how collaborations are begun with the trust of co-constructing something with others
- Elicits the joyful and playful experience of offering and yielding (like gift giving) in collaboration

The 'where to next' with the Practice

Consider:

- Giving people in the team a small collaborative task where they explicitly use the language of offering and yielding.
- Allow people to reflect on the process of offering and yielding, and what they feel is working or not working when they a begin to collaborate.
- Use cards or tokens to encourage everyone to offer and yield in future collaborative discussions or tasks.

Yielding

Offers happen throughout the collaboration process as ideas and actions are developed and undertaken. Not everyone's offers are undertaken, but in the process of yielding, offers are developed, built on or discarded. Yielding is the accepting of offers, but it is not 'submitting' or 'conceding' to an offer. To yield provides something in response to an offer. Like a 'crops yield' it makes something productive from offers.

Yielding to other people's ideas is to connect, proceed and profit from offers. Rather than giving way, yielding is being receptive to generate something further. It is not simply saying yes to another offer, it is taking an equal share of responsibility in supporting or shaping the focus of the offer. A yield is 'yes and . . .' or 'yes but . . .' It is not blocking, shutting down or ignoring someone else's offer. Yielding links or builds your thinking to someone else's previous offer, even if it means going in a new direction.

Yielding is a responsive process that requires engagement and commitment from everyone in the group. Active listening is critical for yielding, and it is developed by repeating others' ideas, asking questions about them, and elaborating on or reasoning with what has been said or done. The interaction of offers and yields is when ideas begin to be shuffled, added to, or moved to the side as people come to a shared understanding of what they are creating or solving together.

Leading through yielding is to show respect and empathy for others by deeply listening and engaging with other's ideas. It is making an active commitment to the ideas or actions of the group. The gift practice (4.2) is an empathic and deep listening experience of yielding to someone else's ideas and building on to those ideas. Yielding continues to build trust and respectful dialogue in a group and values the contributions of everyone in a group.

Yielding is also to take responsibility for your actions by committing to the shared endeavour of the group and clarifying your role within it. Yielding is engaging with and making a commitment to the endeavour, and Practice 4.3 Committing to Actions is an example of how team members make explicit their responsibility to the team through the process of yielding.

Reflection questions about yielding for leaders:

- How do you habitually respond to other people's offers?
- How do you develop active listening in yourself and others?
- How do you encourage and support engagement and commitment in a group?

Practice 4.3 Committing to actions

The 'how' of the Practice

When collaborating a simple strategy to focus people on their commitments to action is to get everyone to write their actions on small, sticky notes. Team members then commit to their actions by naming them and placing them on a team timeline.

Throughout the collaboration, the sticky notes can be returned to by the group, and taken off the timeline when done, or moved along the timeline until they can be done.

The 'why' of the Practice

- makes visible and communicates the actions people are committed to take
- organizes the actions and their connections with other's actions on a team timeline

The 'where to next' with the Practice

Consider:

- reflecting with the group on the effect of the communicating actions on a team timeline.
- reflecting on and addressing why actions could not be undertaken by team members.

Leaders lead by acknowledging and elaborating on other people's ideas through yielding. However, this does not mean that ideas are not challenged. In fact, collaborations thrive when there is challenge, evaluation and extensions of other's ideas and actions.

Challenging, evaluating and extending

Ideas and actions in collaborations are constrained if they are not challenged, evaluated and extended. Making the processes of challenging, evaluating and extending explicit in the process of collaboration is about how respectful voices of dissent and a questioning of ideas and assumptions are necessary for a group to work effectively and achieve the best outcomes (see chapter 3 on Critical Reflection).

Challenging and evaluating are to investigate, probe and extend ideas and actions. It encourages divergent and reflective thinking which supports the team to come up with better ideas and results.

Challenging, evaluating and extending is a more sophisticated and rigorous form of offering and yielding. It is a process that explicitly recognizes and employs different people's perspectives and ideas to interrogate assumptions and biases embedded in our default thinking, ideas and actions. Shared goals are critical for collaborations but so is creating a climate where people can question, examine, rethink and expand the direction of the team's collaboration.

In groups, there is often a fear of conflict, and challenging and evaluating are mistaken as conflict. Challenging, evaluating and extending allow for robust, respectful, constructive and playful debate and questioning, always with the shared goal of the group in mind. Collaboration needs social cohesion and acceptance of everyone's ideas, but it also needs individual differences in thinking and working. This diversity is what makes collaborations so powerful.

Trust in the group is further developed when challenging and evaluating are explicitly understood as critical to collaboration. Social dynamics that can negate trust are conflict, 'agreeing to disagree' and indifference. The collaborative process focuses on shared understandings and interests, but this is not to say collaboration is without challenge and struggle. If there is a climate of trust and confidence developed in the group through the processes we describe, ideas and actions should be stimulated rather than debilitated.

Challenging in the collaborative process can create the spark for latent ideas and for opportunities to emerge. Evaluating as a reflective and analytical practice is like a mirror that provides constructive feedback to the group as ideas are developed. The following 'card game', Practice 4.4, can be used by leaders to experience and explore how to challenge, evaluate and extend with their team. By challenging and evaluating, ideas and actions are constructed and extended to their potential, which brings us to the last aspect of Collaboration Circles: advancing co-constructions and connections.

Reflection question about challenging, evaluating and extending for leaders:

- What do you observe in yourself and your team when people challenge and evaluate?
- How do you encourage and support others to constructively challenge and evaluate without conflict, defensiveness and fear?
- What processes do you use to ensure there is challenging, evaluating and extending within a team?

Practice 4.4 The card game (Challenge – Evaluate – Extend)

Figure 4.5 Assorted playing cards

The team uses this strategy when working on a collaboration together.

The 'how' of the Practice

After initial ideas have been generated through offers and yields, the team explicitly challenges, evaluates and extends using three deck cards that represent these aspects of Collaboration Circles. The cards are used in the following way:

- Hearts represent challenge, as 'you have a courageous heart to challenge'.
- Spades represent evaluation, as 'you evaluate by calling a spade a spade'.
- Diamonds represent extension, as 'you extend ideas by refining and polishing the diamonds', or you 'may find a diamond in the rough'.
- Club cards may be added as well if needed. They represent offers and yields, as 'offering and yielding is to be part of the club'.

Team members play their heart, spade and diamond cards at an appropriate time to discuss the ideas and actions generated by the group. They can only play their three cards once, and only speak to what the cards represent, that is, 'My challenge is . . . My evaluation is . . . My extension is . . .' Once they have used all their cards, they cannot speak until everyone has played their cards. The discussion can continue 'normally' after all the cards are played.

The 'why' of the Practice

- Encourages team members to be metacognitive about the role of challenging, evaluating and extending.
- Rigorously deepens the ideas and actions being generated by the group.
- Develops trust and confidence in the group to challenge, evaluate and extend.

The 'where to next' with the Practice

Consider:

- Reflecting with the team on what happens to the ideas during this process
- Reflecting with the team on the effect on individuals and the group when challenging, evaluating and extending with the cards
- Asking what people see as their strengths and yet-to-be-strengths in the processes of challenging, evaluating and extending

Advancing co-construction and connections

Collaboration is more than co-operating or working together. It specifically involves a group of people co-constructing and connecting something. Collaborative co-constructions happen in a sports team, music ensembles, team teaching in a classroom or leadership teams in schools. Co-construction means everyone should have a sense of joint ownership of what has been created from the collaboration. This is why the group having clear, shared goals and roles is integral to collaboration.

To identify with the co-construction through shared ownership is a powerful motivator for people. The mutual sense of purpose and social cohesion that is generated by collaboration encourages intrinsic and autonomous extrinsic motivation, and a sense of agency to achieve (see chapters 7 and 8 on joy, motivation and agency). In Google's research into the essential dynamics for team effectiveness, they describe ownership in collaboration as 'meaning' and team members 'finding a sense of purpose in the work'.

Advancing co-construction and connections clarifies collaboration as not just an agreed goal and product, but an experience and achievement that develops or influences future collaborations and connections. This refers to people's connection with each other in the collaboration and to further ideas, actions and relationships beyond their collaboration. Apart from a result or outcome, collaboration can achieve social cohesion and a sense of group identity, as well as a sense of purpose and confidence in the individuals and in the team.

If collaborations in a school are connected by positive feedback loops, as explained by complexity theory earlier in the chapter, the outcomes or co-constructions of groups can advance or influence each other as a ripple effect throughout a school. The experience of advancing co-constructions and connections (and all the stages of Collaboration Circles) can be explored through Practice 4.5 Advancing Lazy Susan.

Reflection questions about advancing and co-constructions and connections for leaders:

- How do you know everyone feels connected to co-constructed ideas and actions when collaborating?
- How do you keep growing and connecting everyone's learnings and achievements from collaboration?
- How can groups continue to influence each other through collaboration, and affect your context and culture?

Practice 4.5 Advancing Lazy Susan

This strategy is an experience in using all aspects of Collaboration Circles and demonstrates how ideas and actions can be advanced by being developed, connected and shared. The team may be responding to a problem or generating ideas.

The team sits around a table and passes on large pieces of paper that have the four stages of the coherence maker around the four sides. Everyone begins with a piece of paper and writes down their offer. They then pass the piece of paper on (like a 'lazy Susan' on a restaurant table), and yield to the previous person's offer with a 'Yes and . . .'. They pass on again and challenge, evaluate or extend on the previous offers and yields they receive by writing 'My challenge is . . .', 'My evaluation is . . .' or 'My extension is . . .'. They then pass on to advance co-constructions and connections from all the ideas made across the group. This process can continue to cycle around the table, with further ideas and connections being made.

When finished, people can look at their original offers and discuss the connections advanced through the 'lazy Susan' process of sharing ideas.

The 'why' of the Practice

- Metacognitively understand and experience advancing co-constructions and connections in the process of collaborating.

- Recognize the diversity and divergence of ideas in a group that can be shared in collaboration.
- Experience the non-linear and lateral way ideas and actions can be developed and connected in a group.

The 'where to next' with the Practice

Consider:

- Discussing with the group how the 'lazy Susan' strategy may illuminate but also limit the process of collaboration, and why.
- Reflecting on how collaborations advance ideas and actions and connect people.
- How you might use Collaboration Circles to be used more seamlessly in on-going practice.

In summary, leading through collaboration involves encouraging, supporting and developing others:

- *to offer* – to initiate and communicate ideas or actions towards a shared goal
- *to yield* – to generate further ideas and actions with the group
- *to challenge, evaluate and extend* – to probe, analyse and promote new perspectives and feedback to generate and deepen ideas and actions.
- *to advance co-constructions and connections* – to take joint ownership of a shared process and continue to harness the collective genius of groups.

Concluding reflections

The metalanguage and processes of the coherence maker Collaboration Circles can be developed and embedded by courageous leaders. Collaboration as a leadership practice can influence the 'sayings, doings and relatings' of a school culture. Leading through collaboration is powerful for courageous leaders because it empowers others. When Aristotle said, 'the whole is something beside the parts, there is a cause', the 'cause' in schools is the empowerment of others to make learning, teaching and leading effective, satisfying and joyful. The 'totality' that Aristotle refers to is the combined power of motivated people in collaboration with each other.

Early twentieth century organizational theory and behaviour pioneer Mary Parker Follett was ahead of her time when she advocated for collaborative leadership practice that involved 'power-with' rather than 'power-over' people. She wrote at a time when authoritarian regimes were in the ascendency across the world, and when Frederick Taylor's 'science of management theory' (the hierarchical, 'one way of doing things', factory-like efficiency approach) had enormous influence in organizations and schools.

Mary Parker Follett saw 'power-with' as 'genuine power' that through collaboration enables people, and 'power-over' as 'pseudo power' which stifles them.[21] The process of collaboration empowers people with agency through the sharing of leadership, which Follett describes as 'coactive power'. She argues that a leader's responsibility is to garner all available forces so that power is exercised within and by a team. Follett writes, 'Our task is not to learn where to place power; it is how to develop power . . . Genuine power can only be grown, it will slip from every arbitrary hand that grasps it; for genuine power is not coercive control, but coactive control. Coercive power is the curse of the universe; coactive power, the enrichment and advancement of every human soul.'[22]

Leading through collaboration is about everyone developing agency for coactive power so that schools are enriched and advanced through collective action. A school's organizational culture and capacity for evolution and transformation is influenced by collaborations if they are connected by positive communication feedback loops and a shared vision.

The next chapter explores how communication supports leadership for school transformation.

Key actions

1. How would you introduce Collaboration Circles and continue to use it as a collaborative tool?
2. Where might you place the schema to remind you to use it regularly to embed it into your practice?
3. What practices could you use in your context to develop skills and habits in collaboration?
4. How do collaborations across your context connect and advance a shared vision or goal?

Leading through communication

5

Figure 5.1 The Sydney Opera House celebrates Indigenous Australians' artwork through the projection of songlines onto its sails[1]

Songlines and dreamings

What are the stories that shape the culture in the country in which you live, and how are they told? Are your stories told in songs, family stories, cinema, social media, books, television, photographs, sport or something else? A place that tells stories in Australia is the Sydney Opera House. It tells stories through music, theatre, opera and dance, and sometimes through the images that are projected on its impressive sail-like roof. The projected images often reflect the national stories that Australians tell of themselves.

In 2016, the Vivid light festival lit up the Opera House by celebrating the artwork of Indigenous Australians through the projections of 'dreaming stories' or 'songlines' (see figure 5.1). We begin with a description of Australian Aboriginal songlines as they resonate with us[2] as authentic and profound communication that creates knowledge and culture. Songlines provide insights into leading with communication that is sustaining, empowering and connected by feedback loops of emergent knowledge.

As the longest living culture, Australia's Aboriginal people have been telling stories for thousands of years. Their songlines are continuing, complex narratives told about country and culture through song, dance and art. Indigenous knowledge researcher Margo Neale (from the Kulin nation and Gumbayngirr clan) and science educator Lynne Kelly write about Indigenous ways of knowing in *Songlines: The Power and the Promise* and explain how songlines communicate cultural knowledge of Country and the Dreaming.

> Everything starts and ends with Country in the Aboriginal worldview. Yet there are no endings in this worldview, nor are there any beginnings . . . Everything is part of a continuum, and endless flow of life and ideas emanating from Country, which some refer to as the Dreaming.
>
> In the Dreaming, as in Country, there is no separation between the animate and the inanimate. Everything is living – people, animals, plants, earth, water and air . . .
>
> Songlines related to Dreaming or Dreaming tracks, connect sites of knowledge embodied in the features of the land. It is along these routes that people travelled to learn from Country.
>
> Country holds information, innovations, stories and secrets – from medicine, engineering, ecology and astronomy to social mores or how to live . . . It is the wellspring from which all knowledge originates and give rise to the expression 'Our history is written in the land'.[3]

In Aboriginal culture, the songline cycles (or spirals) are passed on across different Countries in Australia by people who may specialize in certain parts of the

Figure 5.2 Aboriginal songlines in Australia embody knowledge of Country and culture

story for their Country. The songlines describe customs, obligations, stages of knowledge, ceremonies and history so people can 'navigate' Country and live their lives. As the stories are passed on to neighbouring peoples and Countries across Australia, the story changes, and the next 'chapters' are told. Songlines crisscross and weave across the country, acknowledging the connections and differences in cultural knowledge. According to the Indigenous Gay'wu group of women, Yolngu elders from far north Australia, songlines are infinite in their knowledge and learning:

> They spiral, connecting and remaking. They twist and turn, they move and loop. This is like all our songs. Our songs are not a straight line. They do not move in one direction through time and space. They are a map we follow through Country as they connect to other clans. Everything is connected, layered with beauty. Each time we sing our song spirals we learn more, go deeper, spiral in and spiral out . . .[4]

We use Aboriginal songlines to illustrate that leading through communication:

- enables an interaction and joint 'story' of learning between people
- empowers others by making coherence of context and culture
- generates authentic connections, feedback and actions
- is multimodal and embodied

The type of communication we discuss, is a capability that empowers individual leaders and their teams to generate 'stories', action and agency together.

This chapter is about how communication and storytelling in leadership practice is vital to creating, sharing and motivating people towards a collective vision and culture for transformation in schools. In the Leadership Lantern (see chapter 2), transformative leadership depends on communication as a 4C capability that generates agency in courageous leaders and co-agency in the social conditions of leadership-as-practice. We explore the significance of leading through storytelling and use complexity theory to explain how feedback loops communicate and create knowledge in a school's eco-system.

Communication through storytelling and feedback loops are integral to galvanizing people's values and emergent knowledge in a school's culture. *How* leaders do this in practice will be explained through our coherence maker, the Communication Crystal. The Crystal describes the skills and social processes leaders can harness for effective and agentic communication. To begin we define our understanding of communication and the significance of leading through stories.

The significance of leading through stories

Our definition of communication is based on a critical constructivist approach[5] which explains communication as continually shaping our 'reality' of the world and our experiences in it. Communication combines our individual internal psychology with the external social environment and thereby creates human culture and knowledge. Communication theorist Milton N. Campos explains:

> Communication should be understood as a transversal discipline that crosses all others because it is both psychological and social and because it accounts for necessary and particular contingent knowledge. Communication is the foundation of all scientific disciplines and all forms of human expression (e.g. art, common sense codes) because it is simultaneously a condition and result of all possible human knowledge.[6]

Communication is fundamental to both understanding and generating knowledge, and often humans do this through storytelling. Communication is more than just storytelling; it is interpretation, analysis, data gathering, evaluation, discussions, statistics, reports, observations, research, inquiries etc. All these forms of communication are critical tools for leaders to create knowledge to transform schools. However, we can learn from Indigenous peoples that storytelling, even in the oral form, is critical to creating and sustaining culture.

Storytelling creates a narrative that makes meaning and coherence of ideas and shared experiences in a cultural context. Stories have been doing this for humans throughout time. Stories create structure, order and meaning of often complex ideas, experiences and undertakings. Stories with their sense making structures (beginnings, middles, ends, and to be continued) and their elements of engagement (tension, characters, mood etc.) make sense of complexity in the world. Rather than being reductionist and simplifying ideas, stories help us to understand, remember and explore ideas and actions. This was explained by cultural anthropologist Mary Catherine Bateson when she said, 'The human species thinks in metaphors and learns through stories.'[7]

Storytelling is constantly upheld by management and psychology experts as integral to successful leadership communication. Howard Gardner in *Leading Minds: An Anatomy of Leadership* argues, 'It is important for leaders to know their stories; to get them straight; communicate them effectively, particularly to those who are in the thrall of rival stories; and above all, to embody in their lives the stories that they tell.'[8] Gardner views leadership as a process that occurs within the minds of individuals who live in a culture, and that creating, understanding and evaluating stories is integral to the process of leadership. The stories that become predominant in a culture are the ones that are timely and create a sense of identity for the people who live within that community or institution.

Creating an overarching narrative in school transformation is crucial for leaders supporting others to understand and share values, and to develop new ways of 'seeing, doing and relating'.[9] Stories help us to learn and change, and they create our identity and how we see how ourselves in our cultural context. Gardner explains the role of storytelling for leaders and their 'followers' (which he also describes as 'collaborators') in this way:

> We deliberately use the terms *story* and *narrative* rather than *message* or *theme*. In speaking of stories, we want to call attention to the fact that leaders present a *dynamic* perspective to their followers; not just a headline or snapshot, but a drama that unfolds over time, in which they – leaders and followers – are the principal characters and heroes. Together, they have embarked on a journey in pursuit of certain goals, and along the way and into the future, they can expect to encounter certain obstacles or resistances that must be overcome. Leaders and audiences traffic in many stories, but the most basic story has to do with issues of *identity*. And so it is the leader who succeeds in conveying a new version of a given group's story who is likely to be effective.[10]

Storytelling in leadership practice, however, should be authentic, truthful and transparent, or as Gardner says, leaders must embody the stories they tell. If leaders don't lead by example or 'walk the talk', their stories are illusionary or vacuous. Truth, ethics, wisdom and action should inform the stories of leaders, and critically these stories should include and empower others if communication is to build action with agency. Like the songlines we began with, leading through communication isn't one directional communication, it is about enabling interactions and connections that create a shared 'story' between people. Leading through communication is to empower others by making coherence of the context and culture through shared understanding and sense making.

The power of communication and storytelling is that there are many modes that can be used to engage and interact with people. For example, one school we work with in a professional learning partnership created their on-going story through a web-based video channel called 4C TV. Every few weeks at this primary school, students and staff created videos about new approaches and ideas they were experiencing in the classroom. Over time, these videos built a narrative of their shared culture. In another example, a high school we partner with had students with community artists create murals around the school exploring their shared identity and new educational ideas. Leaders can consider the Practice 5.1, Building the Story, to explore how they could use storytelling to frame a narrative with others that creates and sustains transformative action and agency.

Practice 5.1 Building the story (school narratives and metaphors)

This is a process that begins by reflecting on the stories already told in a school and considering how they could be enhanced, reversed or amplified.

The 'how' of the Practice

Ask everyone in the team to think about two examples (one positive and one negative) of part of the school's story. Everyone then finds or draws an object that may be a metaphor for their story. For example, if the school story is that sport is strong but the arts less so, the object may be a big branch and a small branch from a tree. Individual team members then tell their school stories using their object or drawing. In our example, the long branch could tell a story that sport has had a long history at the school but overshadows the newer story of arts learning symbolized by the small branch. The question raised is how the arts at the school can be as equally important as sport in the school's storytelling. How can both stories be told to change the overemphasize on sports learning at the school?

After hearing all the stories, the team discuss:

- what they notice about the stories
- what the similarities and differences are
- who are in the stories
- how the objects or drawings affect the storytelling

The 'why' of the Practice

- Reflects on the stories of the school, what they tell and who is in the stories.
- Begins an awareness and analysis of how much the stories are *shared* across the school.
- Explores the power of storytelling and the effect of metaphor in messaging.

The 'where to next' with the Practice

Consider:

- What stories need to be told, and why?
- How can the stories be shared?
- Who should be telling the stories of the school?
- What embodied and multimodal ways could the stories be told?

The interacting of stories across a school can create a cultural narrative. The stories should be authentic and constantly reframed and retold to reflect the dynamic of change and transformation happening over time. The stories of change and emergent knowledge usually occur in different areas of a school, and these stories can also connect and enrich other parts of the school. We use complexity theory to understand how communication can be effective in networking stories and knowledge across a school through feedback loops.

The dynamics of authentic connections and feedback loops

What we can learn from Indigenous songlines is that communication *is* knowledge. And knowledge can grow and expand as it is woven in and out, and fed back and forth, with other knowledge through communication. Complexity theory explains how knowledge can emerge and evolve from collaborative groups interconnected by feedback loops[11] (see chapter 4).

Interconnecting feedback loops depend on effective communication processes. *How* this communication happens and is connected is critical for leaders who want new knowledge to emerge and evolve in their school. If key groups of teachers are working on innovations and improvements across a school, they can influence each other by being connected by 'positive' or 'amplifying' feedback loops.

Positive feedback loops are characterized by communication that is regular or timely, and engaged with authentically and genuinely. Like the songlines, feedback loops should spiral in and out, deepening, expanding and strengthening knowledge being passed back and forth between people, and within people. 'Negative' or 'regulatory' feedback loops maintain stability by monitoring what people are doing and are about keeping people on a predetermined path.

In essence, a positive feedback loop of communication is when people want to know what others are doing, so they can support, learn from and challenge them. Feedback loops like these should be features of classrooms that have dynamic (that is, interactive and effective) learning feedback between teachers and students. A negative feedback loop is communication when people are disinterested, don't believe they can support or learn from others, or are happy to continue and maintain the status quo. The dynamism of positive feedback loops is communication that continues to expand knowledge and innovation in schools.

Margaret Wheatley is a researcher and management consultant who uses recent discoveries in the sciences (such as biology, quantum physics, chaos theory, neuroscience) to inform organizational leadership practice. She describes how positive feedback loops can amplify and circulate knowledge, and shape an organization to be self-organizing, adaptive and resilient. Wheatley argues communication as feedback loops should encourage and contribute to the genesis of ideas, not manage and control them. On communication, knowledge and feedback loops she says:

> The literature on organizational innovation, creativity, and knowledge management is rich in lessons . . . not surprisingly, they describe processes that also characterize the natural universe. Innovation is fostered by information gathered from new connections; from insights gained by journeys into other disciplines or places; from active, collegial networks and fluid, open boundaries. Knowledge grows inside relationships, from ongoing circles of exchange where information is not just accumulated by individuals, but is willingly shared. Information-rich, ambiguous environments are the source of surprising new births.[12]

When communication feedback loops are combined with processes from the other Cs, creativity, critical reflection and collaboration, they become authentic and richer learnings and feedback for the people involved. We will give two examples of 4C 'infused' feedback loops, one is a 'macro' example of groups across a school feeding back to each other, the other is a 'micro' view of feedback looping between individuals.

The macro example is leadership with teachers across a school creating and collaborating on a transdisciplinary study of something complex like climate change. The transdisciplinary team are devising an integrated area of learning, and they are also problem solving how they can address issues of climate change in their school context. By using and learning about a range of disciplines they are connecting and flowing different ideas and skills back and forth between each other using creativity and collaboration to expand their knowledge.

The micro example of a 'flowing' feedback loop is leaders giving 'performance feedback'. This is an example of communication as a feedback loop being enhanced by critical reflection. If performance feedback begins with a leader asking a reflective question to a teacher (rather than launching straight into feedback), then the discussion begins with the teacher's self-reflection. That self-reflection is already creating internal feedback in the teacher but also feedback for the leader and what they should ask next to continue the flow of self-reflection in the teacher. The leader is also reflecting on the teacher's responses which informs the performance feedback they give.

The following Practice 5.2, 4C Feedback Loop Infusions allows leaders to examine how they may infuse and enrich connections across the school through communication that involves collaboration, creativity and/or critical reflection.

Practice 5.2 4C Feedback loop infusions

Consider an area in the school you are responsible for (e.g. performance reviews, professional learning, curriculum development, student well-being, faculty or learning stage teams etc.) and frame it as a feedback loop. Explore how the interactions could be infused with creativity, collaboration or critical reflection to make the feedback loop more dynamic, connective and self-perpetuating.

For example, how could performance reviews be more collaborative and critically reflective? How could well-being meetings be more creative and collaborative etc.?

In the macro or big picture view of transformation, a systems thinking 'knowledge-to-action' approach[13] (turning knowledge into action) that uses complexity theory explains how leading through communication can play a key role to support and

Figure 5.3 The Communication Crystal

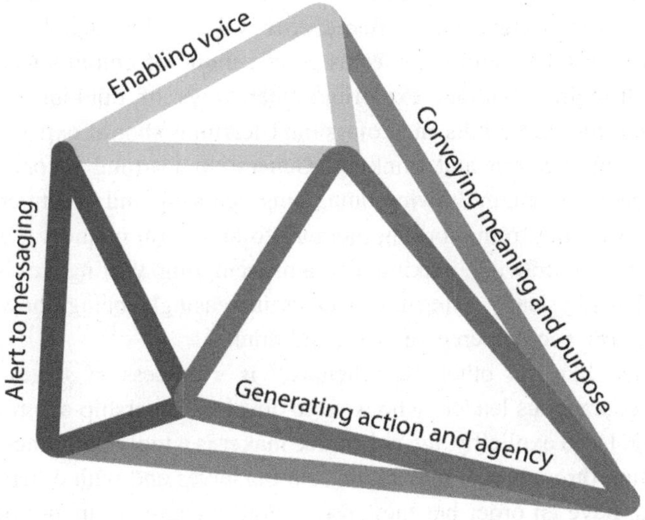

stimulate change in schools. Across a school, leadership can collaborate and create non-linear processes and feedback loops of communication that connect:

- Strategic and effective interventions across multiple sites
- People's capacity and readiness with those initiatives
- Teams with leadership through collaborative support
- Strategies that catalyse, co-ordinate and support change

Communication is the 'web' that connects the complexity of change in schools, and it is the *how* of communication that strengthens the web of those connections. We will now discuss our Communication Crystal coherence maker as a tool to support leadership to understand and develop capacities and practices to lead though communication.

The Communication Crystal

Often, we introduce the Crystal (see figure 5.3) in schools by asking why communication may be likened to a crystal and get groups to express their ideas through a tableau (a frozen image using their bodies). The ideas leaders and teachers explore are that communication can be multifaceted, multidirectional and multimodal. Communication can reflect and refract ideas, it should be transparent, enlightening, clear and coherent, structured and purposeful with a 'point', it can be simple but complex etc.

By presenting their thoughts through collaborative group tableaus they illustrate how communication can be multimodal and embodied. They also realize how using metaphor allows for different and often deeper ways of thinking. Too often school leaders limit themselves and their teams to one mode of communication (usually talking and listening) without exploring other ways of thinking.[14] Students in classroom learning and adults in professional learning should experience varying modes of communication and thinking. Generative learning theory shows how strategies such as mapping, drawing, imagining, teaching and enactment contribute to processing learning from working memory to long-term memory.[15] Embodiment (such as enactment, drawing, making diagrams, sculpting, writing etc) is rarely used with adults but physically using the body is increasingly being shown to have a major role in how people perceive, learn and think.[16]

The Crystal, like our other 4C schemas,[17] is a process of stages that can be practised by courageous leaders who want to develop leadership-as-practice in their school setting. Used explicitly, the coherence maker is a tool that frames how we can develop leading through communication – in ourselves and with others. The stages of the Crystal have an order but they also 'spiral' recursively in and out with each other in practice. The Communication Crystal comprises:

- Alert to messaging
- Enabling voice
- Conveying meaning and purpose
- Generating action and agency

The communication described by the Crystal is essentially about leaders enabling or empowering action and agency, rather than commanding and controlling. As a seemingly 'simple' scaffold the Crystal coheres the complexity of communication. The Crystal begins with 'alert to messaging' and this is the first step towards generating action and agency.

Alert to messaging

Alert to messaging is having a heightened awareness of the messaging we and others create. Rather than just being aware of sending and receiving messages, the 'alert' in alert to messaging is an elevated and reflexive internal state of being. Reflexivity is to see ourselves critically and being mindful of what and how we (and others) say and do things.

Alert to messaging is being aware of how we and others communicate verbally and non-verbally – what we and others say, what tone is used, facial expressions, body language, proximity to other people, how emails and texts are expressed, how technology is used, what behaviour is being expressed, how we use pictures, what words we use etc. It is about being actively and metacognitively aware of how messaging affects others, and what we can do about it.

Being alert to messaging is a complex thing to do but with practice we can learn to notice more about ourselves and others when we communicate. Deeply noticing communication often requires making the 'familiar strange', and this means disrupting the patterns and dynamics of communication that have become normalized or habitually ingrained in our practice

For example, in a team discussion you may be working on your laptop and say, 'I'm still listening'. You may well be listening, however the speaker in the discussion will communicate better if you as the listener are more attentive by using eye contact, nods and questions. Working on the laptop also messages to the speaker and to others in the discussion that whatever you are doing is more important than what the speaker is saying.

Another example of being alert to messaging is noticing the communication patterns in team discussions. You may realize that you always begin team discussions and with that awareness you may wonder if it is a habitual pattern that you and your team have established. You may ask yourself, what does this ritualized behaviour mean about the dynamics and habits of the group? Why do I always begin discussions? Should others start the discussions? Why do I always lead? How can I empower others to lead?

To lead through communication that empowers others begins with introducing some simple discussion processes that develop you and your team to be more alert to messaging. You can:

- Encourage people to face each other to improve communication across the group.
- Use eyes and attentive and empathic listening skills (nods, elaborating, questioning, writing down thoughts etc) to support the person speaking, especially when online.
- Sit in a circle if you want to create a sense of community and equality.
- Only use tables if they are needed during the discussion as they don't allow for flexibility to different discussion configurations (e.g. pairs, threes).
- Introduce ways in which everyone has an opportunity and responsibility to contribute.

In whatever form of communication – listening, emailing, reading, using social media, giving an instruction, taking a photo etc, being alert to messaging is about 'noticing' (see Practice 6.3 in chapter 6 on creativity). When leaders and teams develop a deeper awareness of their messaging, the communication between them can become more complex.

Leaders and teams who are practised in complex communication have deeper and more rigorous discussions and are better at collaborating, and more creative and critically reflective (the other Cs).[18] Communication studies researcher Abran J. Salazar describes what a group with complex communication may look like:

> Whenever we see group members changing their interaction patterns, whether by changing the frequency and directional flow of communication, using new procedures to solve problems or make decisions, displaying little or no discussion typical of group member roles, or questioning or supplanting assumptions about what counts as good or bad information, the group is showing evidence of operating in a complex state.[19]

As a leader, you may wonder whether your team's communication is complex, and consider: how often does everyone contribute in the team? Do they always see things the same way? Do they always make the same assumptions? Do the discussions feel predetermined? Do I need to disrupt the patterns of our communication and how we do things?

Practice 5.3, the Bus Stop that we describe in the breakout box may be a way of disrupting established patterns and ruts in the group dynamics of communication. The Practice is an example of being both 'alert to messaging' and the next step of the Communication Crystal, 'enabling voice'.

Practice 5.3 Bus stop practice

The 'how' of the Practice

The team is asked a complex question to respond to and discuss it in pairs or just think individually. Then a few people (depending on numbers) nominate themselves to respond to the question based on their pair or individual thinking. They stand up as if they are standing at a bus stop. Those standing respond to the question in any spontaneous order. The rules of the bus stop are that:

- You can only speak once.
- You can speak at any time.
- You must allow others to speak.
- You cannot repeat anything already said as your idea must be new or an elaboration of something already said.

When you have spoken, you sit down, you are on the bus.

The 'why' of the Practice

- When to speak requires being alert to the messaging of others.
- Not repeating and having to add on to ideas requires deep listening and possibly thinking differently.
- Voices not normally heard are enabled as others are alert to messaging and allow everyone an opportunity to contribute.
- Encourages a deeper and more rigorous discussion.

The 'where to next' with the Practice

Consider:

- Reflecting on the Practice and how the constraint of the bus stop process heightens people's awareness of being alert to messaging.
- How the Practice can be used to enable different voices in discussions.
- When you would use a bus stop and for what purpose.

Enabling voice

Enabling voice is leading by creating the conditions that allows people to express their thinking, and to be open to receive others' thinking. 'Having a voice' and respecting other voices is critical to creating self-confidence and self-identity, complex thinking, and building trust and empathy in others.[20] By voice we don't just mean when we speak, voice refers to who we are and how we express ourselves through whatever mode of communication.

Having opportunities to express our thinking affects how we perceive ourselves and develops confidence and complexity in our ideas. Enabling and developing people's confidence and self-belief through communication is critical for leaders who wish to develop the potential of the people around them. Agency and collaboration in a team can only be realized through communication strategies that encourage all voices to be enabled. However, to do that we need to examine what factors constrain voices to be heard.

One constraint to enabling voice is often time pressure, that is, there's not enough time to hear from everyone. Rather than just always having a group discussion when a few people can speak in the time available, leaders could consider productive strategies that enable all voices. This may be getting people to share in a pair or smaller group first and then feeding back their ideas to the larger group (known as a jigsaw practice). Or leaders and teams may use a practice like brainstorming with sticky notes and then organize and categorize the ideas for further discussion.

Another constraint to enabling all voices can be the ritualized patterns in communication. This may be the same person leading the discussion, or someone who always has the final word, or another who always waits to be asked to contribute. These habits can be disrupted by using new communication strategies. Practices already described such as jigsaw, bus stop and tableau can disrupt communication patterns and create more inclusive and more complex interactions. Other examples are working online for a group brainstorm or using tokens and cards to limit and encourage people to speak (see Chapter 4 on collaboration).

Fear of contributing and fear of judgement can be as much a problem to ritualized patterns of communication as voices that continually dominate. Encouraging people and developing their confidence to contribute can be scaffolded over time through processes like bus stop, or 5.4 the Practice Donut Conversations described in the next breakout box.

Practice 5.4 Donut Conversations

This Practice is for at least six people.

The 'how' of the Practice

Sit everyone in two concentric circles, people facing each other in pairs. Construct a set of questions that will deepen people's thinking on a particular issue. Ask the first question and let pairs discuss their ideas for an appropriate amount of time. You can stipulate 'protected time' if necessary, which is when each person has a set amount of time to express their thoughts. Move people in one of the circles so different pairs are constructed and ask the same question or the second question and let the new pairs discuss. Move the circle again and ask another question for a new combination of pairs to discuss. After all the questions have been asked, have a plenary discussion by nominating people to report back what has been discussed in response to the issue. The ideas reported back can be the 'sprinkles or icing on the donut'.

The 'why' of the Practice

- Promotes intimate one on one exchanges that allows less guarded and performative responses.
- Enables everyone to voice their ideas in a more personal way.
- Allows for different perspectives and how ideas can be synthesized.

The 'where to next' with the Practice

Consider:

- Reflect on how this communication process is different to an open plenary discussion.
- Evaluate how productive the donut Practice is as a discussion process.
- Consider how donut discussions may be appropriate for critical reflection.

Just as we can be constrained by ritualized communication patterns, we can also be constrained by the habits of our thinking patterns. More complex communication processes are critical if you wish to develop creativity and thinking laterally to solve problems in a team. Communication strategies can be deliberately used to break away from our usual, habitual ways of thinking and open new perspectives. For example, you might create a drawing to make your thinking visible in a fresh, more visual form. You could find an image and use it as a metaphor to represent a complex idea, helping others to see it in a new light. Alternatively, you might take part in a role play to experiment with different ways of responding to a situation, allowing you to explore ideas and emotions from another person's point of view. How we message affects the ways we think, and exploring news ways of enabling voice develops greater complexity in our thinking.

Enabling voice can only be achieved with new communication strategies if the processes themselves are reflected upon. Leaders and teams should reflect on how new strategies affect the patterns and dynamics of their communication. Reflective processes are communication feedback loops that allow leaders and teams to be metacognitive and aware of how processes are affecting the dynamics of their communication.

Practices for communication should be fit for purpose and not just randomly used. The Practice a leader or team uses should be appropriate to the desired outcome of the communication. For instance, a brainstorm gathers everyone's ideas, a tableau can put ideas into the body, a bus stop may be used to encourage less heard voices, a jigsaw harvests and distils everyone's ideas, a donut allows for a more intimate discussion etc. A communication process is precise and focused when the 'why' of a Practice is linked to the 'how'.

As with all the stages in the Communication Crystal, leading by enabling voice takes time, practice and on-going reflective feedback loops with teams to build trust and confidence in the value and worth of everyone's voices being enabled. Practice 5.5 Meccano Connections in the breakout box is an example how voices can be enabled and connected in a discussion. Meccano Connections also illustrates the next step in the Communication Crystal, 'conveying meaning and purpose'.

Practice 5.5 Meccano connections

The Meccano Connection process illustrates how teams can develop and sharpen the meaning and purpose of their messaging towards shared understanding. In the process, people have a visual way of displaying the intent and meaning of their ideas by connecting their thinking to others.

The 'how' of the Practice

This Practice is named after the children's toy which uses small nuts and bolts to build metal structures. Like the nuts and bolts, Meccano as a communication Practice is about the connections between people's ideas. Connections are shown in a visual way, such as physically expressed by people using their proximity to each other, or making connections using pictures or ideas on sticky notes etc.

In response to a complex question, reflection or issue, a person begins with their idea or response, and then others build around that idea by making connections.

Each time an idea is explored through these connections a visual Meccano is built that represents the discussion. The Meccano Connections are like well-constructed paragraphs that link ideas in a structured and thoughtful way.

The 'rules' of Meccano are:

- You can only speak by making a genuine connection to something someone has already said and it does not necessarily connect to the last idea articulated.
- The connection can be big or small, and possibly link to several ideas, but the connections must be shown visually as well as explained orally.
- Once connected, you can't speak again.
- When the connections are exhausted, the Meccano visual representation of the discussion is dismantled, and a new idea for another Meccano can begin, and people can connect again if they wish.

The 'why' of the Practice

- Enables voices and awareness of messaging across a group.
- Connects ideas and different perspectives across a group in an efficient and mindful way.
- Heightens the meaning and purpose of what people say.

The 'where to next' with the Practice

Consider:

- Reflecting on how the Meccano process affects a group's communication.
- What actions can be developed from the connecting ideas in the group.
- Reflect on the sharing and connecting of ideas, and how that can work towards a shared vision.
- Imagine other creative ways that ideas can be connected and how they could be used as positive feedback loops across a team.

Conveying meaning and purpose

When a message is conveyed there must be a shared understanding between people. It is not enough to be alert to messaging and enable voice if nobody understands what is being communicated and why. The meaning and purpose of communication and how it is conveyed strengthens the shared understanding and connection between people.

For courageous leaders, conveying meaning and purpose is critical for motivating and empowering others when creating and achieving a shared vision. It involves leaders asking the following questions about their communication:

- Meaning – What do I want to message?
- Purpose – Why am I messaging this, and who is my message for?
- Conveyance – How do I get my message across, and when? And how does it create shared understanding?

An example may be a leader wanting to recognize a group of teachers who have had success with students on a learning project. It would be easy to just stand up at a staff morning tea break and congratulate these teachers. However, when applying the above questions, the leader may realize they really want other staff to have some insights into what the project has achieved and empower the teachers by talking about the project. The leader decides to congratulate the teachers but also asks questions to allow them to speak about the project. The staff are also encouraged to ask any questions to the teachers about the project. The leader's choice in communication is more precise in conveying the intended meaning and purpose of her messaging.

This example also illustrates how successfully conveying meaning and purpose requires leaders to:

- deeply know their context
- authentically connect with people
- cohere and craft a shared message

Context, connection and coherence are critical for leaders to choose, craft and deliver their messaging.

Leaders should consider communication as an exchange and integration of meaning between people that continually spirals and expands like a feedback loop. Everyone in the communication has responsibility for the quality of the shared understanding they create. Courageous leaders need to be clear and genuine about the meaning and purpose of their communications but also develop the conditions for others to be effective communicators.

A common language or meta-language contributes to enhancing the feedback loops and conditions for effective communication. One of the reasons we use coherence makers like the Crystal is to provide leaders and their teams with a common language for communicating the processes of the 4Cs so they develop a shared understanding of what the 4Cs mean in action. For instance, they can ask, are we being alert to messaging, are we enabling voice and what is the meaning and purpose of our communication?

Conveying meaning and purpose is critical for school leaders endeavouring to involve their teams in a shared vision towards change. Continually explaining and exploring the 'why' of a vision clarifies meaning and purpose of a school objective and endeavour. We have already discussed the power of authentic storytelling to continually structure and convey a shared vision with others. The significance of conveying meaning and purpose for leaders is being able to connect authentically with people and creating coherent communication that leads to generating action and agency.

Generating action and agency

Communication in our view should be a humanizing and dynamic exchange that leads to generating action and agency rather than disempowerment and compliance. Leading through communication occurs when leaders actively support and develop people's sense of identity, meaningful relationships, positive behaviours and wisdom to act. Leading through communication is making and embodying choices to support others in acting for the common good.

Education philosopher Paulo Freire in *Pedagogy of the Oppressed* argues that communication can profoundly underpin agency and be a potentially transformative and humanizing force. Freire explains that authentic communication is dialogue that empowers and liberates people. He says, 'Human existence cannot be silent, nor can it be nourished by false words, but by true words, with which men and women transform the world . . . If it is in speaking their word that people, by naming the world, transform it, dialogue imposes itself as the way by which they achieve significance as human beings.'[21]

Leading through communication involves genuinely connecting with others by building trust, demonstrating humility and being reflective and ethical in our words and actions. Treating communication as a means of generating action and agency changes the way people lead. It is communication that humanizes but also empowers and challenges the status quo. Leaders can only transform schools if they realize that motivating others to act beyond the status quo depends on engaging with the values of people and what drives them (see chapter 7 on joy and motivation).

To connect and engage with peoples' values, leaders need to recognize and reflect on their perspective and be open and empathic to other people's viewpoints. Leading through communication is to support the identity and agency of others and foster belief in what they can do. Leaders can motivate and challenge people towards a shared vision of action through communication that encourages the continual emergence and expansion of knowledge and new ideas.

We argue that processes, choices and structures in communication often combined with the other Cs, creativity, critical reflection and collaboration, lead to generating action and agency. Some examples of processes, choices and structures for leading through communication that can generate action and agency are:

- Allowing others to take ownership of leading a team discussion (collaboration).
- Instituting formalized reflective discussions with individual members of the team (critical reflection).

- Encouraging and supporting creative ideas in the team but also challenging, refining and evaluating those ideas with them (creativity).
- Engaging with other faculties or learning stages and establishing with them clear questions and objectives to discuss their challenges and achievements (critical reflection).
- Scaffolding authentic opportunities for students to lead communication processes in the school, for instance, greeting school visitors, explaining teaching and learning, leading student conferences with parents etc. (collaboration).
- Recognizing and connecting any staff and student initiatives across the school through genuine communication feedback loop structures (creativity).

Often, a realization for school leaders is that much of the communication in schools is one-way and not a dynamic feedback loop of shared understanding that generates action and agency. Practice 5.6, Communication Audit, allows leaders to assess their communication structures and processes through a communication audit that applies all the stages of the Crystal.

Practice 5.6 Communication audit

Consider communications in your schools, such as school assemblies, parent newsletters, email directives, executive meetings, student wellbeing meetings, parent and teacher interviews, performance reviews, school reports etc.

Ask how do these forms of communication:

- Develop alertness to messaging?
- Enable voice?
- Convey meaning and purpose?
- Generate action and agency?
- How can they be positive feedback loops?

Like other processes we have already discussed, these school communications may have become ritualized patterns that may need re-imagining so that communication is agentic.

The Communication Crystal is a guide for courageous leaders to reflect on their communication behaviours and implement processes and structures for communication as leadership-as-practice. In summary, the Communication Crystal involves leaders scaffolding and empowering themselves and others to:

- *Be alert to messaging* – being hyper-aware of how we affect others by what we say, how we say it and how we receive messages.
- *Enable voices* – creating opportunities and capacities for all voices to be expressed.
- *Convey meaning and purpose* – crafting skills in communication so that messages have clarity and coherence as shared understanding and intent between people.
- *Generate action and agency* – using communication as a dynamic to empower the efficacy of identity, relationships, knowledge and action in others.

Concluding reflections

Schools are institutions that enable communication and knowledge in a community. How that communication is led shapes the culture. The songlines or spirals that began this chapter demonstrate the deep and challenging way communication can be conceptualized as a dynamic and authentic relationship between people, culture and emergent knowledge.

Leading through communication is developing ways in which people can share in a joint narrative towards transformation. This isn't a straightforward process; it is complex developing your own capacity and the capacity of others through communication processes. Communication is critical in schools because it creates culture and knowledge, and this shapes the experiences, beliefs and actions of everyone in that community.

The Gay'wu group of women elders we referred to earlier say this about what their song spirals communicate:

> It is all the feelings, the songs and ceremonies, the things that go beyond us, that anchor us in eternity, in the infinite cycles of kinship, sharing and responsibility.
>
> Country is the way we mix and merge, the way we are different and yet become together, are part of each other. It is all the messages, languages and communication from all beings to all beings. And Country is the song spirals. It is milkarri.[22]

We acknowledge the powerful way of knowing that is deeply woven into the communication and culture of First Nations' peoples, and feel we have much to learn from them about sharing, responsibility and making deep connections between people. The next chapter explores Creativity that is also deeply woven into the practices and history of Indigenous cultures.

Key actions

1. Apply the Communication Crystal to the ways you communicate with others.
2. Explicitly frame new communication Practices by using the Crystal.
3. Explore and experiment with new communication Practices with the purpose of creating effective feedback loops, supporting people's agency and creating more complex communication processes.
4. Explore Indigenous cultures' ways of knowing and reflect on how they resonate with or challenges your values and beliefs about communication.

Leading through creativity

6

Figure 6.1 Melanie Perkins CEO of Canva

Ideas into Action

Schools are full of dreams, ideas and challenges. The task of leadership, especially in times of change, is to turn these ideas into wise action. As management consultant Peter Drucker noted, 'Ideas are cheap and abundant; what is of value is the effective placement of those ideas into action.'[1] Creativity in leadership is a powerful way to turn ideas into context-relevant, evidence-based actions.

Melanie Perkins (figure 6.1), co-founder of Canva, is an example of creativity for transformative leadership. In 2007, Perkins started a small business from her parents' living room in Perth, Western Australia that would eventually revolutionize online graphic design. Her journey shows that creativity can drive meaningful change in any context, from business to education.

Perkins' inspiration came from her teaching experience at the University of Western Australia, where she found existing design programs like Adobe Photoshop too expensive and complex for students. She wanted to make design software 'simple, online, and collaborative'. In response, she launched Fusion Books in 2007, enabling schools to create yearbooks easily and efficiently, turning noticing into creative action.

As she explains, Fusion was a creative response to a school-based need. The little company that began life in her parents' home emerged from a noticing:

> My Mum is a teacher and had always been responsible for the yearbook at her school which took her hundreds of hours. Often the yearbook coordinator is a teacher trying to oversee a major project (pulling together a book!) while still teaching full-time, and with no prior design experience. The huge need for a better solution was obvious.[2]

Flash forwards over a decade, and this niche start-up has evolved into Canva. It has surpassed more than 20 billion designs with 170 million users, (mostly using it for free), including 60 million students and teachers from 190 countries. The evolution of Canva from a niche business to a household name worth more than $26 billion is a tribute to leading with creativity.

This chapter explores how creativity enables leaders to drive meaningful and sustainable transformation. It introduces the Creativity Cascade as a practical framework for leading change through creativity, a systematic approach that moves from Noticing the challenges and opportunities within each school's context, to Asking why? Really why? through deep inquiry, to Playing with Possibility through collaborative experimentation, and then to Selecting and Evaluating creative actions that generate transformative change.

We define and discuss creativity and its relationship to courageous leadership, the willingness to embrace uncertainty and challenge status quo practices, and leadership-as-practice, where transformation becomes collaborative work embedded in the everyday culture of schools. This chapter discusses how agency and creativity are mutually reinforcing. When school communities are engaged, their creative potential grows. When creative processes are embedded in practice, collective agency strengthens.

We examine the substantial benefits creativity offers to school leaders navigating 'postnormal times'.[3] marked by 'chaos, complexity and contradiction' where status quo approaches are inadequate. In these times of relentless change in culture, society, technology and politics, creative leadership becomes not just nice to have but essential for transformative work. Let's begin by defining creativity.

What is creativity?

While there are several ways of defining creativity, this definition is especially relevant to school leaders and aligns with The Leadership Lantern we introduced in chapter 2:[4] 'Creativity is the interaction among aptitude, process, and environment by which an individual or group produces a perceptible product that is both novel and useful as defined within a social context'.[5] Aptitude, process and environment are approximations of the dynamics we identify in the Lantern namely *capacity* (aptitude), *agency* (process) and *context* (environment).

This relationship between capacity, agency and context emphasizes creativity is not the result of any single factor but rather a dynamic interaction among these three components. This interaction is synergistic, meaning that creativity emerges not from any single component being strong, but from how effectively these three elements combine and influence each other. For example, even strong capacity may not lead to creativity without agency or a context that is open to creative action. The absence or weakness of any one of these can diminish the capacity for creativity in leadership. If they are all present, they will reinforce and support each other to make leadership through creativity possible.

For leadership teams, consider a situation where team leaders possess diverse expertise and strong collaborative skills (capacity) but operate in a systemic culture that discourages risk-taking (restrictive context) and lack processes for collective decision-making or innovation (limited agency). Despite their individual and collective capabilities, the team is unlikely to develop creative solutions to complex challenges. Conversely, when leadership teams combine their collective expertise with systematic collaborative processes within a culture that supports experimentation and learning from failure, creative leadership approaches emerge and make transformation possible.

For school leaders, the product of the interaction of these factors could be innovative teaching strategies, the development of collaborative interdisciplinary projects or more effective and meaningful ways of communicating student progress to parents. These examples are shaped by the ongoing interplay of creativity i.e. context, capacity and agency.

Understanding creativity through context, capacity and agency helps leaders use their strengths to develop creative, innovative and practical solutions to the challenges and opportunities within their learning communities. This works because creativity is deliberate and systematic. It can be understood and mapped to help schools and leadership notice where it is present and absent.

This approach recognizes that effective creative leadership isn't simply about generating new ideas. This approach:

- Responds to the unique context of each school.
- Uses existing capacity and strengths as the foundation for developing innovative yet practical approaches.
- Brings change through deliberate, collaborative processes that recognize creativity as systematic and methodical rather than spontaneous.[6]

By integrating context, capacity and agency, leaders can ensure their creative initiatives are both innovative and practical. In the school context, a useful or novel product could be a program to improve student engagement or retention, or a strategy for enhancing pedagogy across a stage/year level. Context provides situational awareness to identify the dimensions of problems and opportunities. Capacity ensures ideas can be implemented with available resources and support, and agency empowers leaders to take meaningful action and adapt strategies. In the school context, this integration enables leaders to develop context relevant innovation. For instance, transform student engagement or retention, or generate strategies for enhancing pedagogy across a stage/year level. Context, capacity and agency create the foundation for creative leadership. Leadership teams can explore this interaction of aptitude, process and environment through Practice 6.1.

Practice 6.1 Mapping creative leadership

This Practice will help you map creativity in your school.

- Divide your group into three groups
- Provide each group with an A3 map of the school
- Ask each of the groups to map one of the following:
  - Group 1: Where do they notice creative leadership in the *context* of the school? For example, is it occurring in the science labs, the music rooms, the staffroom or on the sports field? Does it apply to a particular year level or extracurricular activity. Remember, leadership is not necessarily positional.
  - Group 2: Where do they notice the creative *capacities* for leadership in the school? For instance, the administrators in the office and the students who meet for debating club.
  - Group 3: Where do they notice creative leadership and *agency* evident in the school? For instance, the musical, the science expo, the maths Olympiad, staff meetings.
- Ask groups to look at each other's maps and identify the crossover areas and where the opportunities might be for creative leadership.

Having discussed the definitions of creativity let's explore its qualities. In other words, how creativity exists in the real world of school leadership.

The qualities of creativity

Vlad Glăveanu's research can deepen our understanding of the qualities of creativity. He argues that engaging with the possible recognizes real constraints while still imagining creative paths forward. In our view engaging with the possible is an active ingredient to grow critical hope[7]. Glăveanu nominates fifteen qualities of possibility.[8] We have chosen five that we think are especially relevant to leaders of transformation.

1. Creativity is distributed

   Possibility is not the property of a single individual. Leadership for transformation relies on collaborative engagement; exploring what is possible should be a collective process. Effective consultation and genuine collaboration are at the core of creativity. For example, when addressing the digital divide among students, seeking perspectives from teachers, IT staff, students, parents and community members can uncover a wider range of solutions. Leadership teams might ask:

   - How might our current problem-solving processes limit the possibilities we consider?
   - Who might we involve who is not currently part of these conversations?
   - Are our consultation processes genuinely inclusive, or just formalities?

2. Creativity is intertwined with the actual

   Playing with Possibility requires leaders to stay connected to their context. The phases of Noticing and Asking why? Really why? draw evidence from the specific context, anchoring the process in actual needs and constraints of each school. For instance, if a school is experiencing high early career teacher attrition, leaders who notice that teachers lack support can avoid simplistic solutions. In this instance, teachers may feel they have little agency, potential for professional growth, effective mentoring etc. By grounding creativity in the actual, leaders ensure that their strategies are authentically responsive. Questions to explore this might include:

   - How might our existing assumptions prevent us from seeing new possibilities in our context?
   - In what ways can our evidence-gathering better inform our strategic planning?
   - What are the underlying patterns or trends in our current reality that we may be overlooking?

3. Creativity depends on constraints

   Constraints are an inevitable part of any context. As Glăveanu points out,[9] constraints are not solely obstacles – they can focus creative energies and act as motivators. Constraints are dynamic, and their shifting nature encourages leaders to stay flexible and adaptive. Facing budget cuts, for example, a school may engage local community resources or partner with other schools to maintain arts programs. Constraints guide and shape creativity, often giving rise to solutions that would not have emerged in more abundant circumstances. Leadership teams could reflect on:

   - How might budget, staffing, or policy constraints prompt creative solutions?
   - What challenges in our school could help spark new, practical initiatives?
   - How might collaboration help us navigate chronic constraints to create sustainable improvements?

4. Creativity is mediated

   Human creations and tools mediate what can become possible. Technology, for example, enables actions and solutions that were unattainable in previous decades. The adoption of video conferencing in schools reduced the need for travel and freed up time and resources. Reimagining a school library as a flexible 'Imagination Hub' can allow for new teaching and learning practices, supported by mediated spaces like podcast or film studios. Leadership teams might consider:

   - How can technology or other tools help us play with possibilities for traditional practices and spaces?
   - What forms of mediation could address specific challenges or constraints in our environment?
   - How might current resources, such as the library, be leveraged to generate new possibilities?

5. Creativity is grounded in difference

   Diversity of perspectives expands the range of possibilities in any context. Creative leadership thrives on dialogue and inclusion, as multiple viewpoints reveal novel and sometimes unexpected options. As Glăveanu notes the:

   > . . . possible emerges in human experience whenever there is a multitude of perspectives available for individuals, groups and societies to draw upon in understanding themselves and their environment . . . Minds and societies defined by diversity and dialogue are, consequently, open to new possibilities in ways that monological, fixated, and totalitarian worlds and mindsets are not.[10]

For example, a school that values and promotes staff and student diversity creates a possibility for innovative ideas. Encouraging debate and collaboration across differences can lead to instructive projects, such as student-led initiatives in sustainability that arise from group inquiry. Teams could ask:

- How can we actively incorporate a broader range of viewpoints to foster creativity?
- In what ways could open dialogue and debate generate transformative possibilities for our school?
- Who is contributing and who is not in decision making? How might we change that?

In addition to these qualities, agency is central to the success of leading through creativity.

Creativity and agency

To realize the transformative potential of creativity in schools, as Glăveanu suggests,[11] leaders must also attend to the conditions that enable it. Agency is central to this, as highlighted in the Leadership Lantern (chapter 2). Without a sense of autonomy and empowerment, creative leadership cannot take root or support the changes in culture needed for schools to truly flourish. Leaders need some freedom to experiment, make decisions and adapt their approaches based on what they learn about their context. When leaders lack autonomy, they become constrained by rigid hierarchies and bureaucratic processes that stifle innovation and prevent them from responding dynamically to emerging challenges or opportunities. Empowerment enables leaders to take calculated risks, try new things and create the culture necessary for others to contribute creatively.

This relationship between agency and creativity is well-supported by research and practice. Psychologist Teresa Amabile[12] found that creativity flourishes when individuals feel empowered with autonomy and control, fuelling the drive to explore and innovate. In a school, for example, teachers who have autonomy to design and implement innovative approaches to assessment or curriculum are more likely to experiment and generate novel solutions. Likewise, psychologists Ryan and Deci[13] established that agency enhances intrinsic motivation: as autonomy grows, so too does the internal drive to create, leading to richer and more transformative outcomes.

For individuals, agency manifests as courageous leadership, which involves the willingness to embrace uncertainty, question conventions and make difficult decisions to achieve transformation. Courageous leaders demonstrate agency through their capacity to stand up for their values while wisely balancing the need for stability with the imperative for meaningful change.[14] Courageous leaders understand that transformation requires skill, determination and particularly courage to move beyond the relative 'comfort' of the status quo. Research on transformational leadership confirms that leaders who exhibit courage and moral conviction are more effective at inspiring organizational change and fostering innovation among their teams.[15] However, individual courage alone cannot sustain transformation; it must be coupled with systemic change.

Agency also operates at the cultural level through leadership-as-practice, where transformation becomes collaborative work that extends beyond individual capability. This approach recognizes that sustainable change requires shifting the 'sayings, doings and relatings' that make up a school's culture discussed in chapter 2. Research on distributed leadership demonstrates that schools achieve greater innovation when leadership practices are embedded across multiple levels and roles rather than concentrated in individual positions.[16] For instance, while individual teachers might learn innovative pedagogical approaches, lasting transformation requires changing the underlying systems from curriculum delivery and assessment methods to resource allocation and reporting that can enable or constrain innovation and creative action.

Agency also allows leaders to challenge the status quo and foster real innovation.[17] When school leadership teams are empowered to make decisions – not simply to comply with external demands – they can identify and implement contextually relevant solutions that address the actual needs of their community. This process can be practiced in schools through explicit reflection and collaboration. Practice 5.2 demonstrates how agency and creativity are mutually reinforcing by engaging participants in collaborative challenges.

Practice 6.2 Leading through agency and creativity

In this Practice, participants make autonomous choices while working within constraints, they experience how agency can generate creativity and how creative processes can build agency.

Materials needed:

- Building materials: paper, tape, straws, blocks
- Timer or stopwatch
- Flip chart paper and markers
- Index cards

Process

Step 1 Agency Self-assessment (10 minutes)

Participants position themselves physically on three lines marked on the floor:

- **Autonomy**: 'I follow rules exactly' to 'I create my own approaches'.
- **Risk-taking**: 'I prefer safe methods' to 'I experiment with new ideas'.
- **Influence**: 'I wait for direction' to 'I initiate change'. Share briefly with a partner why they chose each position.

Step 2 Team Challenge Rotation (25 minutes)

Teams of 4–5 rotate through three stations, spending 8 minutes at each:

- **Student Engagement Challenge**: Design a new approach to increase student participation in school decision-making with limited budget and time.
- **Communication Challenge**: Develop a strategy to effectively communicate a major curriculum change to parents, staff, and students.
- **Innovation Challenge**: Redesign how your school conducts staff meetings to make them more collaborative and productive Teams must make quick autonomous decisions and adapt their strategies.

Step 3: Barrier Mapping and Solutions (15 minutes)

Teams identify their biggest barrier to creative leadership from four categories:

- Individual barriers (personal habits, fears).
- Team barriers (communication, trust issues).
- System barriers (policies, structures).
- Cultural barriers ('the way we do things' or 'I don't have permission') then identify three creative actions they could take in the next 30 days to address it.

Step 4: Action Commitments (10 minutes)

Participants move to different corners of the room representing timeframes:

- **This week**: Actions within 7 days.
- **This month**: Changes within 30 days.
- **This term**: Longer-term systemic changes. At each corner, state one specific commitment aloud to the group.

Reflection Questions for Debrief

1. How did your sense of agency change during the challenges?
2. What connections did you notice between feeling empowered and generating creative solutions?
3. Which barrier feels most limiting, and which solution most actionable?
4. What surprised you about your creative leadership capacity?

Let's now turn to the benefits of creativity for school leaders.

The benefits of leading through creativity

The benefits of leading through creativity extend beyond the bringing new ideas into schools. In a world where rapid technological, social, and cultural changes are the norm, school leaders are uniquely challenged to both respond to their immediate environment and build the capacity for long-term transformation. Philosopher Ziauddin Sardar aptly describes the era we face as *postnormality*, a time characterized by 'chaos, complexity and contradiction',[18] with relentless changes in media, technology and science presenting both obstacles and opportunities for creative engagement. For leaders, this climate can seem bewildering, but it also highlights the necessity, and opportunity, of embracing creativity as a guiding force.

Postnormal times also create significant opportunities for school leaders. The transformation of student wellbeing support exemplifies this potential: it represents not merely a policy adjustment, but a paradigm shift that demands creative leadership to implement meaningful change. Key to this transformation is the ability to recognize and act on emergent needs: as adolescent mental health challenges intensify and social media fundamentally reshapes peer dynamics, visionary school leaders identify opportunities to democratize emotional support for students previously marginalized by stigma and inadequate resources. These leaders reframe traditional disciplinary systems and fragmented support services as obstacles to be overcome rather than accepted constraints. They transform these barriers into catalysts for innovation, developing integrated wellbeing hubs, peer mentorship programs and community mental health partnerships that fundamentally reshape school culture. Such leadership demonstrates how creativity becomes not just a response to change but a strategic tool for harnessing uncertainty itself.

Creativity becomes not just a response to change but a way to harness it. Educational psychologist Vlad Glăveanu highlights that these conditions require educators to act imaginatively to 'reshape our futures'. He writes:

> Living within uncertain, complex and difficult environments defined by a fast pace of change, our responsibility is to educate individuals and communities who can envision and enact new possibilities in a reflective, proactive, and ethical manner. Twenty-first-century education needs to rise to the challenge of helping students and teachers go beyond the world 'as it was' and 'as it is' and enrich it with imaginations of how it 'can and should be'.[19]

Glăveanu argues here that imagination and creativity are fundamental to meeting current and future challenges in schools. Creative leadership is necessary not only to ensure learning is transformational and relevant but also to shape schools into places where meaningful change occurs continuously, so they become places of true flourishing. The 4C coherence makers and in this case the Creativity Cascade provide the how of imagining, designing and animating change in schools.

The Creativity Cascade

As we discussed earlier, 4C coherence makers provide a process to enact often vague or mystical concepts such as creativity. This makes them suited not only for understanding but also for enabling creative processes in any aspect of schooling, such as teaching and learning, but it is critical for transformative leadership. These coherence makers can be especially potent for school leaders as they navigate the challenges and opportunities that transformation brings.

Our coherence maker for creativity, the Creativity Cascade offers school leaders a framework for leading through creativity and generating transformative change in schools. The Cascade breaks creativity into four interrelated processes that can be employed by leaders to generate thinking and doing towards transformation. It is metaphorically structured as a cascade with four interconnected stages or 'pools', suggesting a continuous flow where one process leads dynamically into the next. This signifies that creativity is not an unstructured or discipline-free activity, but rather a structured and iterative process. The Creativity Cascade directly supports courageous leadership by providing a structured way for leaders to embrace this inherent risk-taking and iterative approach to problem-solving and innovation.

In this section, we explain each stage of the coherence maker and then provide Practices for leaders to use the Creativity Cascade (figure 6.2) as a structure to enable beneficial change. We begin with the foundational skills of creativity, noticing.

Figure 6.2 The Creativity Cascade

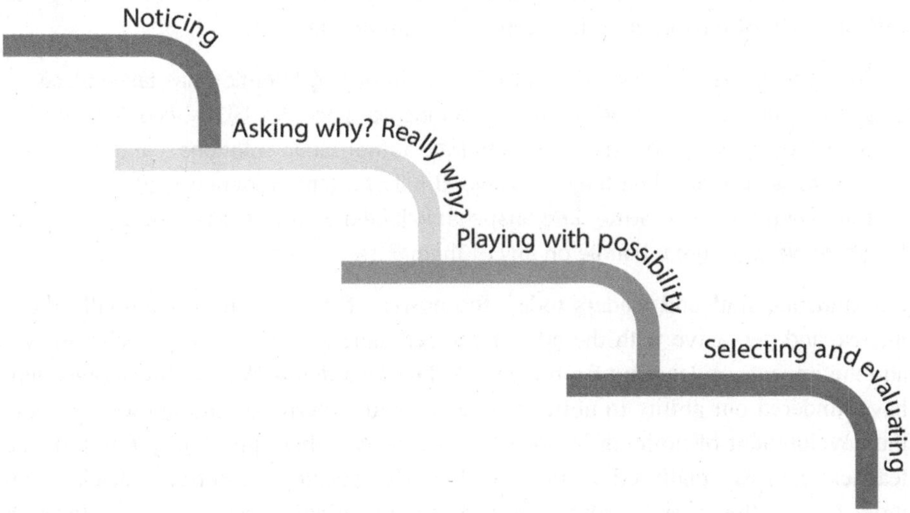

Noticing

Noticing provides a bridge between everyday observation and creative possibility. While many leaders see 'what is', creativity provides capacity to notice the possible. In the Cascade noticing goes beyond problem identification; it involves recognizing the creative potential inherent in challenges and seeing opportunities where others may see only obstacles. Noticing becomes the catalyst that transforms routine observations into innovative insights, making it the essential first step in any creative leadership process. Whether it is Melanie Perkins noticing that design software was 'expensive and complicated and didn't suit the needs of students', or a school leader recognizing that an outdated timetable is hampering innovation, the starting point is the same. Transformative leadership begins with close and purposeful observation. It involves actively identifying and naming the challenges and opportunities present in each school's unique context. In any field, and especially in education, the ability to notice, to listen, observe and critically reflect is the foundation for generating creative responses that can truly reshape what is possible. Noticing is the art of paying attention.

The concept of the 'attention economy' emerged in the 1960s. It was economists Thomas Davenport and John Beck[20] who reinterpreted the concept in the early 2000s with the rise of the internet and seemingly unlimited information and distraction. They argued that human attention had become a scarce commodity. Rather than an information economy, they argue we now live in an attention economy. For leaders, and particularly leaders in schools, the constant bombardment of information means they are often swamped by 'noise'. In the face of the multiple demands on a leader's attention, noticing needs to be a deliberate practice to discern the signal from the noise.

In *Stolen Focus*,[21] journalist Johann Hari argues that an absence of noticing (he calls it a lack of paying attention) can have profound impacts:

> I don't think it's a coincidence that this crisis in paying attention has taken place at the same time as the worst crisis of democracy since the 1930s. People who can't focus will be more drawn to simplistic authoritarian solutions – and less likely to see clearly when they fail. A world full of attention-deprived citizens alternating between Twitter and Snapchat will be a world of cascading crises where we can't get a handle on any of them.[22]

For students, staff and leaders today, the power of distraction is potentially more intense and pervasive with the advent and refinement of 'distraction technologies' and the impacts on learning from the COVID-19 pandemic. While distractions may have hindered our ability to notice the details and patterns around us, we can view the development of noticing in our schools as a valuable opportunity for students, teachers, and especially educational leaders. By focusing on noticing, leaders can move beyond the everyday routine and identify meaningful insights, cutting through the noise of distractions.

The capacity to notice forms the foundation of both courageous leadership and leadership-as-practice. For courageous leadership, noticing provides the essential 'problem-finding' capability that enables leaders to identify challenges and opportunities that others might miss. Noticing allows courageous leaders to recognize when bold action is required and to understand the shape and size of challenges before them. When leaders notice patterns of inequity, ineffective practices or untapped potential within their schools, they can respond with the determination and bravery that characterizes courageous leadership.

Leadership-as-practice requires a noticing that attends to the sayings, doings and relatings that constitute the cultural fabric of schools. Through systematic observation of how people interact, what they say about their work and how they conduct their professional activities, leaders can identify opportunities to shift from individual heroic leadership models towards more distributed and collaborative approaches.

In our experience, leaders who notice are more likely to create a cohesive culture in their staff. Noticing rather than simply acting on impulse, emphasizes the use of reflection on evidence. These noticings might be from experience, observations and research. In a noticing culture, leaders can consider opportunities from many perspectives. They broaden their understanding of the challenge or the opportunity by considering student, teacher and community perspectives before acting. These noticings have the potential not only to impact classroom practice but also to build the quality of decision-making and strategy across the school.

In a US-based study, educational researcher Joseph Johnson observed the noticing practices of fourteen leaders of high-performing urban schools. His findings reflect leaders who can notice from multiple viewpoints (student perspectives, teacher perspectives, etc). He found that when these leaders observed classrooms, they noticed:[23]

- Issues related to student engagement and understanding and classroom atmosphere.
- The extent to which students actively participated in learning activities.
- The extent to which students were talking, explaining and describing in ways that gave teachers an indication of each student's levels of understanding.
- The climate, atmosphere or tone of the classroom.
- Classroom environments that were academically and intellectually stimulating, warm and welcoming, and orderly without being rigid.[24]

This study did not look at other aspects of the school, but this focus on learning provides some critical indications for how noticing can be an effective first step in leading through creativity. The leaders here didn't go in with a checklist or a series of preconceptions; rather, they spent time observing and engaging with their school's context. In our view, the same is true for all school leaders. If leaders are unable to notice the complexities of their context, they are unlikely to make meaningful innovation or transformation a reality. Noticing is the first step in leading through creativity by sensing the challenges and opportunities in each school's context. Practice 6.3 provides one strategy to develop a culture of noticing.

Practice 6.3 Developing a culture of noticing

In the following Practice, you might consider some ways that you can generate more noticing in your leadership practice and build noticing in the culture of your school.

Figure 6.3 'Las Meninas' by Diego Velázquez

1. Look at the artwork 'Las Meninas' by Diego Velázquez (1656) (figure 6.3).[25] Take time to 'take in' the image without analysing the work. Now, spend time noticing. What do you notice about:
   a. your reaction to the image?
   b. the interactions of the characters?
   c. the use of light, the position of the figures, etc?
   d. the power dynamics at play?
   e. the story this picture might be telling?

Discuss your noticings in the group.

2. In the second part of the Practice, do a reflective walk around the school or a certain part of the school. Again, the aim here is not to analyse but to notice.
   a. What do you notice about what you see, hear and smell?
   b. What do you notice about the way you feel about different parts of the school?
   c. What do you notice about the different behaviours of students and staff in different parts of the school?

3. Using these noticings about the school, build a 'noticings map' using keywords associated with the different areas of the school where the noticings occurred. Use this as the basis for a group discussion about:

   a. What surprised you?
   b. What concerned you?
   c. What excited you about these noticings?

Noticing in the Creativity Cascade is the act of focused attention to details, events, and interactions in each school's context. Noticing can create a bridge between everyday observation and creative possibility. Effective leaders take the time to focus intently on what is occurring in their schools and develop the capacity to notice what could be. Noticing can transform routine observations into innovative insights. This allows leaders to move from simply maintaining the status-quo to transformation and making their schools places that generate change rather than merely respond to it.

Asking why? Really why

The Asking why? Really why? deepens potentially simplistic observation into generative exploration. While noticing captures what exists in the present moment, Asking why? Really why? opens pathways to understanding the complex web of relationships that shape school contexts. Good ideas don't just appear magically; they emerge from the deep thinking that inquiry requires. It often takes time for patterns to surface and connections to become visible. This inquiry process becomes creative through its capacity to reveal unexpected connections, challenge assumptions and generate multiple interpretations in the patterns discovered in the noticing process of the cascade. The result of the Asking why? Really why? process is not just analysis but creative synthesis that reveals previously hidden opportunities for transformation within each school's context. When a school leader noticed patterns or cultural features about a school, the next step is to understand deeply the 'Really Whys?' that emerge from their noticings. This phase of the cascade is an invitation for more than questions, it invites leaders to engage with inquiry.

This deep inquiry approach reflects what School Principal Alison Rourke and Educational Researcher Kelly Freebody argue for in *How Schools Transform*. They emphasize that meaningful change requires moving beyond surface observations to engage with complex, adaptive approaches to learning challenges.[26] They argue: 'Inquiry is not about a packaged solution in search of a problem. The issues we face are complex, so they require adaptive approaches. Most of the significant learning challenges at a school will require experimentation, discoveries and shifts in some established practices . . . Working in this inquiry space is serious work that makes a difference in increasing students' achievement and improving school outcomes.'[27]

The process of Asking why? Really why? creates a bridge between individual courage and collective practice. For courageous leadership, this inquiry process develops analytical thinking crucial to leading complex and dynamic places like schools. Leaders who engage deeply with questioning their assumptions and examining root causes develop the intellectual courage necessary to challenge existing systems and practices. This form of inquiry enables leaders to move beyond symptomatic responses towards addressing fundamental issues that require transformative action.

From a leadership-as-practice perspective, the Asking why? Really why? process becomes a collective endeavour that shifts leadership from individual decision-making toward collaborative sense-making. When leadership teams engage together in systematic inquiry, they create what leadership researcher Joseph Raelin[28] calls collaborative agentic practice. This approach distributes the work of understanding complex problems across multiple perspectives and expertise areas, reducing reliance on single leaders while building collective capacity for transformation.

When leaders engage with Asking why? Really why? through inquiry, they go beyond superficial noticings or taken-for-granted assumptions. In the Asking why? Really why? process, leaders identify the root causes of the patterns and cultural features they have noticed. They also examine the broader context in which these elements occur. For instance, how does a system's after-school program funding affect families in regions where safe, supervised environments are critical during parents' working hours? Inquiry encourages leaders to ask deeper questions, such as:

- What are the underlying assumptions that shape these patterns?
- How do cultural features influence student learning and teacher practices?
- What external factors might be impacting our school?
- How do challenges relate to and influence one another?

The inquiry process (aka Asking why? Really why?) is iterative. As leaders explore and answer these questions, new questions will inevitably arise. Complex problems in schools are not disconnected from other problems. For instance, student engagement is often affected by social media use, that is linked to peer group effects, connected to pedagogical approaches that generate student agency and so on. So, as one question arises, several other questions are likely to emerge. When this happens, the Asking why? Really why? process has likely begun, as the complexity and interconnectedness of the questions start to form a network of related inquiries. This ongoing cycle of questioning may feel frustrating at first, but with these questions, clarity will begin to emerge. Practice 6.4 illustrates the process of digging deeper through inquiry.

The practice of posing probing questions based on noticings fosters a culture of inquiry. This process encourages collaboration to explore complex issues and engage with emerging opportunities, ultimately deepening collective understanding and driving meaningful change. As we have discussed in our other books, inquiry is an essential skill for student learning as it builds curiosity and discovery skills. Inquiry is also essential in school leadership to generate creativity and meaningful change.

Practice 6.4 Asking why? Really why? (Why tree)

This Practice is designed to develop an understanding of the Really Why? The Practice follows on from the noticings you created in Practice 6.3. It is intended for you to dig beyond superficial impressions or unevidenced assumptions.

- Take three or four noticings from the previous Practice.
- Create a 'Why Tree' (figure 6.4). The purpose of the tree is to generate as many responses as possible to deepen, broaden and connect the 'Asking why, Really why?' of your challenge or problem.

Figure 6.4 The Why Tree

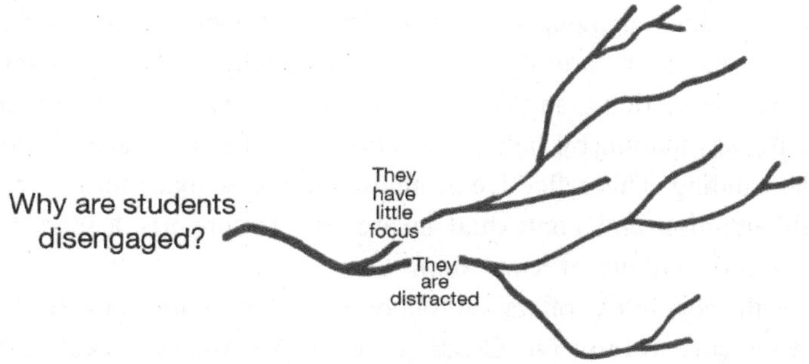

This tree can be extended with more branches as needed and linked to other trees. When you have completed your tree each participant circles one of the responses in the tree to explore further by playing with possibility and then Asking why? Really why?

The relationship between Asking why? Really why? and Playing with Possibility reveals creativity as both analytical and imaginative work. While Asking why? Really why? deepens understanding through systematic inquiry, Playing with Possibility transforms that understanding into innovative action. These processes are interdependent: without the contextual insights that emerge from sustained questioning, possibility thinking can become disconnected from context and constraints. On the other hand, without the creative experimentation of playing with possibility, deep inquiry can remain trapped in analysis without generating transformative outcomes.

Together, they demonstrate that leading through creativity requires both rigorous investigation of what is and bold imagination of what could be. The questioning phase creates what Anna Craft calls the foundation for 'possibility thinking' by revealing the assumptions, constraints and relationships that shape current practice. This groundwork then enables play with alternatives, knowing that their creative experiments are anchored in contextual understanding rather than wishful thinking. The interplay between these processes shows that creativity emerges not from inspiration alone but from the dynamic relationship between deep understanding and imaginative exploration. Which brings us to playing with possibility.

Playing with possibility

Leaders engaged in transformation adopt a 'what's possible?' mindset. In this phase of the Cascade, they explore creative options through play by combining unlikely ideas, thinking around constraints and energizing their teams. As James Biddulph and colleagues explain, play offers 'the necessary prompts, structures and holding environment to enable school leaders to expose themselves to the complexity of the "task at hand"'.[29]

For school leaders, engaging with possibility isn't about making reckless leaps. Possibility is grounded in careful noticing and deep inquiry. The early stages of the Creativity Cascade, noticing and Asking why? Really why? lay the foundation for meaningful transformation by helping leaders move from surface observations to deeper understanding. This reflective groundwork makes space for exploring possibilities with intention and contextual awareness. It supports leaders to develop courage and build a culture of leadership.

Playing with possibility offers an opportunity for courageous leadership and leadership-as-practice to converge. Creativity researcher Anna Craft called this 'possibility thinking'[30] – the transformation from what is to what might be. For courageous leadership, this phase requires creative risk-taking behaviour. Leaders must be willing to move beyond status quo solutions and imagine approaches that respond to or transcend existing constraints. This demands both intellectual courage and the emotional intelligence to explore ideas that may challenge established practices or expectations.

Leadership-as-practice approaches possibility through collaborative creativity, where diverse perspectives combine to generate solutions that no single individual could imagine. This distributed approach to possibility thinking generates creative emergence where novel solutions arise from authentic collaboration within schools rather than being imposed from above. When leadership teams engage collectively in playing with possibility, they model the collaborative innovation they seek to cultivate throughout their school communities.

Playfulness in school leadership helps to create environments where creativity, experimentation and engagement can thrive.[31] Leaders who embrace playfulness are more open to new ideas and view setbacks as learning opportunities, which encourages innovation and flexibility in navigating complex educational challenges. This approach helps leaders to take creative risks and move beyond traditional limits, fostering a 'what's possible?' mindset that is essential for transformative leadership. Throughout this book, we offer Practices that use playful strategies to stimulate creative thinking and transformative action. Practice 6.5 will help leadership teams to engage, explore and critically play with possibility. These Practices support leaders to tackle the complex challenges and tangles[32] of transformation in imaginative and motivating ways. As Biddulph and colleagues note, 'Rather than the grey murky ambiguity that can drain the spirits and leave people exhausted and overwhelmed, school leaders are more likely to experience the rainbow of progress, possibility and positivity – because they engage with a mindset that is playful'.[33] Playing with possibility also means putting ideas into action. Leaders need the agency to test their ideas in real-world conditions, where constraints and opportunities shape innovation.

In many educational settings, structural barriers and compliance cultures contribute to school leaders hesitating to embrace playfulness and creativity. In these places, leaders can feel pressured to maintain strict control, fear judgement, and avoid risk.[34] Additionally, many educational leaders lack the experience of playfulness in leadership. The restrictive nature of some accountability heavy education systems establishes risk-averse climates where leaders perceive playfulness as frivolous rather than strategic.

Play can create the psychological safety necessary for creative risk-taking while fostering the thinking necessary for creativity.[35] When school leaders' model playful experimentation with challenges, they can generate a culture in the school where teachers and students feel empowered to play with possibilities. Establishing a culture of playfulness requires deliberate changes: scheduling regular 'possibility session' where teams explore challenges through creative constraints, reconfiguring spaces to support collaborative thinking, and consistently demonstrating that learning from failure is valued over perfect implementation.

Practice 6.5 Playing with leadership possibilities

This Practice explores Playing with Possibility by inviting leaders to engage with challenges through creative, collaborative action. The Practice can assist school leaders to move beyond status quo solutions by experimenting with small, imaginative shifts in practice. By making space for playful exploration, the activity cultivates the courage and contextual awareness needed for transformational leadership. It requires the following resources:

- Challenge cards (pre-written or created by participants)
- Constraint cards (for playful limitations)
- Remix prompt cards (to shift thinking)
- Large sheets of paper or flipcharts
- Sticky notes
- Markers or pens
- Optional: Props, tactile materials (LEGO, string, objects), music

1. The challenge card draw (5 minutes)

Each team selects a challenge card representing a real leadership tension, such as:

- Staff burnout is rising
- Student voice is tokenistic
- Innovation is blocked by compliance
- Parental engagement is low
- Communication across teams is unclear

Optionally, teams could write their own challenge from their school context.

2. Constraint role play – the challenge gets tougher (10 minutes)

Each team draws a constraint card that adds a playful limitation to how they approach their challenge. For example:

- You can't speak. Only draw or act
- Solve this as if you're a group of Year 6 students
- You have no authority, no budget, and no email
- Pitch it as a 30-second TV ad or dance move

Teams act, draw, build, or otherwise show a playful first attempt at engaging with their challenge using the assigned constraint. This step removes pressure and invites playfulness.

3. Remix with random prompts (15 minutes)

Each team now receives a remix prompt card designed to shift or expand their perspective. Examples include:

- What would an artist do?
- Shrink the idea – what would it look like in 15 minutes?
- Make it joyful or surprising
- Involve someone unexpected — a student, a cleaner, a neighbour

Teams revise or reimagine their original idea using the remix prompt and prepare a new version. They may sketch, role-play, build a model or describe it in a short narrative. The goal is to stretch thinking beyond familiar approaches.

4. Test the possibility (15 minutes)

Now, each team selects one idea or approach from their revised version that they could try in a small way within the next two weeks. This is not a full program – it's a small, low-risk step toward enacting the idea in real school life.

Teams complete an action sketch, which helps them move from imaginative play to practical action.

Action sketch template

What part of your idea are you trying out?

Describe one small element you can try immediately.

a. Who needs to be part of it?

List the people or roles involved.

b. Where and when will it happen?

Be specific – a particular place, time, and situation.

c. What will you look or listen for?

Identify signs of engagement, curiosity, disruption or response.

d. What's your next move after that?

Note one thing you'll do based on what happens – build on it, adjust it, or rethink it.

This step grounds possibility in real-world action and helps leadership teams begin testing creative approaches with intention and purpose.

5. Gallery walk and reflect (15 minutes)

Teams post their action sketches around the room.

Participants walk around the space, reading the sketches and leaving sticky notes with:

- 'Yes, and . . .' suggestions
- Thoughtful questions
- Comments on what excites, challenges, or surprises them

Bring the whole group together for a short reflective discussion.

For discussion

- What shifted in your thinking today?
- How did play help you see your challenge differently?
- What's one small possibility you'll carry back to your leadership practice?

The transition from Playing with Possibility to Selecting and Evaluating marks a shift from imaginative and playful exploration of possibilities to deliberate action. This phase is essential in a transforming school, where ideas need to become embedded and made into action. At this point, leaders begin to recognize which possibilities are most aligned with their values, context and capabilities. Some ideas may remain as provocations that stretch thinking. Others are shaped into strategies that can be trialled and refined. This stage invites courage to move forward in uncertainty and calls for wisdom in choosing where to focus collective effort. It is also a moment for collaboration, where leadership teams identify the ideas with the greatest potential and begin the shared work of bringing them into practice.

Selecting and evaluating responses

The selecting and evaluating stage supports school leaders to translate possibilities into action. It requires making wise choices from numerous ideas and continuous, iterative evaluation (both self-reflection and external feedback) to refine strategies. This process empowers leaders by enabling evidence-based practice, ensuring initiatives are effective and continuously revised. It fosters useful innovation aligned with context, supports strategic planning and monitoring for wise decisions through ongoing reflection and adaptation, leading to effective initiatives and a culture of innovative transformation.

This final process in the Creativity Cascade is also a test of courage. Courageous leadership is not only about taking bold leaps, it is also about knowing when to act, how to adapt and when to respond to what is emerging. For school leaders, selecting from a range of possibilities often requires letting go of status-quo practices in favour of new, uncertain directions. This involves risk, and with it, the possibility of failure. Courage lies in acting and remaining open to learning from what happens.

At the same time, selecting and evaluating must extend beyond the actions of individual leaders. It should be embedded in the culture of the school. This is where leadership-as-practice becomes critical. Evaluating the success and relevance of creative initiatives is not a solitary act. it is embedded in the collective rhythms of the school community. In schools working towards transformation, this process is not reserved for formal review cycles but is present in everyday conversations, planning meetings, student reflections and community discussions.

Leadership-as-practice transforms evaluation into a distributed form of agency. Rather than depending on a few leaders to assess possibilities all in the school community can have a voice. This collaborative and distributed approach also creates the conditions for sustainable transformation. When creative actions are selected collectively and evaluated collaboratively, they are more likely to stick. People see themselves in the work. They are invested not only in the outcomes, but in the processes of inquiry and adaptation that shape those outcomes. This reinforces a school culture where everyone contributes to the ongoing refinement of practice, and where innovation is not a one-off project but a continuous, evolving commitment. A way to make this process a reality is through the Selecting and Evaluating Pathway.

Selecting and Evaluating Pathway

The Selecting and Evaluating Pathway is inspired by Participatory Action Research[36] and supports inquiry, collaboration and creativity in decision making. It is not only a space for reflection but also a generative process where creative leadership can take shape. Leaders use the pathway to move from imaginative ideas to deliberate, context-aware actions. Selecting is not only about narrowing options. It is a creative action that involves selecting possibilities that are courageous enough to shift practice yet realistic enough to be taken up in the context of the school. In a similar way evaluation is not the end of a process but part of an ongoing cycle of inquiry.

Figure 6.5 The Selecting and Evaluating Pathway enables action and innovation

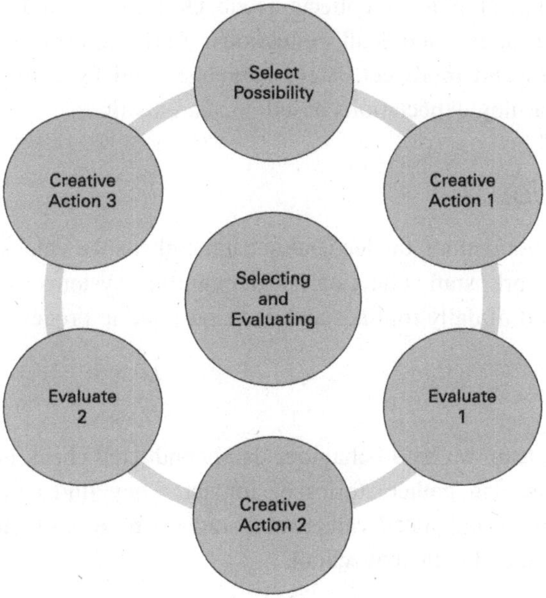

In this way, the Selecting and Evaluating Pathway becomes a structure that supports creative experimentation, builds collective agency and helps teams bring ideas to life in ways that are thoughtful, responsive and capable of generating transformation.

Here's how the Selecting and Evaluating Pathway might be applied in a school working to embed its core values into everyday practice.

Select possibility

After recognizing that the school's core values are not consistently reflected in daily practice, the leadership team explores possibilities such as revising the values to ensure relevance, embedding them into curriculum and behaviour processes, and co-developing values-led practices with students and staff.

Creative action 1

Following community consultation and review of school data, the leadership team chooses to relaunch the school values with a focus on shared ownership. They work with staff and student leaders to co-create clear definitions and real-life examples of what each value looks like in learning, behaviour, and relationships.

Evaluate 1

The new values are introduced through assemblies, classroom dialogue and visual displays. The leadership team collects feedback through student voice forums, classroom walkthroughs and staff reflections. Early indicators show increased student awareness and more consistent language used by staff when discussing behaviour and learning expectations based on shared values.

Creative action 2

Building on this momentum, the leadership team embeds the values into the school's behaviour framework, staff induction and recognition systems – ensuring that the values became part of daily routines and decision-making processes.

Evaluate 2

After a term, the team reviews behaviour data, conducted check in interviews with staff and students, and gather stories of impact. They find enhanced alignment between staff actions and stated values, and students reported feeling clearer about what was expected and valued at school.

Creative action 3

To deepen the cultural shift, the leadership team establishes student and staff values ambassadors who facilitate peer workshops, lead weekly reflections in mentor groups, and curated examples of values in action to share across the school community.

The evaluation could lead to this approach being adopted in other areas such as curriculum change, staff professional learning etc (select possibility), regenerating values embedded practices across the school and initiating a new pathway. Practice 6.6 Planning with the Selecting and Evaluating Pathway explores this process.

Practice 6.6 Planning with the selecting and evaluating pathway

As discussed, selection and evaluation are an iterative and interactive process. This Practice may unfold over several sessions. It acts as a dynamic process to help leadership teams plan, frame, refine, reframe, and act. The Selecting and Evaluating Pathway (Figure 6.6) provides a scaffold that can be revisited throughout your creative action. It becomes a living document. In essence a visual record of your evolving thinking and leadership.

Let's revisit the example of how this might work in a school leadership context.

Your leadership team has identified a desire to embed the school's core values – curiosity, inquiry and wisdom – more intentionally across the life of the school. This becomes your central possibility:

> 'Bringing the values of curiosity, inquiry and wisdom to life in teaching, learning, and leadership.'

Using the Selecting and evaluating Pathway, map your imaginings on a large sheet of paper (A3 or larger). Use words, diagrams or images to represent your ideas, showing how key actions and evaluation strategies connect to your central possibility.

- ***Select possibility***

  In the top circle, write your possibility:

  > 'Bringing the values of curiosity, inquiry and wisdom to life in teaching, learning, and leadership'.

  This may have emerged from staff conversations, strategic planning processes, or noticing a disconnect between stated values and daily practices.

- ***Creative action 1***

  Based on your selected possibility, plan the first round of actions. This might involve:

  - A professional learning program exploring how to embed the values into pedagogy and classroom culture.
  - Co-designing and co-teaching units of work that explicitly build inquiry and curiosity.
  - Creating reflective tools for students and staff to engage with the idea of wisdom in learning.

- ***Evaluate 1***

  In the next circle, choose an evaluation method aligned with your focus. This might include:

  - Focus groups with students and teachers across different year levels.
  - A review of curriculum documents and lesson plans to identify where the values are present or absent.

These strategies help gather early insights. For example:

- Are students encouraged to be curious in their learning?
- Are inquiry-based approaches being used?
- Do staff feel confident in fostering wisdom through reflective practice and ethical decision-making?

- *Creative Action 2*

  Identify the changes to be made and implement again. These changes (emerging from Evaluate 1) might include:

  - Limiting the inquiry approach to specific year levels.
  - Adjusting the professional learning program based on teacher feedback (fewer sessions that go deeper).
  - Partnering with students to design new approaches or practices that reflect these values.

- *Evaluate 2*

  Plan how this second phase will be evaluated. Consider using:

  - Student-led learning reviews
  - Collaborative peer observation
  - Samples of student work demonstrating the values in action

  Your evaluation method should suit the nature and scope of your updated creative action.

- *Creative action 3*

  Use the findings from Evaluate 2 to generate new ideas and refine your leadership strategy. Perhaps the work leads to a new school-wide focus: 'Positioning wisdom as a hallmark of our school'. This becomes the start of another cycle, using the Selecting and Evaluating Pathway to scaffold the next phase.

You can repeat this process for other initiatives. Leadership teams might develop multiple Selecting and Evaluating Pathways – one for professional learning, another for student agency, another for pedagogical transformation. These can be visualized in a 'creative galaxy', where each map links to others.

For example, you might notice that embedding curiosity and inquiry in the curriculum is supported by staff professional learning in questioning techniques. Or that student reflection on wisdom connects with your school's wellbeing and leadership programs. The 'galaxy' view helps teams visualize how distinct strategies support and reinforce each other. This kind of visual mapping supports understanding, planning, and communication across the school. It can also reveal new possibilities – connections that deepen your insight into how things work, and how they might evolve over time.

Concluding reflections

Leaders in schools confront challenges that resist traditional leadership approaches, requiring creativity. The adaptive capacities that creativity offers can support leaders to respond dynamically to shifting social, cultural and technological landscapes. Rather than viewing creativity as an optional extra, educational leaders can recognize it as a fundamental requirement for navigating uncertainty and fostering sustainable transformation. The Creativity Cascade can assist here by transforming abstract ideas into tangible actions, enabling leaders to bridge the gap between visionary thinking and practical implementation within each school's context.

The framework presented here in the Cascade provides school leaders with some ways to enable the 'how' of transformation. Noticing develops the contextual understanding necessary for informed decision-making, while Asking why? Really why? reveals the interconnected nature of educational challenges. Playing with Possibility throws up new ideas from playful exploration and selecting and evaluating generates the feedback loops essential for iterative transformation. Together, these elements have the potential to create a coherent approach to leadership that recognizes each school's context and values.

The transformation from status quo leadership to leading for transformation through creativity represents more than a shift in a few leadership techniques. It requires a fundamental change in how educational leaders understand their role. Creativity encourages them individually and collectively to embrace complexity, engage in sustained inquiry, foster collaborative innovation, and maintain commitment to wise and beneficial change. In our interconnected and rapidly evolving world, such creative leadership becomes indispensable for creating schools where every member of the learning community can develop agency and fulfil their potential.

In the next chapter we discuss how transformative leadership can encompass joy and motivation.

Key actions

1. Develop a culture of noticing for yourself and as cultural practice in your school: Encourage leaders to actively observe and interpret their surroundings, interactions, and experiences within the school environment.
2. Engage in deep inquiry: Foster a habit of asking 'why, really why?' to explore root causes, underlying assumptions, and broader contexts of observed patterns and cultural features in the school.
3. Play with possibilities: Create opportunities for collaborative possibility thinking and experimentation, allowing for the exploration of diverse perspectives to challenges while considering the contextual features of the

school. This becomes possible when creativity is developed and applied in leadership and elsewhere in the school.

4. Select and evaluate: Based on noticing, deep inquiry and playing with possibilities act. Generate some achievable transformative strategies that you try in your school. Use the Selecting and Evaluating Pathway to evaluate them.

Leading through joy and motivation

7

Figure 7.1 Artist Francis Alÿs' short films of children playing games was exhibited at the Venice Biennale in 2022. Here is featured film #29 'La roue' (2021) from the Democratic Republic of Congo

Children's games, or are they?

Francis Alÿs is a Belgian artist living in Mexico who makes short films[1] of children playing games from around the world, mostly from the Global South. The thirty-plus films have an extraordinary impact when they are screened simultaneously in art exhibitions such as Venice's Biennale. In figure 7.1 we see an image from a Democratic Republic of the Congo film where a boy pushes a large tyre up a slag heap with great determination and then thrillingly rolls inside the tyre all the way down the enormous hill.

In all Alÿs' films, children use ordinary objects and their bodies to create their playful worlds. The films evoke a poignant humanism that is hopeful and joyful, even in the direst social and economic conditions. In Iraq, children play leapfrog in the desert, in a refugee camp they play hopscotch, in Belgium they race painted snails and in the Democratic Republic of the Congo children hum at a particular pitch to attract and kill mosquitos. All the videos show the dexterity, determination and delight of children, and their overwhelming capacity for resilience through creative and collaborative play.

We use one of the games called Nzango (see figure 7.2, film #28, 2021, from the Democratic Republic of the Congo) to provide insights into human behaviour and what that could mean for joy and motivation, and leadership-as-practice in schools. We argue throughout this book that leadership is a practice that can be developed and supported in everyone in a school community. Leadership-as-practice sees leadership everywhere, in anyone, at any time. It focuses on what we can accomplish together rather than what one person thinks or does.[2] Leadership-as-practice is developed in a school culture through embedded social practices in the way we say and do things and relate with each other.

In chapter 2, we introduced a coherence maker, the Leadership Lantern, which encapsulates what needs to be considered for transformation to happen in schools. The lantern as a metaphor describes how its illumination provides direction in transformation, but the lantern is also a light that should create joy and motivation. This chapter is about the significance of joy and autonomous motivation in developing the potential, engagement, learning and well-being of people in schools. How leadership is practiced in schools affects how teachers teach which affects how students flourish, learn and achieve.[3]

The engagement of students, and the low morale and well-being of teachers are widely recognized as issues (and in some places a crisis) for schools.[4] Disengagement and low morale is related to a lack of joy and autonomous motivation in schools.[5] How then can leadership-as-practice develop joy and motivation? We return to the children's game Nzango to deepen our understanding of joy and motivation.

The game Nzango involves girls imitating and anticipating the leg movements of the facing player as a mirror image. The pace is fast and set by both teams singing and clapping in unison. To an outsider watching the game, the lightning speed movements of the girls seem impossible to mimic and predict. The game is subtle and mesmerizing, and suggests a deeply shared understanding, almost telepathic

Figure 7.2 In the rhythmic children's game Nzango, played in the Democratic Republic of the Congo, the girls mirror each other's lightning-fast leg movements

connection between the girls. They communicate and 'mirror' each other through imperceptible movements.

What do we notice about the game?

First, we notice the skills of the young girls, they have exceptional competence in rhythm, movement and mimicry. Mirroring or mimicking people's actions and behaviours is called limbic synchrony, and it's an unconscious function hardwired into human brains.[6] The game is fast and competitive and all the girls in the circle are in what can be described as a 'state of flow'. Psychology researcher Mihaly Csikszentmihalyi explains 'flow' as the feeling of 'an almost automatic, effortless, yet highly focused state of consciousness'.[7]

What we also see in Nzango (and all the children's games in Francis Alÿs' videos) is that there are no adults directing the play. The children are self-motivated and self-regulated in their play. In Nzango, the girls play because there is inherent enjoyment in their desire to challenge themselves with the dance moves. The girls are actively committed to learn and extend themselves through the game.[8] What we see is intrinsic motivation.

There is also evidence of collaboration, that is, the girls are co-constructing the game together as a shared endeavour. There is also creativity, as they try to challenge their opponent with novel and faster ways to do the dance moves. As they play, they consider or reflect on what is working and what isn't, to adjust their tactics in the game. The rhythmic clapping, dancing and playing of the game is a form of communication that creates meaning and purpose for these young girls. In other words, the 4Cs: creativity, critical reflection, communication and collaboration are evident in the game.

Who is the leader in the game? Leadership appears to be constantly changing, shared and emergent. It is not leaderless; the game works because it is 'full of leadership'. Everyone is demonstrating leadership for the game to work, it is 'leadership-as-practice'. According to leadership researcher Joe Raelin, 'leadership is directly tied to the practices to which people are dedicated. Through their practices, they decide on what they hope to accomplish and organize the tasks that need to be performed to achieve their mission. They commit to one another as a working body dedicated to a useful outcome.'[9]

What might this children's game mean for schools?

Imagine if . . .

Imagine if the practice of leadership in schools feels like a state of flow, that it feels effortless, highly focused and creative. Imagine if you feel joy and delight in most of the work you are doing, and that positive relationships and collaboration drive the direction of the school. Imagine if others around you feel just as joyful, highly motivated and engaged with the achievements and challenges of your school. Imagine students being engaged and self-motivated to learn. Imagine finding fun in what you do, and knowing anything is possible for your students, staff and community. Imagine that you can pursue goals and ignore distractions, and that working with others leads to joyful discoveries.

Is the practice of leadership in your school as joyous as the children playing Nzango, or is it, weighed down by the stress and burden of workload, imposed reforms and policies, accountability systems, disruptive students and staff and parent concerns? Does joy and play belong only to children playing games or can it exist in classrooms and in the world of adults, and in the practice of leadership?

We would love teachers in schools to have the joy and motivation evident in the children playing games that introduce this chapter. Is that, however, a utopian dream that can never be realized because of the systemic realities of schools? Can this be a reality when teachers are concerned that even students may not be experiencing much joy in the classroom? Before discussing why joy matters to the practice of leadership, we must consider how joy is essential to the core business of learning in schools.

Why joy matters in the classroom

The experience of positive emotions such as joy, happiness, optimism, self-belief, confidence and hope improves learning outcomes. Research in psychology and neuroscience finds that emotions and cognition are inextricably linked, and that positive emotions enhance the attention, memory and motivation of learners.[10]

Neuroimaging and neuroelectric-recording studies of the human brain show that three main structures in the brain architecture (the anterior cingulate, the orbitofrontal cortex and the amygdala) deeply connect our emotions to the processes of cognition and are heavily connected to pleasure and reward. According to education neuroscientists Li, Gow and Zhou:

> Positive emotions and feelings are mainly manifested in increased learning opportunities – creating a state where more learning is able to take place – and this increase is completed through successive activations of enhanced psychological schemas, a pattern of thought or behaviour known for organizing information and showing relationships. Put simply, because a learning process is going well, the learner is able to visualize it continuing to go well and so continues in this way.[11]

Students who experience learning with more positive emotions such as joy and happiness tend to be able to self-monitor and self-regulate their learning. Students who experience negative emotions such as unhappiness, boredom, anxiety, lack of self-worth or confidence, tend to be less self-motivated and rely on being externally monitored by someone else, such as a teacher, to learn and perform.

Positive emotions experienced in learning also enhance attention and memory. Negative and even neutral emotions can inhibit or jeopardize memory, engagement and motivation. Therefore, students in a positive emotional state can drive towards higher levels of attainment and are more likely to adapt to more self-regulated, flexible and innovative learning strategies.[12]

Joy and other positive emotions are deeply connected to student motivation in the classroom. Despite this knowledge about positive emotions and learning, student engagement and well-being are problems for schools, particularly in the middle to high school years. The COVID pandemic and the move to online learning exacerbated these issues, but the problems with student engagement were already evident well before the pandemic.[13]

We argue that leadership-as-practice can create an environment for joy and motivation, and contribute to closing the joy, engagement and well-being gap in schools.

The joy and wellbeing gap in schools

We will focus on practices of leadership that can enhance joy and motivation, but in doing so, we acknowledge the impact that education systems and policies have on joy and motivation in schools. Reviews across a range of countries and school systems have shown that educator (and student) well-being is at an all-time low.[14] Morale, energy and renewal are critical, and require a reimagining of how we do things in schools. Research educators Dennis Shirley, Andy Hargreaves and Shaneé Washingtin-Wangia found:

> that sustainable change in regard to educator's well-being must address and transform the core aspects of their work in ways that draw on their aspirations

> for moral purpose and their quest for collaborative professionalism with their colleagues. Add-ons like mediation or yoga classes outside of schools are popular amongst educators, but they are incomplete without redesigning the everyday ways that their work is organised and supported.[15]

The premise of this book is that leadership-as-practice developed in a school culture can transform schools. However, governing education bodies and systems must support schools in doing this. Education systems that oversee schools must examine how they contribute to ill-being (such as the over reliance on standardized testing and accountability administration overload) and how they can support schools with coherent and consistent strategies for well-being.

It is not just schools that have a joy problem. In a survey[16] of 500 workers across a range of companies, industries, ages and countries, 90 per cent of workers expect to feel joy at work, but only 37 per cent report it as their lived work experience. There is a substantial gap between the expectation of joy in the workplace and the actual experience of working. But does it have to be like this? We explain why joy is critical in leadership-as-practice and describe some approaches and strategies that can be used to encourage it. Then we will look at the relationship between joy and motivation in leadership-as-practice.

Why joy matters in leadership practice

First and foremost, experiences of joy affect our well-being. Joy lifts our spirits and our energy because it is generated from situations that relate to our sense of meaning, goals and desires in life.[17] Joy can bring a sense of internal harmony and unity within ourselves, and a sense of vitality, potency and aliveness.[18] Leadership as a practice cannot be instigated by burnt-out, hollowed out human-beings in a constant state of busyness and distraction. How can we motivate, support, develop and learn from others when our tank is empty or constantly overflowing?

Joy is fundamental to a human's life and well-being. The 'broaden and build' theory[19] in positive psychology explains how repeated experiences of joy expands our thoughts and actions to facilitate the learning of new modes of thoughts and behaviours. Feeling joy opens us up to new possibilities and provides us with the opportunity to learn new cognitive and behavioural skills, and to forge new social relationships and skills. Moments of joy have long-lasting consequences in our lives as they help us to build capacities that allow us to navigate and develop resilience for future challenges and obstacles. Joy and other positive emotions build enduring physical, intellectual, psychological and social resources in us.

Joy is described as a positive emotion, mood or disposition, and theologians, philosophers, poets and artists have long known the profound effect of feeling joy. Nobel Prize winning poet Seamus Heaney said in an interview, 'I've always associated the moment of writing with a moment of lift, of joy, of unexpected reward'. Joy is often associated with creativity and achieving an outcome that is hoped for but not presumed.

Joy is also primarily felt as an affiliated or social phenomenon, that is, it is often experienced with other people in the fulfilment of a shared desire.[20] For instance, you may feel affiliated joy with your team when you are involved in a particular school event that goes beyond expectations. Or, when a student triumphs over adversity with your support, or it can be an exciting new idea you come up with others. It can simply be the joy felt when a loved colleague returns to work after some time away. Leaders can explore the nature of joy with their teams through the reflection Practice 7.1, Where's the Joy?

Practice 7.1 Where's the joy?

Figure 7.3 Children dancing with an orange in Copenhagen, from one of Francis Alÿs' short films, *Children's Game #34: Appelsindans* (2022)

The 'how' of the Practice

This is both an individual and group Practice.

Reflect on a time that you felt joy in your life or work. Individually write, draw or find an object that captures that joyous moment. Then describe that joyous moment with others, and why you found joy in it.

After people have shared their experiences of joy, discuss what you notice about these experiences. What are the features across these experiences, what is common, and what is different?

The 'why' of the Practice

- Develops metacognition of joy through awareness and focus on joyful experiences and considers how joy may be cultivated more regularly.
- Influences feelings of joy through transference, i.e. joy is contagious and we can spread and share joy.
- Supports understanding in how joy can help to potentiate action in ourselves and others.

The 'where to next' with the Practice

Consider:

- How your disposition for joy can be developed.
- How being metacognitive of joyful experiences can transfer feelings of joy to others.
- How aspects of school life can be reframed through the 'joy lens'.
- How this reframing could become embedded culturally in your school rather than a one-off action that is soon forgotten.

Joy is crucial for leadership-as-practice as it encourages action. Joy is energizing and gives people the motivation to act, to intervene and improve.[21] People sharing and experiencing moments of joy together also deeply connects them.[22] Leadership-as-practice needs experiences of joy to encourage people to take the many steps to achieve goals that may be challenging and visionary.

A multidisciplinary project at Yale University, the Theology of Joy and the Good Life project defines joy as 'a positive, affective response to an objective external good, construed rightly and about which one is rightly concerned'.[23] In other words, joy is both affective and cognitive, that is, we feel joyful when we perceive and evaluate situations as a gift to us. This means we can develop a disposition for joy and construe and create situations as more joyous. Like a gardener we can find the potential for joy by cultivating it in our environment. But how?

Based on positive psychology research,[24] we offer some practical strategies that can foster joy in leadership-as-practice. We frame and make coherence of these ideas through the lens of the 4Cs: creativity, critical reflection, communication and collaboration. The 4Cs are foundational capabilities to cultivate practical experiences in schools that can create or contribute to an environment that recognizes and encourages experiences of joy. To begin, joy in creativity means leadership as a practice needs to be playful and bold.

The 4Cs: how the practice of leadership can find joy

Joy in creativity means playing and being bold

Joy in creativity means needing to play, and that means making opportunities for experiences that are lively, rigorous, purposeful and absorbing like a children's game. This can be a creative task that is used to address a school challenge or ambition. For example, we know a school where the staff, students and parent community created a sculpture to represent their school vision. They individually contributed and collaborated over time to construct a tree sculpture made from branches, colourful wool, paper and other materials. Making the sculpture was a playful and creative way for the school community to engage with and contribute to the school's direction. The tree itself was a symbol and expression of joy and helped to inspire them to drive change in their school.

Finding opportunities for playing and creating is rejuvenating and reawakens the feeling of joy, sometimes only associated with childhood for some adults. Years ago, in a professional learning workshop, we remember a principal becoming visibly upset that the creative task we had given him had sparked a feeling of play and joy he had never felt in his leadership practice. He realized these were the very things that had attracted him to teaching in the first place. The pressures, stresses and expectations in his leadership role had switched off his capacity to play and derive pleasure from his work. His epiphany was that joy and delight in leadership-as-practice were just as significant as they were for learning in the classroom.

In children, play facilitates the development of social competence, emotional capacities, resilience, creativity and problem-solving skills.[25] Neuroscientists argue that although play is abundant in children and young animals, it is also present in adults. Throughout life, play may contribute to the continued development of our physical, social, cognitive and emotional functions and health.[26] Play can also enhance wellbeing and reduce stress.[27]

Play is critical for leadership-as-practice, for through play and creativity, we can create bold, new ideas and better problem solve 'curly' challenges with greater flexibility and openness.[28] Play is something that we need to practice and make time for. Playing and being brave with new ideas can evoke joyful experiences of discovery, creation and pleasure.[29]

Reflection questions:

- Why is play and creativity valuable for the practice of leadership?
- When did you see adults playing or creating in your school, and what was its purpose and effect on them?
- How could play and creativity be integrated into your leadership practice?
- When have you acted boldly and felt joy in your leadership practice?

Joy in critical reflection means finding and creating joy

Author Eleanor H. Porter said through her character, Pollyanna, '. . . most generally there is something about everything that you can be glad about, if you keep hunting long enough to find it.'[30] Joy can be developed as a disposition by seeing situations as good or as a gift.[31] This means we can look for, find or create joy around us. We can appreciate and see the potential for joy by first being more critically reflective and metacognitive of joy. The Where's the Joy? (Practice 7.1) is an example of developing metacognition to strengthen our awareness and recognition of joyful experiences.

What prevents joy in the school environment can also be examined through critical reflection. For example, consider whether work meetings, workloads and responsibilities prevent joy. How could these things be re-imagined, re-framed and done differently in schools? This is no easy task and will probably take some bold initiatives such as prioritising what is crucial and what can be done more productively.[32]

For instance, we have observed how high school teachers have made joyless faculty meetings focused on administrivia into something more productive and pleasurable. These teachers have reimagined their faculty time as opportunities to pair, share and experience new practices they have introduced in their classrooms, such as a new learning strategy or a novel way to begin a unit of work. Dealing with faculty administration instead was reduced to a strict, stand-up five-minute huddle at the beginning of the week. These teachers re-structured their faculty time by reducing and being more productive with administration and making joy, and learning from each other, a priority.

Reflection questions:

- What is your disposition for joy, and how can you find experiences of joy around you?
- How does your team find joy?
- What can be done differently in your school environment to find and create joy?

Joy in communication means celebrating and finding purpose

A joyful disposition is also developed when situations are reframed in a positive rather than negative light.[33] Joy is primarily a social phenomenon and is therefore contagious.[34] The way we celebrate and frame stories in the positive, effects and motivates others.[35] Often, we observe in schools a negative outlook towards challenges and obstacles, rather than celebrating what has actually been achieved. Practice 7.2 Celebrate and Shift is an example of how challenges can be reframed.

A practice of leadership that celebrates challenges and successes can foster a climate for joy when everyone feels they have purpose and investment in what they are doing. For example, we have witnessed joy with a teaching team in a middle school where they had a strong sense of motivation and determination in what they were doing. They were equally committed to a new integrated teaching program and invested in deeply knowing their students. As a team, they felt enormous joy celebrating the shifts in their students' behaviours and achievements.

In the same school we have seen cynicism and undermining from other positional leaders not involved in the program who didn't want to share in celebrating the team's achievements. What is the sense of purpose and ethics of these positional leaders? Leadership as a practice should find moral purpose, act on what matters and connect with others to spread and celebrate joy. This highlights the moral dimensions of joy and leadership-as-practice. Joy should be to delight in what is ethical and good, and not to delight in others' misfortunes or seek to sabotage other's joy.[36] Leadership-as-practice should be ethical and show moral integrity by enabling others, delighting in what is good and spreading the joy.[37]

Reflection questions

- How can you frame situations in a positive light, and celebrate challenges?
- What is your moral purpose, and what is it for your team?
- How can you communicate purpose and stories of joy?
- Why would people sabotage other's joy?

Practice 7.2 Celebrate and shift

The 'how' of the Practice

This Practice is engaged with individually first and then with everyone in a team.

Each team member is given as many sticky notes they need to individually write down what they perceive as the achievements and gains they can celebrate, and the things that they perceive need shifting. Each celebration or shift is a separate sticky note. When team members have completed this task, they share their celebrations and shifts by placing their sticky notes on a board divided into two columns labelled 'celebration' and 'shift'. As they share their sticky notes, they connect them with other celebrations and shifts already on the board. A facilitator groups and organizes the celebrations and shifts into themes for a further team discussion.

The 'why' of the Practice

- Celebrates the efforts and conviction of a team towards achievements and gains over time (nothing is too small) that often go unrecognized because of the focus on bigger, long-term goals and vision.
- Reframes challenges as on-going shifts that can be achieved over time and with strategy.
- Supports a positive and collaborative outlook for the team and aims to communicate and clarify their vision and goals.

The 'where to next' with this Practice

The team considers:

- What to learn from their celebrations (achievements).
- How to share the joy and celebrate what has been achieved in the school.
- How to prioritize and strategize actions towards the shifts they need to address.

Joy in collaboration means connecting . . . and probably laughing more

Joy is found in human connection. The more we bond with others and have a sense of belonging, the more we are likely to experience joy.[38] Connecting with others gives us a sense of purpose and deeper sense of meaning in our lives. Fostering relationships is critical for leadership-as-practice, so time needs to be invested in making connections with people in a social sense and through collaboration. To do that we build trust and a clear and agreed moral purpose through those relationships. If trust and shared moral purpose don't exist in relationships, there will be no joy in leadership.[39]

For true collaboration in teams, leadership as a practice supports the development of mutual trust, a clarity of shared purpose, equal commitment and respect for everyone's expertise.[40] Collaboration struggles where there is no real connection amongst people, selfish agendas and toxic relationships. Collaboration cannot thrive in a command-and-control approach to leadership or where there is a lack of mutual respect. Sometimes people feel too busy and overburdened to connect and collaborate.[41] If any of these situations are accepted as the cultural norm of a school or team, joylessness will permeate a culture.

Laughter is not the solution to all relational issues, but it helps. People are connected through shared laughter. Laughter lowers stress hormones, increases positive mood and strengthens social connections.[42] Like playfulness and seeing the positive in things, the practice of leadership can authentically cultivate laughter in the work environment by seeing levity and joy in situations.

Reflection questions

- How would you describe the connection with your team? Is their mutual trust and commitment to a shared goal?
- How often does your team collaborate on something as a shared endeavour?
- How often do you laugh with your colleagues? How could you laugh more?

Leading through joy is critical for well-being in a school, but a certain type of motivation in leadership practice also plays a key role in staff well-being, student engagement and school transformation. Our own motivation and how we motivate others defines the type of leadership practiced. Motivation is at the heart of what teachers and students can achieve together in the classroom and how leadership is practiced in a school.

How motivation is inculcated in others is deeply related to how teams experience work satisfaction and joy. We will discuss the significant role motivation plays in leadership-as-practice and how autonomous and intrinsic motivation support teacher well-being, transformation of practices and student learning.

Why motivation matters in the practice of leadership

Motivation is an invisible force that directs, energizes and sustains people's behaviour over time and across changing circumstances.[43] Motivation predicts commitment, work effort, engagement, well-being and job performance in the workplace.[44] Leadership-as-practice is to be motivated and to motivate others.

Leadership can have a proximal external influence on motivation, that is, the social influence of leading affects the perception and motivation of those around us.[45] The practice of leadership has the potential to motivate or demotivate others. Leadership can influence the work environment depending on the type of motivation used. For instance, leadership that uses reward and punishment to motivate people's behaviour can create an environment that feels controlling and constraining. This is described as 'controlled motivation'. Leadership practice that encourages and supports people to contribute to shared goals can foster an environment where people have a sense of autonomy and commitment. This is described as 'autonomous motivation'.

In schools, people need to be personally invested if a genuine commitment to a shared moral purpose is to be created that in turn generates motivated action. Leadership as a practice creates an environment that builds autonomous motivation in people, rather than controlled motivation. But how can we create an environment that encourages and supports people to be motivated of their own volition?

Self-Determination Theory[46] developed by psychology researchers Richard Ryan and Edward Deci[47] is a broad and widely applied theory of human motivation, development and wellness. Self-Determination Theory explains how certain types of motivational behaviours develop autonomous motivation and a greater sense of well-being in people. It describes the conditions that can influence a range of motivational states, from a lack of motivation, to controlled motivation, to autonomous motivation. Motivation varies according to how much people are controlled or regulated externally by outside influences (extrinsic motivation) or regulated internally within themselves (intrinsic motivation).

A lack of motivation happens when there is no regulation occurring externally or internally. No motivation promotes no or little initiative to do anything. Extrinsic motivation can be based on external rewards such as money, status, praise or goals. Intrinsic motivation is based on internal personal satisfaction. The degree to which motivation is internally regulated depends upon how much what people are doing aligns with their personal values, beliefs, needs and capacities.[48] For instance, being internally or autonomously motivated to try a new teaching strategy depends on whether you believe the new teaching strategy is worth trying, whether you believe there is a need for it and whether you think you can do it. If you don't believe any of these things, you either won't do it, or you do it unwillingly with a degree of resentment and without sustained commitment.

Autonomous motivation is when you take initiative and action because what you are doing resonates with your internal belief system or values. You are autonomously motivated to act when you view something as valuable, worthy, relevant, interesting or enjoyable. In the practice of leadership, how do we develop in others, autonomous motivation towards a mutual goal? Self-Determination Theory explores how leadership practice can do this. First, we consider a range of leadership practices or behaviours that don't cultivate autonomous motivation in a team or staff.

Leadership practices that don't build autonomous motivation

In table 7.1 we explain motivation as a continuum from amotivating to extrinsically to intrinsically motivating leadership behaviours. We describe the leadership qualities that typify these different types of motivation on the continuum.

Lackadaisical leadership

A lack of motivation involves leadership '*non-regulating others*' and this is characterized by apathetic or disengaged behaviours. These leaders either don't know how to practice leadership or don't want to lead as they have other priorities. These behaviours are amotivating and produce a lack of motivation in those around them.

Command leadership

'*External regulating of others'* describes transactional leadership behaviours that regulate people using extrinsic rewards and punishments. These leaders use command and control, and compliance to get things done. In these circumstances other people are regulated externally through desire and fear and don't have any autonomous motivation to act of their own volition.

Praising leadership

'*Some external regulating of others (introjected)*' is characterized by using only praise and encouragement as a motivating force. This provides some internal regulation, but the effect on a team or staff is an unconscious adoption of ideas and attitudes rather than the autonomy of consciously taking them on.

These amotivational and controlled motivational leadership practices exist in schools.[49] Telling people what to do *(external regulation)* and giving praise and encouragement *(some external regulation)* are expedient leadership behaviours. They take the least amount of time to implement, and they are simple and straightforward. They are often perceived as 'just wanting to get things done', however, they are forms of controlled motivation and don't support or build autonomous motivation.

Rewards also don't necessarily build autonomous motivation in people. Early experimental work in Self-Determination Theory showed that rewards (especially monetary rewards) for doing an interesting activity could decrease people's intrinsic motivation for doing the activity, whereas positive feedback could sustain or enhance motivation. Further studies and several meta-analyses have confirmed how controlling rewards can negatively affect intrinsic motivation.[50] Self-Determination Theory argues that,

> any factors in social environments that detract from an internal perceived locus of causality, or sense of autonomy, will diminish intrinsic motivation. Not only controlling rewards undermine intrinsic motivation, so can motivational strategies such as controlling praise, threats of punishment, surveillance, controlling language, and grades and evaluations. Even tone of voice can convey control versus autonomy support, thereby undermining intrinsic motivation.[51]

Instead, more positive extrinsic and intrinsic motivational practices support the development of autonomous motivation in staff and teams. However, these behaviours are sometimes viewed as less expedient and more subtle and sophisticated to implement.

Table 7.1 A continuum based on Self-Determination Theory[52] describing leadership behaviours that create different types of motivation in others

As leaders how we do we motivate others?					
Lack of motivation	**Controlled motivation**		**Autonomous motivation**		
Amotivating leadership behaviours	**Extrinsically motivating leadership behaviours**				**Intrinsically motivating leadership behaviours**
Non-regulating of others	External regulating of others	Some external regulating of others (introjected)	Some internal regulating (identified)	Internal regulating (integrated)	Internal regulating
Lackadaisical leadership	*Command leadership*	*Praising leadership*	*High expectations leadership*	*Moral purpose leadership*	*Empowering leadership*
Even though I am a positional leader, I have other priorities other than leading people, or I find it hard to lead. I focus on other things and leave people to their own devices, or I don't know how to lead people.	I lead by telling people what to do and rewarding them with praise and recognition when they do the things I tell them to do, and give negative feedback when they don't. I expect people to follow directions, do their best and to be accountable through compliance.	I lead by making people feel good about themselves and each other by being encouraging and supportive through praise and recognition. I want to impress on them that leadership and teaching is about working hard and effectively.	I lead by setting high expectations and having my team set the goals they wish to achieve. I want them to understand the need to challenge themselves to be effective leaders, teachers and team members.	I lead by raising awareness in my team of the moral imperative and responsibility we have to learn and challenge ourselves to be better leaders, teachers and team members.	I lead by empowering and inspiring the team to discern what challenges fulfil them and their students. I want them to have opportunities to continually grow themselves and others as leaders, teachers and team members.

Leadership practices that build autonomous motivation

There are a range of extrinsic and intrinsic motivational behaviours that can support and encourage autonomous motivation in teams (see table 7.1).

High expectations leadership

Leadership using extrinsically motivating behaviours such as encouraging people to set goals to challenge themselves is *'some internal regulating (identified)'*. This isn't an exercise in compliant goal setting but a process where teams have ownership and a commitment to achieving personal goals that matter to them. The motivation becomes somewhat internalized because it aligns with their personal values. This is when motivation begins to develop a sense of personal awareness and autonomy in people.

Moral purpose leadership

'*Internal regulating (integrated)*' is when motivation is unified with people's personal values and needs. These leadership practices encourage and support teams to be aware of their responsibilities and the benefits of challenging themselves. Teams are motivated to act and take on challenges they consider of worth because it resonates with them and matters to them morally.

Empowering leadership

'Internal regulating (intrinsic)' describes the conditions and opportunities that leaders can provide for others to discover an inherent satisfaction and active commitment in what they are doing. They are motivated because they are stimulated and engaged intrinsically. The benefits of a leadership practice that builds and supports autonomous and intrinsic motivation in people is organizational trust, job satisfaction, self-motivation, less absenteeism, better physical and psychological well-being and effective work performance.[53]

Knowing the different types of motivation supports understanding in the motivational styles in the practice of leadership and how teams operate (see Practice 7.3 What motivating leader are you?)

Practice 7.3 What motivating leader are you? Reflection

The 'how' of the Practice

Begin by doing this reflection on your own or by reflecting with a trusted colleague.

Think of examples of when you have demonstrated different types of motivation in your leadership practice. When have you shown lackadaisical, command, praising, high expectations, moral purpose and an empowering leadership practices?

Which types of leadership practices were easiest and hardest to find examples of? What motivation type do you feel most comfortable with? What would you like to develop?

The 'why' of the Practice

- Understands different types of motivation by finding examples in your own leadership practice.
- Begins reflection of your own motivational style and how you could develop autonomous motivation in others.
- Supports others in understanding and developing autonomous motivation in their sphere of influence.

The 'where to next' with the Practice

Do this Practice with others, but they don't necessarily need to share their examples. The Practice can prompt a team discussion about how to develop practices in autonomous motivation, and how they may be supported as practices in an on-going way.

Leadership-as-practice should cultivate autonomous motivation and encourage people to feel purpose and commitment towards actions that drive change in schools. We can also view autonomous motivation in leadership-as-practice through the lens of the 4C capabilities: creativity, critical reflection, communication and collaboration.

How the 4Cs develop autonomous motivation

The 4Cs and Self-Determination Theory can help to explain how leadership-as-practice cultivates autonomous motivation in others.

Leadership develops motivation through *creativity*,

- by providing opportunities for teams to choose and discover inherent enjoyment and commitment in challenging and creative work practices.

Leadership develops motivation through *critical reflection*,

- by enhancing awareness in teams of their moral responsibilities and the potential impact of challenging their work practices.

Leadership develops motivation through *communication*,

- by acknowledging and addressing a team's achievements and challenges as constructive feedback and encouragement.

Leadership develops motivation through *collaboration*,

- by encouraging teams to set personal and shared goals and actions that challenge their work practices.

In this chapter we focused on the benefits of autonomous motivation in leadership-as-practice, but the benefits are equally significant for teachers and students in classrooms.

Autonomous motivation: What's in it for the students and teachers?

Extensive research demonstrates that intrinsic and autonomous motivation in students promotes human flourishing (well-being) and school achievement.[54] Teachers who support students' intrinsic motivation are the same teachers who support students' rule following and responsible self-regulation. These teachers engage in teaching practices that structure, support and develop autonomous motivation in students.[55] Teachers who support autonomy building in students:

- listen more
- voice fewer directives
- attend to students' interests and questions
- ask questions rather than give answers
- create opportunities for students to take initiative, make choices and to convey their perspectives[56]

Teachers who participate in autonomy supporting workshops and embed these practices in their classrooms report benefits such as reinvigorating their passion for teaching, more teacher efficacy, greater job satisfaction and vitality when teaching, and better relationships with students.[57]

There is also a dynamic relationship between autonomous students and their teachers. The more autonomous the students, the more motivated the teachers to elicit autonomy-supportive teaching which fuels greater learner engagement and community building in the classroom.[58] Teacher autonomy affects the quality of their teaching, professional commitment, job satisfaction and well-being (that is, there is less stress and burnout). The more teachers experience or develop autonomy for themselves, the more teachers can develop skills to support students to be autonomously motivated in classrooms. The more students are autonomously motivated, the more they are engaged in learning and experience well-being.

In a study about the relationship between educational leadership and teacher's motivation, education researchers Ori Eyal and Guy Roth found:

> As educational systems have recently tightened their control over schools, which in turn may drive principals to practice transactional leadership associated with controlled motivation, the role of principals in generating autonomous motivation among teachers cannot be overstated. Although controlled motivation can lead teachers to comply with the system's standards, it is autonomous motivation that transforms jobs into a meaningful experience, drives them to practice autonomy-supportive teaching, protects them from burnout, increases their well-being, improves their effectiveness, and fosters their retention in the system.[59]

Leadership-as-practice can cultivate autonomous motivation and have a positive effect on teachers' experience of joy and satisfaction at work and their teaching in the classroom. Although leadership-as-practice is a key 'part of the puzzle' in affecting motivation in schools, we must recognize that other personal and contextual factors come into play and should not be ignored. These factors can be low teacher wages relative to other groups, a lack of status and community appreciation, work overload, conflicting demands in their role, a lack of support from colleagues, the complexity and diversity of student needs, increased behaviour problems in the classroom and the level of teacher education.[60] Leaders and system administrators must be cognisant of these other possible factors when addressing motivation, well-being and performance in schools. However, joy and autonomous motivation in leadership-as-practice can make a difference to a school's culture.

Concluding reflections

We began this chapter using the game Nzango to explain how joy, intrinsic motivation and the 4Cs are evident in children's play. We argue that joy, autonomous motivation and the 4Cs are also critical to both classroom learning and the practice of leadership in transforming schools.

I (Miranda) worked for many years in a transforming school, and I know that over the years it was driven, in part, by a dogged and committed team of people who had a shared vision for a school that excelled in and celebrated creativity, communication and collaboration. The motivation was to extend students potential in these 4C capabilities through high expectations, a sense of purpose in what they could achieve and skills that empowered them. This vision was sustained by the joy and motivation we all shared as a staff as we realized our aspirations. Without the joy and the autonomous motivation I enjoyed with my colleagues, I could not have contributed to and sustained this long-term vision for transformation.

Joy and motivation through the 4Cs help to drive transformation because they are profoundly linked to people's well-being and capacity to take and sustain action even when there are inevitable difficulties and challenges. The 4Cs are foundational processes or 'ways of doing' that can generate autonomous motivation towards change in schools.

Autonomous motivation and joy are related to another critical concept for the practice of leadership and leading change – the concept of agency. The next chapter examines this relationship and why and how agency is necessary for courageous leadership and leadership-as-practice to transform schools.

Key actions

1. Consider where joy is found in your school life, and why it is there.
2. Initiate and develop on-going joy in your school through experiences and learning through the 4Cs.
3. Consider what sort of leader you are or want to be, and how you can support and develop autonomous motivation your team.
4. Consider your students experiences of joy and motivation in learning, and how it may be related to autonomy supportive teaching.

Leading transformation through agency

8

Figure 8.1 The 'butterfly effect' in a weather system explains how small changes can be related to big changes

The 'butterfly effect'

It is said that a butterfly could flap its wings in Brazil and cause a tornado in Texas. How could such a small thing set off something so powerful and potentially catastrophic from one global hemisphere to another? Could the small change of air pressure caused by the flapping wings of a butterfly really cause a tornado? The flap of a butterfly's wings may not necessarily trigger a tornado, but computer modelling says that something so small can change a weather pattern.

The meteorologist Edward Lorenz used the term 'butterfly effect' to explain how one slight change in the variables that cause weather, changes everything. The 'butterfly effect' highlights how the weather is a highly complex system where tiny events can trigger, cascade and tip into bigger consequences. This is why predicting the weather is tricky and predicting something like climate change even trickier. 'Small' actions by humans can have huge and unforeseen consequences for the planet.

The 'butterfly effect' tells us that small events or actions can be connected and have a non-linear effect in a complex system. In the complex system of a school (and they are complex[1]) small actions matter. Often when we talk of transformation, people become overwhelmed by the enormity of the concept. It is vital to know that transformation can involve many small actions, and that in many cases, the small things are in fact the big things. When you realize small actions matter, transformation seems more doable. Small actions can be processes you use in a meeting or professional learning, the way you phrase something or the way you structure a lesson. These small things scale up to the 'sayings, doings and relating' practices of a school culture.

In our experience, transformation in schools is incremental, it has fits and starts, cascading effects, feedback loops and tipping points when change happens. These are features of a 'complex adaptive system',[2] a social system that continues to learn, evolve and transform as people's actions and their environment dynamically interact. In other words, transformation is not linear and there are many small 'butterfly effects' that progress positive change. In this complexity towards transformation, people are doing many small actions and working together to make a difference. To do these small actions and work together, people need to be everyday 'agents of change'. People are agents of change when they act with agency.

Agency is transformative leadership

Agency describes how human beings are agents of influence who can create and change their environments. Agency is the capacity and opportunity to produce and shape our experiences by exercising judgement in the interest of others and of ourselves.[3] According to leadership and creativity researchers Alfonso Montuori and Gabrielle Donnelly, transformative leadership involves everyday activities and small incremental actions that can be transformative. They describe transformative leadership as '. . . an active decision to acknowledge the current transformative moment, to develop agency by consciously participating in it, and to give this change a direction that allows individuals to embody higher values. In other words, *to lead by creating the future in the present*'.[4]

This chapter examines why agency is at the core of transformative leadership. We argue agency is in an inseparable relationship with an individual's capacity for courageous leadership and developing a culture of leadership-as-practice in schools. Agency is not a synonym for autonomy, but autonomy is essential for developing agency in people. In the previous chapter we discussed how the autonomy of our choices and values are linked to motivation and *why* we may take action. However, agency is more than autonomy and motivation, it is the power of acting and leading in the world because we have the skills and supports to do so. This chapter and the following chapter (on the Leadership Wheel) focus on the skills and supports for developing agency and leadership in schools.

The Leadership Lantern coherence maker in chapter 2 describes how a person's individual agency for courageous leadership cannot exist without developing 'co-agency' (or collective agency) through leadership-as-practice. We use Self-Determination Theory to introduce concepts of how we can build agentic leadership both in the individual and in a school culture. We discuss what hinders agency in schools and what can be done to begin to overcome these challenges. Developing understanding and belief in agency are the first 'small' steps and actions that leaders can undertake to lead transformation in people and their environments. Before exploring those small steps, we begin by imagining and describing the big picture of what agentic leadership might look like in a school.

The big picture: What can agency look like in a school?

Courageous leaders have agency when they have a shared vision with a team or staff, are aware of their own influence and can navigate the cultural and political structures of schools and systems to make change happen. To do this they engage deeply with professional discourse in education and use their learning to engage and actualize their community's potential.[5] Courageous leaders boldly take action to develop other's agency and leadership through leadership-as-practice.[6]

Agency becomes practice in a school's culture when leaders and teachers (and ultimately students) collaborate and learn together in exploring and discovering effective approaches to teaching, learning and leading. Agency is when all voices (their ideas, opinions and questions) are heard and enabled towards actions that continue to make the school (and world) a better place.

In a classroom setting, agency is when students have the skills to be metacognitive, self-regulated and self-determined in their learning.[7] They experience deeper learning, are more interested and less likely to give up on learning challenges. Students (and teachers) with agency go beyond compliant learning engagement by making learning something that matters to their personal growth and the growth of others. Agentic learners experience more authentic, socially relevant learning and enact real-world decision making, solve novel problems and create possibilities.[8]

Without agency, students are passive or disengaged learners whose potential for self-regulated and self-directed learning is unrealized. They may be underachieving, or they could be achieving by 'performing' on measures such as literacy and numeracy tests or high-stakes exams but do not have the confidence, interest, commitment or skills to pursue learning independently or collaboratively.[9]

Agency is the freedom but also the responsibility to act of our own volition. Having little or no agency means being coerced, subjugated or passive in an environment where you can't (or don't) make choices to take action and lead. Social cognitive theorist Albert Bandura explains how agency allows humans to transcend the dictates of their immediate environment and shape their life circumstances. He says, 'People who develop their competencies, self-regulatory skills, and enabling beliefs in their efficacy can generate a wider array of options that expand their freedom of action, and are more successful in realizing desired futures, than those with less developed agentic resources'.[10]

Agency is a big idea for schools, but it takes many small actions and connections between people to build agency in classrooms and as working practices in schools. Self-Determination Theory provides research and a model for us to clarify how we can build agency in ourselves and in those around us.

Self-Determination Theory: building the conditions for agency

Self-Determination Theory[11] is a motivational theory of personality, development and social processes that examines how social contexts and individual differences facilitate different types of motivation to affect learning, performance, experience and well-being. Developed by psychology researchers Edward Deci and Richard Ryan, Self-Determination Theory proposes that all human beings have three basic psychological needs – the needs for autonomy, competence and relatedness – that if satisfied, leads to better life functioning and wellness. These human needs are the 'nutrients' that provide the optimal conditions for people to develop agency. In brief these three basic needs are described as:

- Autonomy – being able to choose and instigate our actions
- Competence – having mastery and confidence in our situation
- Relatedness – sensing a feeling of connection with others

Agency is not 'given' to people, nor is it 'done' to people. Self-Determination Theory explains how agency is what people develop naturally if there are the right supports and nourishment in the environment around them. Edward Deci uses the metaphor of growing an avocado to explain this:

> If you put an avocado pit in a pot of earth it will probably grow into a tree, because it is in the nature of avocados to do that. It happens naturally. But not all pits become trees; some shrivel and decompose. They fail to thrive because the climate is inadequate, or the necessary nutrients are lacking. They need sun; they need water; and they need the right temperatures. Those elements do not *make* trees grow, but they are the nutriments that the developing avocados need, that are necessary for the avocados to do what they do naturally.[12]

The metaphor explains that for human beings to develop agency they need the psychological nutriments to do what they do naturally. They must experience satisfaction of their basic psychological needs – for autonomy, competence and relatedness – to be able to internalize and integrate aspects of society that are important for their own success in life.

Self-Determination Theory explains that human development depends upon how the self assimilates, co-ordinates and regulates influences from our external environment (families, schools, workplaces, social culture etc.) with our internal environment (drives, emotions and needs). The three basic psychological needs – autonomy, competence and relatedness – if developed in people by the conditions around them, leads to both the development and expression of their capacity to act and lead in the world with agency.

Figure 8.2 The nutrients that an avocado seed needs to grow into a tree can be likened to the conditions that are needed to build agency

A lack of support for building people's autonomy, competence and relatedness hinders psychological growth, integrity and well-being.[13]

Self-Determination Theory frames the Leadership Wheel coherence maker discussed in the next chapter. The Leadership Wheel is used as a tool to explore how autonomy, competence and relatedness are cultivated in practice in ourselves and in those around us. This chapter continues to deal more broadly with the concept of agency in schools and why it is necessary for leading and transformation. To develop agency and leadership, we need to recognize what hinders agency in schools, and what we can do about it. The challenge to build agency in schools is best illustrated by Mark Priestley, Gert Biesta and Sarah Robinson's research in *Teacher Agency: An Ecological Approach* (2015)[14] where they discuss the introduction and implementation of Scotland's Curriculum for Excellence in 2010.

The challenge of agency in schools

The Curriculum of Excellence policy in Scotland expected teachers to be agents of change and active developers of their own curriculum. However, many teachers found the implementation of this new approach to curriculum development difficult. Priestley, Biesta and Robinson argue that this expectation of teachers' agency was problematic due to preceding policies in education. It was problematic, they argued, after years of policies that regulated the work of teachers through tight prescriptions of content and teaching methods, and external inspections and judgement of a school's performance based on attainment data, which had effectively eroded teacher autonomy.

Priestley, Biesta and Robinson surmised that, '. . . it is problematic to expect that teachers become agentic, when in their practical contexts they are unable to do so. It is one thing for policy to demand that teachers have agency; it is quite another for this to occur in practice.'[15] Their research illustrates how you cannot suddenly give people agency when their context and work culture has not allowed agency to be developed. Although the new initiative for curriculum development valued teacher agency as desirable, it failed 'to address the cultural and structural conditions that effectively limit or deny that agency. Thus, the changing policy landscape raises new issues and problems, demanding new ways of theorizing the work of teachers and the ways in which schools and teachers operate.'[16]

Expecting individual teachers to have agency can only be achieved if cultural and structural conditions support and build agency. We can begin to understand how to support and build teacher agency in a school culture by examining what Priestley, Biesta and Robinson's found were the issues that prevented agency. Agency is hindered in schools when:

- Leaders and teachers see the purpose of education as a short-term and narrow view of getting through the day and keeping the students interested, rather than having longer-term aspirations for students and schools.

- Leaders and teachers are not able to explore a sophisticated and rigorous discourse about educational practice and theory, so that they can make informed and considered professional judgments about school initiatives.
- One-way information predominately flows top-down in schools and where there is a lack of professional relationships vertically and horizontally across a school.
- League tables, and other accountability and performance indicators, are used to monitor and surveil school attainment, leading to a 'tick-a-box' or compliance mentality towards education policy.
- Systemic top-down policy agendas are implemented, and teachers and leaders as key actors have no intellectual or practical input into educational initiatives.

Some of these problems are systemic and structural and must be addressed at a system and policy level (for example, league tables and accountability measures). However, leadership can address aspects of these challenges within the school context by deepening the professional learning and discourse in schools and being explicit (and reflective) about the building of agency in their context. We argue the conditions for developing people's agency (their autonomy, competence and relatedness) can be cultivated using 4C processes. In the light of Priestley, Biesta and Robinson's research into agency, we frame how leadership can address these concerns through the 4C capabilities and their processes.

Collaboration – deepen the professional and learning discourse

Leadership can role model and influence the professional discourse in schools by encouraging and strengthening continuous, focused and robust explorations of educational theory and practice. This can be achieved through a collaborative inquiry approach relevant to the team's vision, interests and needs (see chapter 4).

Critical reflection – develop a deep purpose for agency

Initiatives can be misunderstood, confused, paid 'lip service' to or discarded when there is no moral purpose or deep understanding why pedagogies and processes that harness agency are being introduced. Through processes in critical reflection, leaders can continue to ask and explore with their teams the purpose of why they are doing what they are doing (see chapter 3).

Creativity – encourage long-term aspirations

Agency is a construct that is temporal and contextually defined, that is, you take action now because you are informed by the past and your context but have an orientation towards what the future could be. Agency doesn't happen once or develop 'overnight' and so longer-term future aspirations, beyond the day-to-day running of the school, must be imagined, encouraged and actioned by leadership. This can be explored through processes that generate creativity (see chapter 6).

Communication – keep telling the stories of agency

Successes and failures should be shared and framed as narratives to clarify and cohere how a team's or a school's actions contribute to the trajectory of shared goals and ambitions in the developing of agency. Constantly telling the story of change allows for the articulation and evaluation of what has been achieved and makes sense of the complexity of 'where we have been, where we are, and where we are going' in transformation. These stories can be told through empowering communication processes (see chapter 5).

Priestley, Biesta and Robinson conclude their findings by saying that agency, although challenging, is critical for the transformation of schools and everything that is good in education.

> [agency] . . . has the capacity to make the operation of the educational system, both at a systemic level and the individual and collective level of teacher practice, more intelligent and, therefore, more able to engage with the complexities and the uniqueness of the here and now in meaningful and purposeful ways. Teacher agency approaches the question of good education from the bottom-up, seeking to enhance the intelligence of the overall operation of the system at all levels and thus offers an alternative that is radically different from the way in which much thinking and policy about educational improvement has been conceived over the past decades.[17]

Agency enhances the overall 'intelligent' operating of a school and dealing with the complexities of education, but it can be a radical departure from past practices. Schools have been influenced (systemically and more broadly socially) by command-and-control leadership, which has been seen as an expedient and clear way of dealing with human anxieties and feelings of uncertainty and possible failure. There are cultural and structural issues that can be addressed in schools over time through the social practices of a schools 'sayings, doings and relatings'. However, misunderstandings about the concept of agency can also make the practice of building it a challenge.

Misunderstandings about agency

Although agency is a hot topic in education,[18] it has often been misunderstood. You cannot develop agency without exploring and understanding what it means and what it doesn't mean. We deal with some of the misunderstandings that people have about agency, and the first is the belief that some people have it, and others don't.

Misunderstanding 1: You are either born with agency or you aren't

People may have different orientations towards agency, but ultimately, we all have a capacity for it. Agency is not something you 'have' or 'give' to people; it is something people learn and 'do'. Agency isn't a power or a fixed ability, it is a capability that is learnt and developed over a lifetime depending on context and culture. Environmental and conditional factors such as our life experience, outlook on life, other people, learning opportunities, resources, social processes and structures give shape to our capacity to take agentic action.[19]

Agency is an emergent phenomenon that is learnt and developed through experiences and practise. As specialists in learning, schools are ideal places for nurturing agency. Agency is a skill that can be cultivated in leadership through relationships, structures, learning and the social processes in which the school operates and functions. It can be nurtured in classrooms through certain pedagogies, learning conditions and social relationships (see Jefferson and Anderson's *Transforming Education: Reimagining Learning, Pedagogy and Curriculum*, 2021).

Misunderstanding 2: Agency means doing as you please

Agency is not a free for all, or 'do as you please' phenomenon, although it is often misunderstood in this way. Acting with agency comes with responsibility and supporting your community. Agency means our actions must have a responsible purpose that considers the effect of our actions on others. Therefore, we must reflect on the intent of our actions, and the impact of our actions on others. Acting with agency requires asking, what is our agency for, or what is someone else's agency for?

The responsibility that comes with agency necessitates considering if acting with agency is in the common good. The intent of acting with agency must address the sometimes complex questions, what is in the best interest, what is the moral imperative, or what is the fundamental issue in this situation?[20] Compassion and social justice are often the values of educators in schools and this is why they are attracted to education in the first place. These values come to life in schools through acts of agency.

Misunderstanding 3: To have agency you can't have boundaries

Agency and action are always bound by the constraints of culture and social structures. For instance, in an education system, leadership and teachers may be bound by bureaucratic, compliance procedures and narrow policy agendas. However, within those boundaries, leaders and teachers may act (with agency) in the best interest of their students by 'acting around' or reimagining the limitations of those procedures and policies. Rather than just efficiently implementing systemic policy agendas, acting with agency requires a more nuanced approach. It requires leadership and teachers to consider what educational values and purpose are important to them, so they act with wisdom for the greater good.

With imagination and persistence, leadership and educators can work within the constraints of systems and policies and build and harness agency to make change in schools. However, restrictive education policies that dictate what schools and their leaders, teachers and students can and can't do, are demotivating or inhibiting for agency to be expressed.[21]

Misunderstanding 4: Agency is all about the individual

We cannot always have the agency to directly control our context and conditions by acting alone. It is only by working with other people or influencing those who have the resources, knowledge and means, that we can affect change beyond our individual control.[22] For example, to transform practices in a school we combine our resources by working with other people to affect change, or we influence people or support advocates to act in our best interests. Schools have considerable potential for agency as they are places of resources, diversity and influence.

The main 'limitation' to individual agency, however, is other people's agency. We can't have our own agency without enabling the agency of others. The individual capacity for agency exists and is developed through the enabling social practices of co-agency or collective agency. These enabling social practices for co-agency are critical to building productive, healthy organizational cultures in schools. Having agency means you can't be a dictator, a bully or person devoid of responsibility to other humans and the planet, as having agency is being responsible for other people's agency.

Agency is co-agency

Co-agency explains how social interactions, relationships and processes are the building blocks for developing agency in practice. Vlad Glăveanu explains that co-agency is not a given but is constructed by groups of people through intentional relational processes in their context.[23] Co-agency explains the interdependent dynamic of how we as individuals can influence our environment through our actions and behaviours, and how the environment and others influence how we act and behave. Glăveanu argues that, 'As a shared phenomenon, people "take part" or "participate" not only in their own agency but also the agency of others.'[24] Implicit in our understanding of agency is the concept of co-agency; that is, there are social processes that work interdependently in developing individual agency. Agency cannot exist without co-agency and vice versa.

Schools have the capacity to shape their social practices (or actions) for co-agency through the ways they communicate, function and foster relationships. For example, co-agency is when teachers, leaders and parents support students' progress and shared goals together.[25] Co-agency is the relationship between teachers and students when students feel understood and supported in realizing a learning aspiration or challenge. Or it can be when students have a voice and are active agents in co-constructing the design of their learning. Or it may be where teachers feel trusted by students and parents to explore a more collaborative approach to learning. However, co-agency can be difficult to foster if people are orientated towards a more command-and-control approach in schools and don't believe in the concept of agency.

Beliefs in agency

Agency cannot be developed in schools without a deep and nuanced understanding of what it is and reflecting on our beliefs towards it.[26] A few years ago, we had two experiences in some professional learning that revealed not everyone desires agency. In one instance, a school deputy at a leadership workshop said, 'teachers don't want agency, they just want to be told what to do'. In another setting where a school community was being moved into new school buildings, a teacher said, 'teachers don't really care about pedagogy and curriculum in the new school, they just want to know where to park their car'.

These opinions may not be widespread but in these instances, agency is not considered as critical to the functioning of a school, nor critical to the development of pedagogy and curriculum. Therefore, it is critical for leadership to explore and question people's understanding and beliefs about agency through learning and metacognition.

Metacognition is being aware of, understanding and controlling our own thinking using forethought and self-reflection. Through metacognition we can gain insight into why we do what we do, and in so doing, are able to shift, adapt and develop our behaviours and actions. Through metacognitive processes people become aware of their thinking and their personal orientation towards agency in a particular context. Practice 8.1 Playground Noticing is a is a starting point for leaders to explore people's understandings of and beliefs in agency.

Practice 8.1 Playground noticing

Figure 8.3 Children in playgrounds

The 'how' of the Practice

This is both an individual and a group Practice.

Without any discussion about agency, reveal the image (figure 8.3) and allow individuals in the group to 'notice' (see chapter 6 on creativity) anything about the image for two minutes in silence. They can write down (or draw) their noticings about the image and how they respond to it.

They then share their noticings in pairs. A Bus Stop Practice (see chapter 5 on communication) can be used to hear back the groups noticings and what they discussed in pairs. The facilitator of the Practice draws out noticings (similarities and differences) from the group and then frames the image as an exploration of agency.

The 'why' of the Practice

- Develops metacognition (awareness) of people's attitudes towards agency.
- Begins a conversation about agency and what it means or doesn't mean.
- Recognizes people's differing attitudes and knowledge about agency.

The 'where to next' with the Practice

Consider:

- How people responded to the images and what it revealed about their perceptions and attitudes.
- How to explore, deepen and challenge people's understandings and attitudes about agency through on-going professional learning and reflective processes.

People's belief in their own capacity for agency depends on their life experiences, work environment and culture, and personal orientation. Sociologists Mustafa Emirbayer and Ann Mische explain how people's agency is shaped by their orientation to look to the future, their influences from the past and their engagement in the present.[27] All these dimensions affect a person's belief and capacity to take initiative and action. Some people tend to look back to the past and reiterate old patterns and habits which may hold them back from engaging with possibilities of action in the present. Or they may realize their imagined future has no relationship to what they can do given their past achievements and experience.[28]

Being metacognitive and learning about our agentic orientations can change or reconstruct the make-up of our beliefs towards agency.[29] By reflecting on past experiences, considering our capacity to engage with the present, and examining our orientation to look to the future, we can support the reframing of our and other's, beliefs towards agency. According to Emirbayer and Mische, 'By subjecting (our) own agentic orientations to imaginative recomposition and critical judgment, actors can loosen themselves from past patterns of interaction and reframe their relationships to existing constraints'.[30] Practice 8.2 Horizon Thinking can be used by leadership to investigate people's awareness of their own beliefs towards agency.

Practice 8.2 Horizon thinking

Figure 8.4 Drawing the landscape

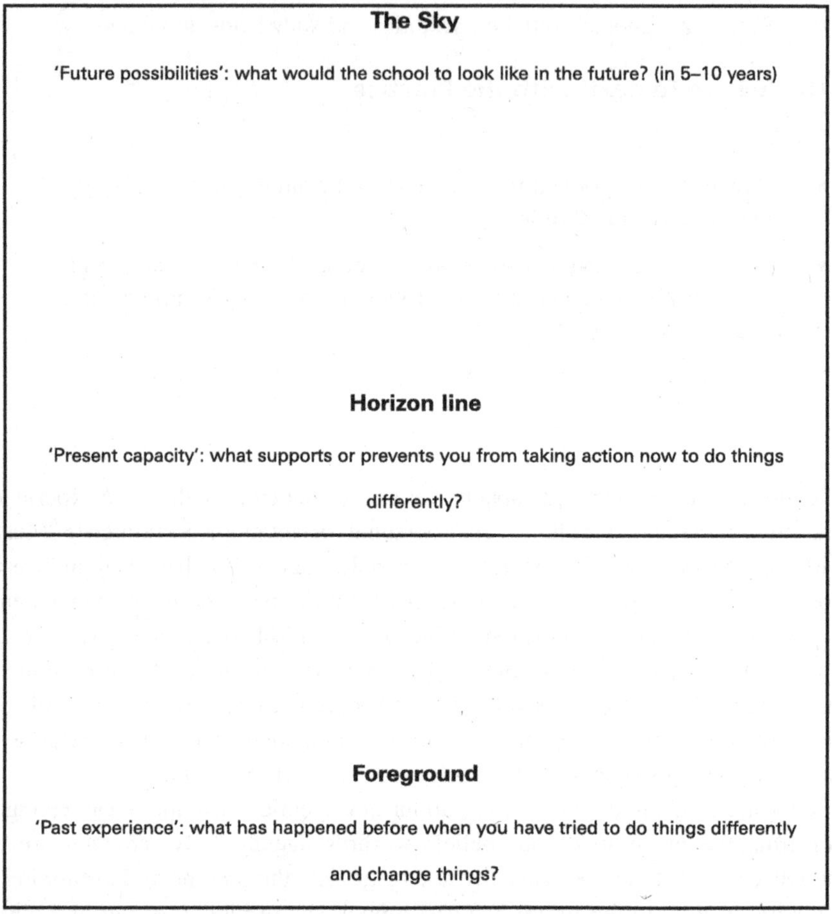

The 'how' of the Practice

This is both an individual and a group Practice.

On a large board or piece of paper draw a horizon line with a big sky and landmass, with the headings and questions indicted in figure 8.4. Ask people to walk around the school or sit in contemplation by themselves (without talking to anyone) for twenty minutes and consider the questions in the sky, foreground and on the horizon. They can write or draw their responses for each question on separate pieces of paper.

As a group, individuals share their responses by placing them in the sky, foreground and horizon through a Meccano Connections Practice (see chapter 5 on communication). After all the groups responses are shared, discuss their noticings from the Practice and about the process (see chapter 3 on critical reflection).

The 'why' of the Practice

- Examines people's perceptions and awareness (metacognition) of past actions that may affect their belief in agency.
- Contributes to exploring and developing a shared understanding of a future vision.
- Reveals capacities and support people feel they need to achieve future possibilities at the school.

The 'where to next' with the Practice

Consider:

- How values and past experiences shape people's sense of agency to do things differently.
- How 'shared' the future possibilities and vision are for the group, and what are the similarities and differences.
- What strategies and first, 'small' steps can be taken as actions towards future possibilities.
- What actions can support people's capacities and develop agency to achieve these first steps.

Agency and leading transformation

Building understanding and belief in agency is critical to leading transformation in schools. The practice of transformative leadership is to create an environment where people believe change is possible, change is necessary and where there are opportunities for people to collaborate towards a shared vision.

Agency is believing change is possible

Without a sense or belief in their own agency, people won't believe they can act towards a desired vision or outcome. Transformation in schools needs people with agency who believe in their capacity to make the possible, possible. Courageous leadership can build people's beliefs in their capacity for agency, and through leadership-as-practice create the environment, resources and supports that they need to be able to take action.

- Reflection question for leadership: Do people feel they have the capacity to make changes towards a desired outcome?

Agency is believing change is necessary

Transformation needs people to believe that change is necessary. Without belief that change is necessary, there will be little incentive or motivation for people to take action towards what is possible. You can tell people what you would like them to do but if they do not believe in what they are doing (see chapter 7), they will have little understanding or commitment to change. Transformation requires people to believe in the desired goal they are seeking. Without that internal belief, transformative ambitions and actions are not sustainable.

- Reflection question for leadership: Do people believe change is necessary?

Agency needs collaboration

Transformation requires the co-agency or collective agency generated by collaboration. The collective efficacy of collaboration brings people together in their common belief they can achieve something together, more than they could alone. Transformation requires collaboration (with the other Cs; creativity, critical reflection and communication) to build collective efficacy and to achieve sustainable cultural change in schools. According to Bandura:

> People's shared beliefs in their collective efficacy influence the types of futures they seek to achieve through collective action, how well they use their resources, how much effort they put into their group endeavour, their staying power when collective efforts fail to produce quick results or meet forcible opposition, and their vulnerability to the discouragement that can beset people taking on tough social problems.[31]

People's perceived collective efficacy towards transformation affects their motivational commitment to their shared goal, their resilience to adversity and what they can achieve. Leading transformation needs collective efficacy and critically, collective efficacy needs to be driven by effective, agentic leadership.

- Reflection question for leadership: How can you support people to collaborate and achieve shared goals?

Concluding reflections

Ultimately, agency in schools is about developing critically reflective, socially engaged and responsible citizens. Agency in individuals (courageous leadership) and agentic practices in a school's culture (leadership-as-practice) are integral to a vision of education that values teaching and learning as a humanizing and active force towards a better future. Agency is key to transformative leadership and continuing to transform education to meet the needs of our communities.

The UNESCO 2022 report, ‘Reimagining Our Future Together: A new social contract for education’,[32] argues that developing agency in children and adults is vital to the transformation of education. It says: ‘Human rights and democratic participation should be key building blocks for learning that transform people and the world. We should prioritize human rights education that supports learners’ agency and offers an entry point into a moral universe committed to the recognition and thriving of all’.[33] We believe schools and leadership have a significant and urgent role in reimagining learning and developing agency to advance human rights and responsible citizenship. This is in a world context of rising inequality, climate stress, growing social and digital polarization, democratic backsliding, dissemination of fake information and the uncertain future of work.

Developing agency and leadership in schools does take time and many small, ‘butterfly’ actions that become the ‘big’ actions towards a culture of agency. It takes many small, connected and persistent actions of agency to develop leadership and transform aspects of schooling. Education researchers Tamar Chen-Levi, Yaffa Buskila and Chen Schechter argue:

> In light of the importance of the agency concept in building school leaders, it is important to promote the practice of agency and develop agent perspective among management talents. Developing agency requires time and effort. It requires thought, reflection, learning through trial and error, creativity, persistence, and courage. In this sense, elements that contribute to this enhanced sense of agency, including opportunities to gain knowledge and apply theory to practice, are important in developing school leaders.[34]

We research and work in schools with a committed belief in the principles of agency and are constantly surprised by the fruits (and labour) of this approach. There are schools that feature the aspirations for agency that we present in this chapter. In these schools there are courageous leaders who believe deeply in their staff, students and community’s agentic potential. They lead by being rigorous in their approach to professional learning, so that educational discourse and action have become a critical part of their school’s culture. Although leaders and teachers commit to the discourse and action at different levels, they still engage.

Cultural shifts in schools are a constant process requiring leadership to be persistent in developing agency and embedding deep and continuing professional learning as the orthodoxy of practice, rather than the exception. Leadership-as-practice is to enable and develop agency in people through continued support, reflection, stimulated challenge, experience and determined focus. As we have discussed in other chapters, the 4C capabilities (creativity, critical reflection, communication and collaboration) are foundational in creating a culture of leadership-as-practice. Agency is also enabled by cultivating the conditions where people experience a sense of autonomy (choice), competence (expertise) and relatedness (belonging), and this is explored in the next chapter through the Leadership Wheel.

Key actions

1. Undertake an 'agency audit' by using reflective processes that explore people's:
   - Understandings (or misunderstandings) of agency
   - Beliefs in the concept of agency
   - Perception of agency in classrooms and in the staff
   - Rationale for agency in education and transformation
2. Evaluate the breadth and depth of professional learning and discourse in the school.
3. Consider how the 4Cs are used to develop agency for courageous leadership and leadership-as-practice in your school.

The Leadership Wheel: Cultivating the conditions for transformative leadership

9

Figure 9.1 Like a crop's yield, leadership in schools depends on the conditions and nutrients in the environment

Liebig's Law of the Minimum

A farmer grows sunflowers to produce oil from its seeds, and every year the farmer uses fertilizer to maximize the growth of her crop, but in one of her fields the sunflowers are less abundant and produce less oil, so she adds more fertilizer to that field. But a year later the sunflowers in this field are still less productive.

The farmer wonders what is going wrong in a field that looks much like her other fields. She does a soil test to measure the nutrients in the field and discovers that the nutritional conditions of this field are different to the others. The field is low in magnesium and sulphur, and the farmer realizes that just adding a general amount of fertilizer was not changing the proportional amount of magnesium and sulphur to the other nutrients.

The farmer had to use Liebig's Law of the Minimum to address the issue of this field's crop yield. Liebig was a nineteenth century German agricultural chemist who formulated the law that crop yields are proportional to the amount of the most limiting essential nutrient. That is, plant growth and health are not controlled by the total amount of nutrients available in the soil but by the scarcest of the nutrients. By adding more sulphur and magnesium the farmer could balance the nutrients in the field and increase the sunflower yield in that particular field. Liebig's Law can be explained through the analogy of a barrel containing water (see figure 9.2). In the analogy, water is retained by different soil nutrients and growth factors, but when the least nutrients are out of balance, the barrel loses it 'yield'.

Figure 9.2 Liebig's Law of the Minimum illustrated through the analogy of a barrel of water

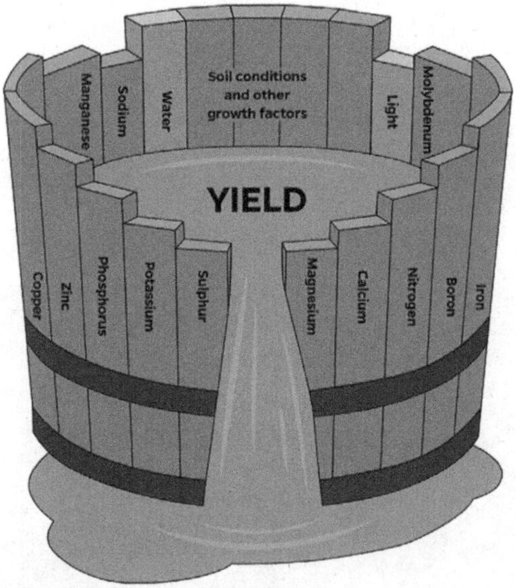

Our farming story is a metaphor to explain how leaders too can cultivate the right conditions to grow leadership and agency in a particular context by considering what 'nutrients' there are less of. We describe these nutrients through our coherence maker, the Leadership Wheel illustrated in figure 9.3. Like Liebig's Law of the Minimum, the Leadership Wheel can be used to diagnose and build the yet-to-be-strengths of leadership in a unique context. Using the analogy of the water barrel, in figure 9.4, we explain how yet-to-be strengths in leadership (engagement and collaboration) increases the 'yield' to develop leadership capacity. This chapter details the capacities and conditions described in the Leadership Wheel.

Figure 9.3 The Leadership Wheel describes the qualities and conditions for leadership to develop and thrive.

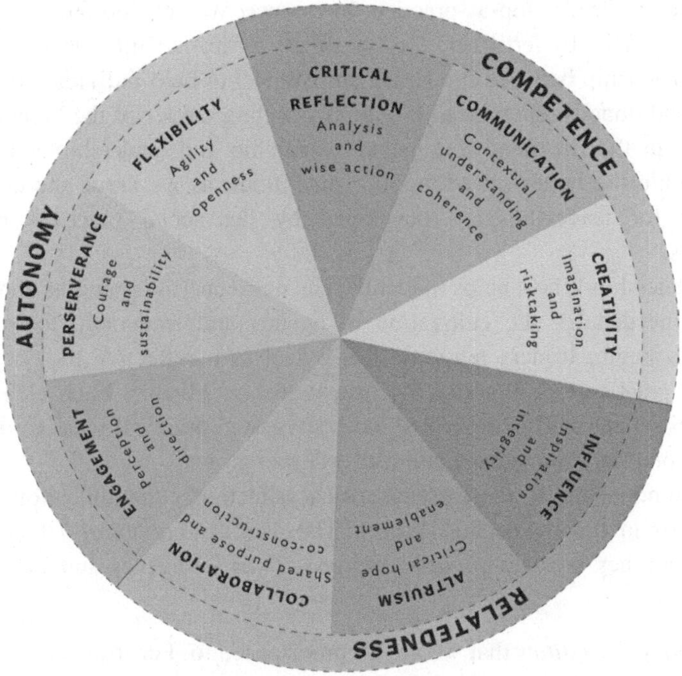

Figure 9.4 The analogy of the water barrel and Liebig's Law is used in relation to developing yet-to-strengths in the Leadership Wheel

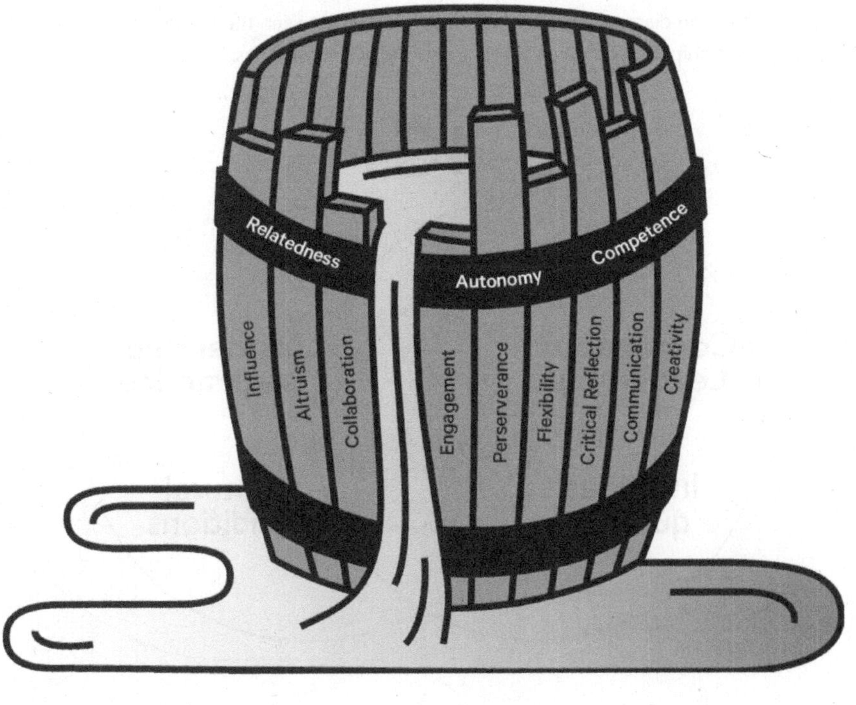

In chapter 2 we discussed the Leadership Lantern and the role of agency to develop courageous leadership and leadership-as-practice. The Leadership Wheel describes both the agentic qualities of individual leaders, and the co-agentic conditions created by leadership-as-practice. In essence, we develop our own individual leadership capacity by fertilizing the conditions for leadership around us.[1]

The relationship between the Leadership Wheel to both individual qualities and cultural conditions is represented by the intersecting circles of the Venn diagram in figure 9.5. In the diagram, courageous leadership and leadership-as-practice are framed within the larger set of the 4C capabilities, as we argue the qualities and conditions for leadership are developed by the social practices of the 4C capabilities.

The Leadership Wheel helps to identify the nutrients (the strengths and yet-to-be-strengths) needed for the cultivation of agency and leadership for a particular context. To begin, leaders may use the Wheel as a reflective tool of their own leadership practice (see Practice 9.1, the Wheel as Mirror). Each element of the Leadership Wheel will be described, with suggested practical ideas to develop the optimum conditions for agency and leadership to grow.

You will notice the 4Cs: creativity, critical reflection, communication and collaboration exist in the Leadership Wheel. The 4Cs are *capabilities* that are social practices, but they are also *qualities* and *conditions* for agency and leadership. The 4Cs are then:

- Individual *qualities* that we are all predisposed to. For instance, we all have the capacity to be creative.

Figure 9.5 The Venn diagram represents the relationship between the Leadership Wheel, courageous leadership, leadership-as-practice and the 4Cs capabilities

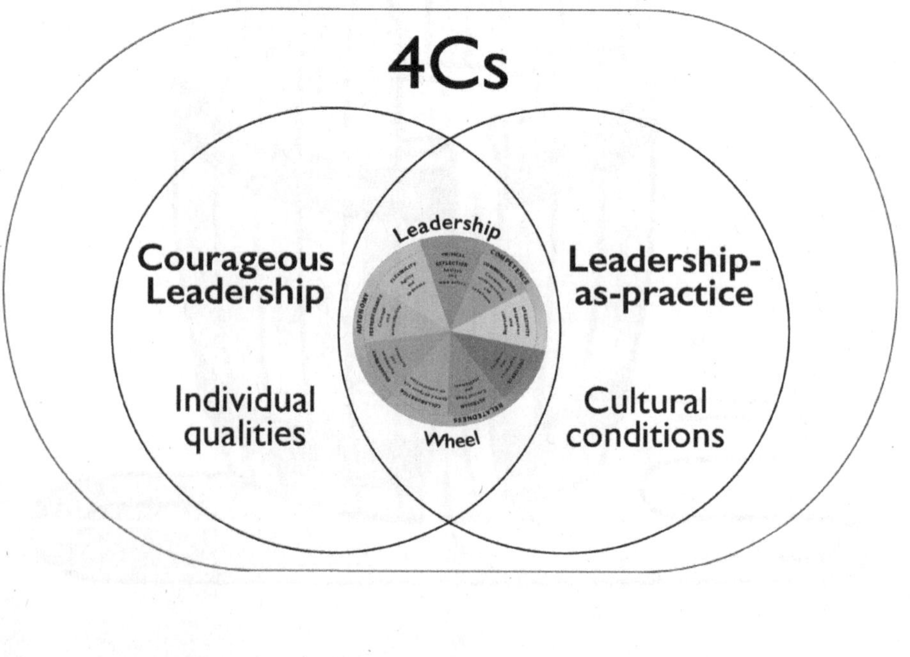

- Social *conditions* of an organizational culture. For example, there can be a collaborative culture in a school or team.
- *Capabilities* that are foundational to the processes and practices for transformative agency and leadership. For instance, critical reflection processes are used to develop the conditions and qualities for agency and leadership.

Practice 9.1 The wheel as mirror

The Leadership Wheel can be used like a mirror to reflect on your own leadership.

Consider the Wheel and firstly recognize and acknowledge the qualities that are your strengths as a leader.

Like Liebig's Law, we become better leaders by focusing on and developing qualities that are our yet-to-be-strengths. Consider the areas of the Wheel that you feel you need to develop further.

By reflecting, acting on those reflections, practising those actions (or behaviours) and reflecting on them again we can develop our leadership capacities. We grow as leaders through a spiral of internal inquiry, experience and reflection, and this process can be formalized through reflective practice discussed in chapter 3 on critical reflection.

The Leadership Wheel

The Leadership Wheel is a schema or coherence maker that helps us to understand both the individual qualities (for courageous leadership) and the cultural conditions (leadership-as-practice) that together cultivate transformative leadership. The Wheel was developed from research in Self-Determination Theory and leadership,[2] and a meta-analysis of human development, learning and differential psychology research from the National Research Council.[3]

The Leadership Wheel makes coherence of the complex conditions that create human agency, but as leadership research continues to evolve so will the Leadership Wheel. However, in the working practice of schools and organizations it has proved to be a constructive and beneficial tool for developing leaders and teams.

The Wheel provides a metalanguage for understanding, and being metacognitive of, our own and others agency and leadership. As a schema or frame, we can deeply reflect on and evaluate leadership development and design practical strategies and processes to cultivate leadership-as-practice. Around the Leadership Wheel are the basic psychological needs (or domains) from Self-Determination Theory: autonomy, competence and relatedness (see chapter 8).

Agency and leadership can be understood as an inter-relationship between building people's sense of:

- Autonomy – engaging in behaviours because it is of personal interest or because it is compatible with your values.
- Competence – feeling confident and having a sense of proficiency and effectiveness in your work.
- Relatedness – feeling connected and interdependent with others and feeling a sense of belonging to a group.

In schools, autonomy is how people experience a sense of freedom and choice when they work and have some level of control in what they do. Competence is to feel effective and successful in their work role and this builds confidence and self-esteem. With greater competence you can be challenged and take on increased responsibilities and mastery of what you do. Relatedness is to feel accepted and cared for by others which creates a sense of belonging in a school community. Authentic, positive and supportive relationships are evident in schools that support people's needs for relatedness,

The three domains in the Leadership Wheel are interrelated, for instance, it is difficult to build autonomy (make choices) without competence (expertise) or relatedness (a sense of belonging). For example, perhaps you know you need to try something new in classrooms because an aspect of learning isn't working well (autonomy), but you don't know what to do. So, developing the ideas and expertise (competence) with someone else (relatedness) helps you to take action (agency) to address this problem.

Or you may be a leader who has the competence and autonomy to address different issues in a school but don't have the relationships and trust (relatedness) to work with other people to solve those issues together as agents of sustainable change. In both these examples, you create the conditions for what is needed in terms of the domains of autonomy, competence or relatedness.

In the Leadership Wheel the three domains are segmented into clusters of three. These clusters are based on the National Research Council's taxonomies developed to align with human abilities and twenty-first century skills for work and life.[4] The nine segments within the three domains are:

Autonomy

- Engagement: perception and direction
- Perseverance: courage and sustainability
- Flexibility: agility and openness

Competence

- Critical reflection: analysis and wise action
- Communication: contextual understanding and coherence
- Creativity: imagination and risk-taking

Relatedness

- Influence: inspiration and integrity
- Altruism: critical hope and enablement
- Collaboration: shared purpose and co-construction

We describe each segment of the Leadership Wheel, and leaders may consider what they want to develop in themselves and what they may explore with their team in a particular context. Through 4C processes, leaders and teams can use the Leadership Wheel to recognize their strengths and identify their yet-to-be-strengths. They can introduce practices and behaviours that explore and create the conditions for developing agency and leadership specific to their needs. An example of using this practice is illustrated in Practice 9.2 Creating a Shared Team Goal.

Practice 9.2 Creating a shared team goal

This Practice uses the Leadership Wheel and Liebig's Law of the Minimum.

Creating a Shared Team Goal for a particular context and problem.

The 'how' of the Practice

The leader facilitates the team in a discussion about a particular problem to be solved or a specific outcome that needs to be achieved. Let's imagine that the issue is with student engagement in a learning area. The group also discuss what they need to do as a team to be as successful in achieving their goal.

The team is then presented with the Leadership Wheel where they individually consider (in silence) what their team really needs in the Leadership Wheel to solve the problem or achieve the outcome based on their previous discussion. They should consider what they perceive as their strengths as a team but recognize the yet-to-be-strengths that may impede their progress.

Each team member then writes a concise question that focuses solely on what they need to do as a team to achieve their task, informed by the frame of the Leadership Wheel and what they view as the main element that is not a team strength (yet). A question rather than a statement frames their actions as an inquiry that needs to be solved. The question stem may be, 'How do we as a team . . .' Someone may write, 'How do we as a team persevere with this issue of student engagement when we get busy with other work?' or someone else may write, 'How do we as a team inspire each other to solve our problem with student engagement?' or 'How do we as a team enable and support each other to solve our issue with student engagement?'

Everyone shares their questions, and after deeply listening to each other, they discuss what aspects of other people's questions resonate with them and why. Everyone then has another go at writing their question again, knowing they want to arrive at a shared goal that is concise and true to their understanding of the team and the issue they are undertaking.

After listening again to the second round of questions, the leader as facilitator makes a suggested 'driving question' that has emerged through the deep listening process. The question should not be an amalgamation of everyone's questions but a question that distils the joint thinking of the group. The question arrived at could be, 'How as a team can we inspire each other and support each other to stay focused on solving issues of student engagement?'

The 'why' of the Practice

- Uses the Leadership Wheel as a metacognitive tool for a team to recognize their strengths and yet-to-be-strengths to solve a problem or achieve a goal.
- Focuses the team on their yet-to-be-strengths to work more effectively and productively to achieve their outcome of a shared goal.
- Evaluates the success and effectiveness of the team to solve their issue.

The 'where to next' with this Practice

As the team embarks on trying to achieve their goal, the group must continue to ask themselves whether they are doing everything possible to contribute to 'answering' the shared, driving question they have created together. If they have forgotten the question, and are not finding ways to answer it, is no longer 'driving them' as a team.

Courageous leaders explain to their teams how to stay true to the 'driving' question' by considering how every decision and action undertaken by the team supports the 'solving' of their shared, team question.

Figure 9.6 The autonomy section of the Leadership Wheel

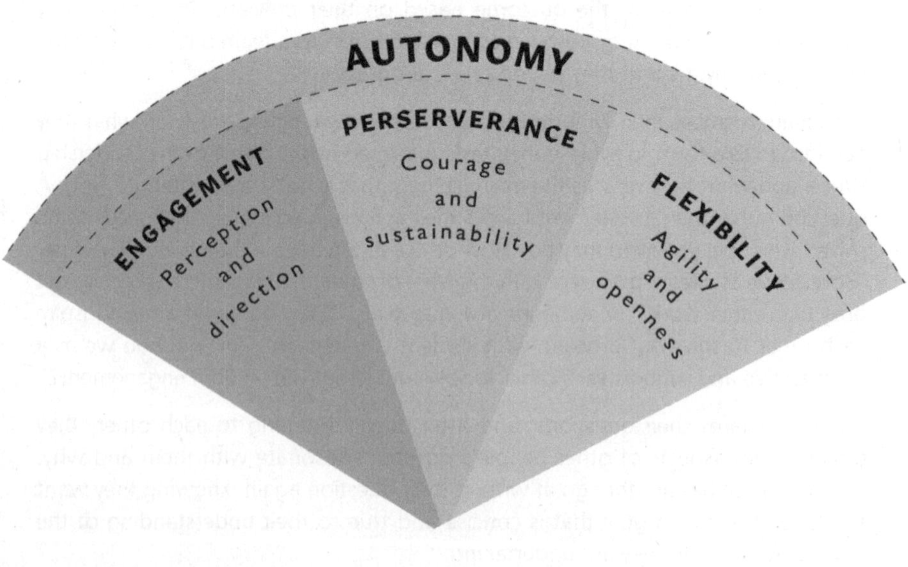

Autonomy

Autonomy focuses on developing qualities and conditions for people to initiate their own actions and achieve desired personal outcomes as part of a shared vision. The qualities and conditions that give expression to and foster autonomy are engagement, perseverance and flexibility. A maze as a metaphor (see figure 9.7) can be used with your team to explore what autonomy and the elements of engagement, perseverance

Figure 9.7 The Maze

and flexibility may mean for leadership. For instance, you may ask what is your intention in a maze, how do you deal with not knowing solutions, why do you continue and how would you lead others through a maze?

Engagement: perception and direction

Engagement describes a leader's commitment to developing and directing a shared vision that is invested in by those they lead. No matter what the leadership role, a transformative leader has a vision for 'what the future should look like, aligns people with that vision, and inspires them to make it happen despite the obstacles'.[5]

Engagement is the passion or moral purpose that drives transformative leaders to have a vision and want to make a difference for a better future.[6] It requires leaders to learn, plan, gain insights and take action to continually develop their leadership capacity to achieve objectives.

By using perception and direction, leaders develop and integrate 'big picture' understandings of moral purpose and vision with the day-to-day life of a school. They must have a keen awareness of who they are leading, what they are leading and why. This is so everyone can understand their values and develop and drive a shared vision and endeavour.

Engagement provides a clarity of purpose and direction for leaders and teams but also develops autonomy by integrating the schemas of people's personal values, needs and perceptions with a shared leadership vision.

Reflection question for courageous leaders

- How do you connect the big picture vision to the day to day running of the school?

Ideas for leadership-as-practice

To create the conditions for engagement, leaders can invest in authentic opportunities for their teams and staff to:

- Express and develop their personal values and needs and challenge them to work towards a vision and purpose they can all share and personally act on.
- Reflect and extend the outcomes of their personal goals in relation to a shared vision.
- Reflect on, recognize and celebrate the learnings from their personal goals and shared vision.

Engagement towards a shared vision requires the determination of perseverance to achieve these objectives.

Perseverance: courage and sustainability

Perseverance is the engine that turns a vision or goal into action. Leaders need perseverance to overcome the distractions, obstacles and setbacks inherent to any challenge. It takes doggedness and tenacity to focus and align people to goals and objectives, but also courage. There is courage in a leader taking on the inevitable uncertainties and complexities when challenging human and cultural growth.

Leaders must develop daring and determination to undertake what corporate leadership expert Simon Sinek refers to as the infinite or unending game of transforming organizations and people.[7] He argues that leaders must be determined to develop an 'infinite mindset' that continues to build trust, collaboration and innovation to lead people into a better future. Transformation is a long, hard but rewarding game that takes courage and perseverance.

Persevering with the long-term goals of school transformation can only be achieved and sustained through persistent and strategic steps.[8] Perseverance to achieve anything resides in thoughtful and sometimes challenging shifts of strategy rather than repeating and persisting with the same actions.

Perseverance can also only be sustained in a well-being sense with collaboration and differentiating the strategies, degrees and timing of challenges for people.[9] Too much challenge, and leaders and their teams can suffer exhaustion or feelings of failure, but with too little challenge there is little growth.[10] Sustainable perseverance is balancing the tension of challenge and long-term goals, by using dynamic, multiple feedback loops between leaders and their teams.[11]

A sense of autonomy is achieved by perseverance through the confidence and self-hood gained by aiming for and achieving goals.

Reflection question for courageous leaders

- What do you do that is challenging, uncertain and/or complex, and how do you stay the course without 'burning out'?

Ideas for leadership-as-practice

To create the conditions for persistence, leaders can invest in genuine opportunities for their teams and staff to:

- Seek out challenges and discuss strategies that develop tenacity in the face of distractions, obstacles and setbacks.

- Develop regular, interactive feedback loops between leaders and teams and staff to focus on and learn from challenges.
- Collaborate on challenges, recognize achievements, and use setbacks as positive, strategic learnings.

Perseverance requires a committed approach to challenges, but flexibility allows for strategic and responsive approaches to those challenges.

Flexibility: agility and openness

Flexibility is being curious and open to learning and experiences and allows leaders to understand a diversity of ideas, perspectives, choices and evidence to inform decision making. Flexible thinking initiates change and demonstrates agility by adapting and responding to opportunities, challenges and changing circumstances as they arise.

Leadership expert Ronald Heifetz argues that 'adaptive leadership'[12] is necessary in organizations to be effective and successful in constantly changing, complex and ambiguous circumstances. All the capacities in the Leadership Wheel support the concept of adaptive leadership but flexibility is the capacity that allows people to adapt and change.

Flexibility reflects an openness and belief that people can change and grow through learning, application and experience. It reveals a 'growth mindset'[13] rather than fixed or rigid thinking that limits the potential opportunities or pathways leaders can discover to make change happen. Openness to ideas and experiences can only occur when leaders and their teams have choice, interest and the resources to pursue those choices.

Flexibility allows leaders and their teams to develop autonomy by discovering their potential by having and being open to choices.

Reflection question for courageous leaders

- Why and when do you allow people to have choice?

Ideas for leadership-as-practice

To create the conditions for flexibility, leaders can invest in varied opportunities for their teams and staff to:

- Develop professional learning structures that allow for choice but are connected to a shared purpose and vision.

- Experience and reflect on a diversity of ideas when making decisions and judgements.
- Question assumptions to open up and allow opportunities for new and adaptive ways to respond to challenges.

The effectiveness of decision-making and the creation of choice enabled by flexible and agile thinking is supported by the wisdom of critical reflection in the domain of competence.

Competence

Competence in leaders and teams focuses on developing capacities and conditions for people to have a sense of expertise and accomplishment in the work they do. The capacities and conditions that give expression to and foster competence are critical reflection, communication and creativity. How might Anish Kapoor's sculpture 'Turning the World Upside Down' (Figure 9.9) be explored with your team to discuss competence and the elements of critical reflection, communication and creativity in the Leadership Wheel? You may ask, what is the effect of reflection on what we see, how does that change how we communicate and what new ideas and actions can emerge when we look at things differently?

Figure 9.8 Competence section of the Leadership Wheel

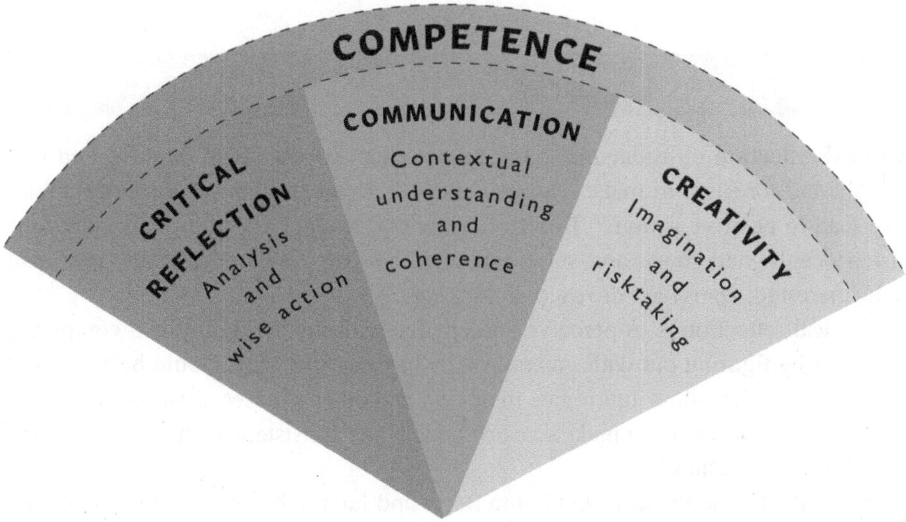

Figure 9.9 Anish Kapoor's sculpture 'Turning the World Upside Down'

Critical reflection: analysis and wise action

Critical reflection in leadership is the development of analytical thinking and with insight and foresight to make reasoned and fair decisions. This process of thinking can lead to positive action.[14] To reflect critically, leaders ask thoughtful questions, listen deeply, and shape and solve problems by going beyond surface, irrational, self-interested, compliant or reactive thinking.[15]

Critical reflection is to perceive and engage with the ambiguity and complexity of issues by figuring out with others, why, what and how they should be addressed. To do this, leaders must interrogate their own and other's biases, assumptions, ethics and positions of power to make reasoned decisions consistent with their articulated transformative values.[16]

Critical reflection researchers Laura Béres and Jan Fook explain critical reflection 'involves learning from and making deeper meaning of experience through a process of unsettling and examining deeply hidden assumptions in order to create better guidelines for action and so improve professional practice and develop a more ethical and compassionate stance.'[17]

The thinking involved with critical reflection interrogates assumptions and power, but it is pragmatic and optimistic. Critical reflection is not 'navel gazing' or 'all talk – no action', but a process of deeper engagement with ideas and problem solving for decisive and empowering action.

Wise analysis and action are informed by leaders acknowledging and learning from their own mistakes and missteps and openly learning from others.[18] To understand and lead through critical reflection means knowing the self and communicating to others what is ethical and in the common good.[19]

Critical reflection develops feelings of competence by providing skills and insights into using better processes and making better decisions to achieve clear and effective outcomes as a leader.

Reflection question for leaders

- What processes do you engage with that develop wisdom in your leadership?

Ideas for leadership-as-practice

To create the conditions for critical reflection, leaders can invest in regular, structured opportunities for their teams and staff to:

- Use authentic processes in learning and decision making that promote listening, transparency, candour, ethical behaviour and trust.
- Discuss how the school's values inform their decisions and chosen actions, and question preconceptions and assumptions.
- Recognize what they have strengths in, identify what they can challenge in themselves as professionals, and take on achievable tasks.

The analysis and wise action developed through critical reflection relies on leaders understanding the contextual needs of their school communities though communication.

Communication: contextual understanding and coherence

Communication is how people in a school organize and interpret their experiences, purpose and aspirations as shared understandings. Communication channels in schools are usually used to organize day-to-day functioning, but they can also be used to motivate, challenge and empower people. This begins with leaders authentically understanding their context through humanizing communication processes that explicitly scaffold and support open dialogue (spoken or written) that value respect, empathy, different points of view and other people's expertise.[20]

Contextual understanding can only be achieved through a culture of communication that is free from coercion, distortion, self-deception and conflict. Rather than transmissive communication, leaders who have contextual understanding communicate and make meaning through processes in participation and negotiation, and use inclusive, audience centred language focused on 'we' not 'I'.[21]

Effective and empowering communication depends on a leader's ability to be coherent, engaging and engaged with others. Communicating with contextual understanding and coherence can be developed by leaders if they ask open questions, actively listen, allow for elaborations in people's responses and receive feedback.[22] Candour and vulnerability in feedback requires a commitment to psychological safety in communication processes. Leaders who are warm, compassionate and empathic gain greater contextual understanding and trust from their teams and communities.[23]

To maintain coherent and effective communication, leaders constantly clarify priorities and organize regular purposeful meetings and communication channels that motivate, challenge and empower people.[24] Making a vision and purpose coherent in a team or school community requires the on-going creation and sharing of an evolving and motivating narrative.[25]

Communication develops a sense of competence in leaders as it creates a constructive feedback loop of understanding and sense making between teams and communities. With contextual understanding and coherence in communication leaders can motivate action with teams and school communities.

Reflection question for leaders

- How do your communication processes empower other people?

Ideas for leadership-as-practice

To create the conditions for communication, leaders can invest in cooperative and collaborative opportunities for their teams and staff to:

- Develop and prioritize participatory processes and structures that explicitly allow for all voices to be heard, respected, encouraged, empathized with and understood.
- Contribute to open, honest and inclusive dialogue for feedback on the effectiveness and organization of communication.
- Cohere and recognize work challenges and achievements as on-going shared sense and narrative making that is affirming, positive and motivating.

A leader's capacity to encourage creativity for innovation is instrumental to continuing the shared narrative in transformative practices.

Creativity: imagination and risk-taking

Creativity is the capacity for leaders to imagine and drive what is possible in schools. Imagining is to go beyond 'what is' to 'what could be' and is essential to a leader's 'finite' or 'growth mindset'. Creativity is the engine for innovation and developing effective leading, teaching and learning.[26] Imagining and achieving what is possible is a disciplined process of developing expertise in the area you want to create in, thinking laterally, being open to ideas, building ideas, learning from and evaluating them. Creativity requires applying high expectations, rigour, practice, a willingness to experiment and being unafraid of questioning orthodoxy.[27]

Leaders who constantly renew and rebuild an organization's innovative capabilities are described by business innovation and strategy expert Gary Pisano[28] as 'creative constructors' who are outward looking, problem solvers, not afraid to be different. What is being created is novel to the creator and therefore creativity requires dealing with ambiguity and uncertainty.[29] Leaders need to take and model intellectual risk-taking and reduce barriers for others to take risks.[30] There is pleasure and joy in creating new, more effective ideas for schools, but they take time and infinite iterating. Leaders should champion their teams and staff who take on big or small creative endeavours, for without creativity, there is stasis in schools.

A leader's competence is built through the learnings and outcomes gained through the risks and imaginings of creative endeavours.

Reflection question for leaders

- How do you encourage and support others to take risks, create and learn from new ideas?

Ideas for leadership-as-practice

To create the conditions for creativity, leaders can invest in supported opportunities for their teams and staff to:

- Imagine and explore what could be possible within an area of expertise and apply rigour and resources to develop ideas and actions.
- Make explicit that creative endeavours need experimentation, iteration, risk-taking and on-going evaluation.
- Make explicit how new ideas strategically serve an objective and vision for effective teaching and learning.

Leaders can model and support the 'riskiness' and rigour of possibility thinking and new ideas when they are perceived to have integrity and a commitment to their teams and staff through influence in the domain of relatedness.

Figure 9.10 Relatedness section of the Leadership Wheel

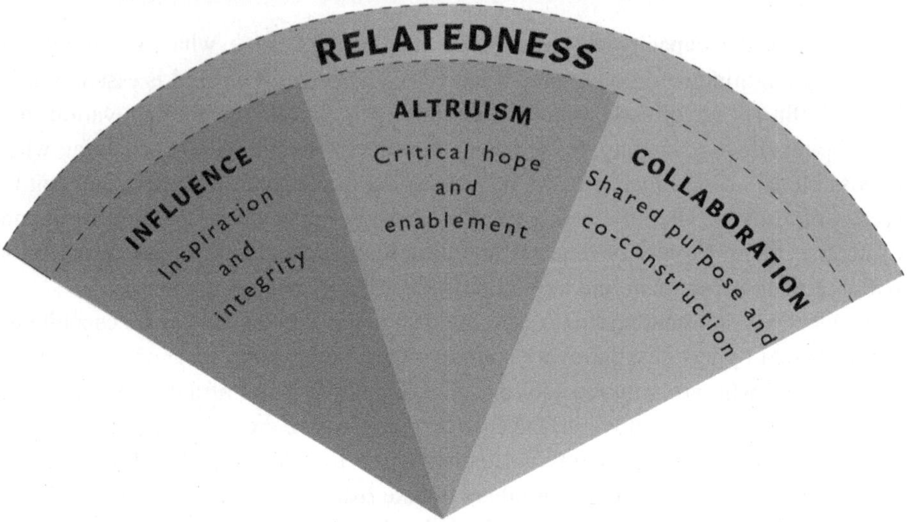

Relatedness

Relatedness in leaders and teams focuses on developing capacities and conditions for people to have a feeling of connection and belonging in a work environment. The quality of social relationships and networks in schools has an impact on how a school and education system functions.[31] The capacities and conditions that give expression to and foster relatedness are influence, altruism and collaboration. Explore with your team how a Catalan community's human pyramid (see figure 9.11) may represent the elements of influence, altruism and collaboration in the domain of relatedness? You might explore why people undertake risky endeavours together, how they achieve their goals, and what do they rely upon?

Influence: inspiration and integrity

Influence is the social effect and impact a leader can have to motivate and mobilize others 'to dream, learn, do, and become more'.[33] Through their influence transformative leaders inspire confidence and belief as they encourage, support and motivate others to actualize their potential.

Leaders inspire by finding the value congruence or common ground that connects people's potential to a shared vision and objective.[34] Respect for a transformative leader comes not from their position, but by the way people around them are empowered and challenged to have a shared purpose and be the best version of

Figure 9.11 Human pyramid[32]

themselves.[35] Leaders are responsible for developing others to initiate actions and be leaders in and beyond their classrooms.

Shared leadership is described by the Carpe Vitam Leadership for Learning project[36] as everyone in a school having the capacity to influence as a person of agency. 'Being an agent or having agency involves having a sense of self encompassing particular values and a cultural identity, and being able to pursue self-determined purposes and goals through self-conscious strategic action.'[37]

A leader's integrity has influence as it demonstrates to others a consistency of ethical and moral behaviours and an authenticity and transparency that develops trust and belief in their leadership.[38] Inspiring leaders build trust by being fair and just when initiating feedback and undertaking difficult decisions. They influence others through their expertise, conscientiousness, consistent valuing of their teams and a commitment to a vision that genuinely addresses equity, opportunity and possibility.[39]

The inspiration and integrity of influence builds relatedness and connection as it develops shared belief and trust between people to achieve something better together.

Reflection question for leaders

- How do you develop shared ethical beliefs, transparency and trust with others?

Ideas for leadership-as-practice

To create the conditions for influence, leaders can invest in appropriate opportunities for their teams and staff to:

- Recognize and develop their own and other's potential as leaders in different work contexts.
- Identify their values and skills in the work context and how that may inspire others.
- Interrogate how moral and ethical considerations inform the capacity to lead, and how their role and actions support or challenge this.

For schools to continue to be better places, a leader's influence must be motivated by critical hope and altruism.

Altruism: critical hope and enablement

Altruism in leadership is pro-social support for people's well-being and the enablement of their agency. Pro-social behaviours can be motivated by egotism (benefiting the self), altruism (to the benefit of others), collectivism (benefit to the group) and principlism (to uphold a moral principle).[40] Altruism as compassionate empathy is to act selflessly and wisely in the interest of others. This requires leaders to enable their team or staff to understand others' needs and points of view.

Transformative leadership acts to the benefit of other people, the group and with a strong, moral purpose informed by critical hope (see chapter 1). Critical hope is the belief in achieving a more just world by having 'a realistic appraisal of conditions, a sense of personal and collective resilience, and the ability to envision a better future'.[41]

The 'critical' in critical hope describes how inequities and power relations must be scrutinized in schools if aspirations for developing agency are to be realized.[42]

Enablement does not mean giving agency but providing opportunities that support and scaffold people's capacity to act for themselves and others. Despite the history, constraints and day-to-day realities of schools, critical hope is acting on the belief that things can change, evolve and empower staff and students over time, through critique, commitment and strategy.

Critical hope and enablement create positive relationships and a sense of belonging through the empowerment people give to each other through altruistic behaviours that are compassionate, efficacious and principled.

Reflection question for leaders

- How do you enable others to believe things can be changed for the better?

Ideas for leadership-as-practice

To create the conditions for altruism, leaders can invest in propitious opportunities for their teams and staff to:

- Scrutinize the established power relations and structures in and outside the classroom and consider how they may align with people's values and purpose.
- Enable others to lead in and outside classrooms.
- Work toward and find long-term solutions to address power relations that create inequities in schools.

A leader's altruism and enablement of others is achieved through successful processes and structures for collaboration.

Collaboration: shared purpose and co-construction

Collaboration is the process of people co-constructing a shared endeavour to achieve a productive and purposeful outcome. Leaders develop people's capacity to collaborate by initiating and developing skills in when and how to collaborate. Successful collaborations are when leaders support teams to know the purpose of what they are doing and that it matters. Without shared purpose, commitment and effort it is difficult for ideas, expertise and actions to coalesce.[43]

In collaborative projects, tasks or goals leaders can support and challenge their team and guide them to sustain their commitment and strategy toward a common objective. Collaborations are motivating in themselves as teams encourage each other by sharing ideas and expertise, and building support and trust as they work towards a goal.[44]

Leaders should also recognize that collaboration can solve the complex and multi-faceted issues of schools. Leaders can encourage diverse and divergent thinking in collaborations and generate increased capacity for creative problem-solving and possibility thinking. Leaders who collaborate demonstrate their commitment to achieving objectives with others. The joint ideas and actions in collaborative co-constructions promote a sense of what social cognitive theorist Albert Bandura[45] describes as collective agency. This is people's co-joint belief in their collective capacity to achieve something positive together.

Collaboration encourages relatedness as it relies on people feeling connected and interdependent with each other and promotes a sense of belonging to a group.

Reflection question for leaders

- When do you have opportunities to pursue and achieve with others a deeply shared purpose and commitment towards a shared goal?

Ideas for leadership-as-practice

To create the conditions for collaboration, leaders can invest in enriching opportunities for their teams and staff to:

- Decide when it is purposeful to collaborate and clarify their roles, processes and intended outcome.
- Share ideas and expertise and recognize unique contributions of individuals to achieve a mutually agreed goal.
- Treat everyone equally and develop clear communication processes and expectations.

Concluding reflections

The Leadership Wheel is a tool that provides a metalanguage and identifies processes for developing transformative leadership and the conditions for fostering autonomy, competence and relatedness. In schools we work with, the Leadership Wheel is a frame that is used by leadership to:

- Diagnose and evaluate what is needed to build courageous leadership and leadership-as-practice in their school context.

- Identify and embed processes and practices to develop the conditions for courageous leadership and leadership-as-practice.
- Develop individual leaders and school cultures towards transformation through metacognitive, focused and strategic action.
- Nurture individual insight, growth and action through reflective practice (see chapter 3).

Based on Self-Determination Theory, the Leadership Wheel allows for the exploration and development of a type of leadership that sport management researchers Angela Lumpkin and Rebecca M. Achen describe in the following way:

> Leaders are visionaries. Through imagination and creativity, leaders translate possibilities into realities in collaboration with others. Leaders are also lifelong learners with personal and professional growth resulting from an eagerness to ask questions, search for new knowledge, and continuously seek greater understanding. Leaders listen, empathize, empower people, and expand personal abilities, while motivating others to do the same . . . a leader's actions can inspire others to dream, learn, do, and become more.[46]

Schools are about growing people so that they thrive as the best version of themselves. It about growing students and staff so that they have the skills and understandings to deal with, influence and shape the complex world they encounter throughout their lives. It is about growing people for the good of others and not just themselves. It is nurturing people so that they feel what they do matters (autonomy), that they feel good at something (competence), and that they feel like they belong somewhere (relatedness). This is what supports people to effectively learn and lead.

Schools can be fertile places for growth, but it is an environment like soil that is nuanced and complex. The Leadership Wheel endeavours to provide a path through that complexity by making coherence of the nutrients that create the conditions for agentic leadership. We conclude the chapter with reflective question for leaders based on the elements of the Leadership Wheel. However, the reflective questions are only valuable if they lead to action.

In the next chapter we conclude by discussing how school leaders might bring all the insights in the Lantern together to generate blueprints for transformation.

Key actions

To develop leadership and agency in your context, continue to ask yourself and your team the following questions and what actions you will take to address them:

Engagement – what do we want to achieve together?
Perseverance – how to we keep going in what we want to achieve?
Flexibility – what are other ways we can achieve it?
Critical reflection – what assumptions have we made?

Communication – how can we tell the story of what we are doing?
Creativity – how can we re-imagine what we are doing?
Influence – how do we inspire others to be involved?
Altruism – how can we enable others to lead?
Collaboration – what other ways can people work deeply together?

Leadership for transformation blueprints

10

Figure 10.1 Blueprints create a map for action

Blueprints, with their crisp white lines etched against cobalt sheets, are more than just tools of construction – they are imagination made tangible. Blueprints date from the nineteenth century,[1] where an idea or a set of drawings could become something real and tangible in the world. They offered a plan to make the complex achievable. A plan that defined and shared a vision that put builders, surveyors, architects and engineers literally on the same page. Blueprints marked the beginning of something, the moment when an idea took shape and became a plan for action.

In schools, the work of leadership for transformation requires a kind of blueprint to move from ideas to action through a shared understanding of the task. A key part of leadership for transformation is to imagine the future with the clarity and courage of an architect – what will be kept, what requires demolition, what needs renovation and what new construction will suit the space and place? The same process is required in leading for transformation. The challenge is to draft a 'blueprint' that inspires action, withstands difficulty, and unites a community around a shared vision for beneficial change. A blueprint in a transforming school is not necessarily drawn- although it helps if it is. It is often crafted in collaborative conversations, decisions, that are infused with critical hope. It is, like all blueprints, a dynamic plan for transformation.

The power and usefulness of blueprints is not only in their clarity but in their adaptability. Very few (if any) buildings are constructed exactly as planned. There are always unexpected twists – yet the blueprint evolves. Transformative leaders in schools face similar realities. A global pandemic, a sudden policy shift, a budget crunch or the changing needs of students can change well laid plans or precisely created blueprints. But effective leaders, like effective builders and designers, respond to these challenges with resilience, revising their designs while keeping their sights on change that will benefit the whole school community.

Central to our exploration of leadership for transformation has been the question of 'how'. How do we move beyond aspiration to make transformation a tangible reality in schools? How do we engage with the many small steps required, navigate systemic pressures, and build the collective capacity for change? We have argued throughout this book that this 'how' lies in understanding and intentionally cultivating specific strategies and practices based in the values and context of each school. To frame the discussion of 'how' school leaders can make transformation real, we return to the Leadership Lantern (figure 10.2) we introduced in the opening chapters of this book.

The Leadership Lantern is our blueprint for school transformation made up of the design features we have seen in the research and in our practice over a more than a decade working side-by-side with schools exploring transformation. The Lantern is, for us, a way to express what we see as critical in transforming schools. It is not meant to be prescriptive or linear but rather a way to shed light and illuminate the direction of travel on the transformation journey.

This concluding chapter articulates a plan for leading transformative action in schools based on the features of the Lantern. We use the Leadership Lantern to frame this discussion beginning with values and context and then explore how leadership-as-practice and courageous leadership create agency. All this action is fuelled by the 4Cs: creativity, collaboration, communication and critical reflection. Let's begin by discussing our first blueprint for change enacting the 4Cs.

ORPHAN HOLD
DO NOT SHIP

H1–000000000455

ISBN 9781350331433

CLIENT	Alternate Sourcing
STATION	TPP Receiving Station 03
HELD	2026–10–08 15:08

SHELF

If its order arrives, scan this label at a receiving station.

Figure 10.2 The Leadership Lantern is our blueprint for transformation

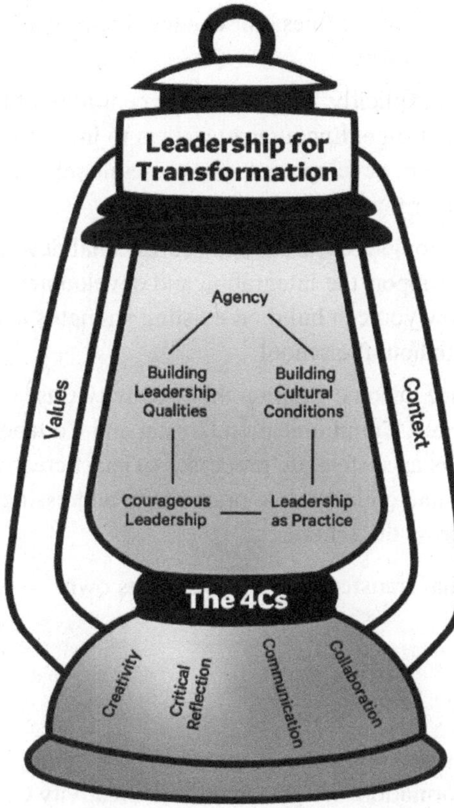

The 4Cs: The fuel for transformation

Leadership for transformation is only possible when the 4Cs are understood and enacted, both in individuals (building leadership capacities) and in schools (building cultural capabilities). They are essential for driving beneficial change, enabling schools to reshape dynamically to ensure student needs are at the forefront of the agenda.

The 4Cs are paradoxical; they are inherent in each of us, yet they require deliberate development and engagement within our context to strengthen our ability to apply them. They make action possible, but only if we continually work to develop them in ourselves and our teams. In these complex and dynamic 'postnormal' times, an understanding and ability to enact the 4Cs are even more critical, shaping our capacity to flexibly imagine, enable and enact transformative change. They provide the capabilities necessary for the 'heavy lifting' that transformation requires. Let's consider how we might embed the 4Cs across practices and strategies and then consider each of the 4C's role individually. When leading for transformation the following actions can embed the 4Cs:

- Assess readiness: Use frameworks like the Conditions for Learning Dial (figure 1.2) to assess where the 4Cs are currently evident in your school and how they contribute to readiness for change. Identify areas for development based on this assessment.
- Integrate the 4Cs explicitly: Emphasize the centrality of the 4Cs in driving transformational change. Encourage teachers to integrate them into teaching practices, curriculum development, and professional interactions. Make them explicit rather than implicit.
- Build capacity: Provide resources and professional development opportunities to support the integration and development of the 4Cs for all staff. Explore how you can build on existing strengths and expand their application throughout the school.
- Use 4C coherence makers: Employ the Creativity Cascade, Critical Reflection Crucible, Communication Crystal and Collaboration Circles coherence makers as systematic processes to enact creative, reflective, communicative, and collaborative practices in addressing challenges and opportunities across the school.

Each of the 4Cs also has transformative power of its own.

Creativity

In chapter 6 we discuss leading through creativity, describing it as an indispensable tool for leading transformation. We presented The Creativity Cascade as a coherence maker that provided the 'how' of generating action from ideas. To recap the Creativity Cascade has four phases: Noticing, Asking why, Really why? Playing with Possibility and Selecting and Evaluating. Here are some ways creativity can generate action in a transforming school.

- Develop a culture of noticing by encouraging leadership staff and students to observe and critically reflect on elements of school life. Exercises like reflective walks or analysing images can assist in the noticing process.
- Engage in deep inquiry by fostering a habit of Asking why? Really why? about observed patterns and cultural features in the school to explore root causes and underlying assumptions. Use strategies like creating a Why Tree that we discussed in chapter 6.
- Play with possibilities by creating opportunities for collaborative possibility thinking and experimentation with challenges, considering the contextual features of the school. Leaders could think more deeply about possibility by approaching challenges and opportunities by actively thinking about what could be, rather than being limited by current realities.

- Generate a selecting and evaluating process to assess and choose viable possibilities, followed by ongoing evaluation and refinement of implemented actions.

Creativity provides the impetus to re-imagine possibilities in a school. Critical reflection allows deep and wise analysis on how these practices and strategies might land in each school's context.

Critical reflection

Critical reflection is a powerful process for leading transformation. It is an active, transformative process where assumptions are challenged, leading to new understandings and action. The Critical Reflection Crucible is presented in Chapter 3 as a schema to support leaders in enacting deep and sustainable action. Here are some approaches to enact critical reflection:

- Embed critical reflection into daily leadership practice. This should be an ongoing practice of questioning 'how and why' or 'why this, why so'. This kind of inquiry practice guards against unfounded assumptions and unconscious bias taking root in decision making.
- Identify and examine assumptions. Generate processes that ensure that leaders, staff and students are considering the evidence for their assumptions. This can be as simple as developing a cultural expectation that all discussions around practice and strategy will be based on evidence.
- Contest, elaborate on, and adapt ideas and practices by encouraging 'what if' questions and exploring issues from diverse perspectives. Create expectations that everyone's strategies and practices can be discussed and enhanced as part of the critical reflection process.
- Re-solve by translating insights into tangible and sustainable action. Plan and engage in transformative action collaboratively, ensuring actions are grounded in evidence and insights from previous phases. Use action-oriented strategies that plan out the actions tangibly on a timeline and include points for regular critical reflection.

Critical reflection provides the space to apply wise consideration to ideas. However, these ideas (when ready) need to be understood by the whole school community. Effective communication can reduce 'friction' as schools transform.

Communication

Communication is vital for creating, sharing and motivating people towards a collective vision and culture for transformation. When communication is effective it can empower all voices within the school creating opportunities for a unified vision for beneficial change. In Chapter 5, the Communication Crystal is presented as a coherence maker to communicate the need and the opportunities for change. Here are some strategies to generate collaborative action that drives transformation.

- Create alertness to messaging, by generating a culture of understanding the expectations of different audiences in the school community. Notice communication patterns and provide appropriate spaces and forums to ensure ideas and challenges can be heard.
- Enable voice by creating processes and structures that give everyone the opportunity and responsibility to contribute. Disrupt ritualized communication patterns using strategies that ensure nobody dominates. This could include debates or other protocols that ensure contributions are respectful and equal.
- Convey meaning and purpose working collaboratively to craft clear messages that resonate with all your audiences. Focus group strategies could be employed to ensure that the is understood by diverse audiences as intended.
- Generate action and agency through communication that is empowering rather than commanding or controlling. Explore and experiment with new communication processes to create effective feedback loops and support people's agency.

As we have explained, the 4Cs are not siloed they interact, overlap and are interdependent. In that sense creativity, communication, collaboration and critical reflection are enabled by each other and all rely on the understanding and practice of each other. For transformative leadership collaboration fuels the opportunity for a 'shared affair of the mind'[2] to move beyond the hero individual as leadership to leadership-as-practice embedded throughout the school community.

Collaboration

Collaboration is the process of co-constructing and connecting to change strategies and practices in transforming schools making them fit for purpose. In chapter 4, we presented the Collaboration Circles coherence maker to structure this leadership process. Here are some strategies to embed collaboration into a transforming school.

- Encourage everyone to offer ideas or actions towards a shared goal, potentially limiting the number of offers initially to ensure participation.
- Support people to yield by modelling and encouraging accepting, developing, or building on offers, generating further ideas and actions with the group. Practice offering and yielding through exercises like the Gift of Offering and Yielding discussed in chapter 4.

- Facilitate challenging, evaluating and extending ideas to probe, analyse, promote new perspectives, and deepen ideas. Use strategies where each person has one opportunity to contest, elaborate or adapt in discussions.
- Advance co-constructions and connections by taking joint ownership of shared processes and harnessing the collective genius of the group. Use the Advancing Lazy Susan (Practice 4.5) featured in chapter 4 practice to connect ideas and experience non-linear development.

The 4Cs provides the capabilities that fuel transformation processes. They are teachable and learnable, and as such they need to be developed and practiced regularly. Returning to the Lantern, the twin structural pillars of context and values hold up the lantern. Context and values are sometimes 'given circumstances' and the 4Cs provide us with the fuel to analyse them and work towards wise transformation. Let's begin with a discussion of how values will influence the design of our transformative blueprint.

Values

Values are another structural component of the Leadership Lantern, crucial for supporting transformative change. They act as a lodestar or guiding star, providing an anchor and guide to ensure school leadership is ethical and has a deep moral purpose. When the complexities and challenges of transformation become overwhelming, values enable leaders to look beyond the tangle of transformation[3] and connect with the rationale for transformation.

Values create a strong set of aspirations, enabling schools to design and act on the necessary changes. However, any set of values is only meaningful when the whole school community is part of their creation (or reshaping) and their implementation.

Here are some ways to integrate values into your transformative blueprint:

- Shape and share values collaboratively: Engage the whole school community in shaping and implementing the values that will guide transformation. Create spaces for communication and collaboration that cater to the specific needs to all in the school community. Create opportunities for genuine collaboration and co-creation with students, parents and staff, inviting them into a shared endeavour.
- Ensure alignment: Use critical reflection to build coherence between the school's stated values and its day-to-day operations and decision-making. Create a values evidence table to track where values are evidenced in practices and strategies across the school. Reinforce this alignment by celebrating it publicly. Continuously evaluate whether actions and strategies are grounded in shared values and where they are not, devise ways to align them.

- Communicate values through storytelling: Use authentic narratives to continuously structure and convey a shared vision tied to values. These stories could be from practice that leaders engage with or observe, from practice in other places or could be imagined. Telling stories about values helps to embed them in the culture of the school.
- Use values as a reference point: When navigating challenges, refer to shared values as a guide for decision-making and action. Use them to anchor shared decision making and drive aspiration.

Values should be sturdy but not inflexible. All values are situated in context and as the context changes, values may need to be re-imagined. Understanding context is critical in the values setting process but also profoundly influences how transformation can be enacted.

Context

Context is a crucial structural element in the Leadership Lantern, signifying that leadership will work differently in different contexts. In other words, what works in one school will not necessarily work in another because the context shapes culture, expectations and responses to transformation. While processes may be applied from theory or other contexts, their timing, sequence and approach must be designed and enacted perceptively to ensure transformation is sensitive to a particular context.

Leading for transformation is shaped by the unique environment of the school, including its history, strengths, and challenges. Here are some suggestions to design your blueprint for transformation considering context:

- Exercise deep noticing: Engage in 'deep noticing' of your school's context. Actively observe and interpret surroundings, interactions and experiences, seeking to actively comprehend, analyse, listen and interpret. Use strategies like mapping and creating collages of images of the context to generate discussions about context.
- Gather diverse perspectives: Use processes like Practice 2.1 a modified Citizen Jury Approach (described in chapter 2) to gather observations and perspectives from diverse members of the school community – leadership, staff and students – about what they notice about the school and its needs.
- Analyse challenges and opportunities: Frame observed challenges and opportunities through inquiry. Identify existing assumptions about the context and challenge them using critical reflection. Ask Why this? Why so? to understand root causes and underlying factors.

- Adapt strategies to context: Ensure that strategies and actions developed are sustainable and relevant to the specific needs and circumstances of your school community. Recognize that knowledge and practices must be adapted, requiring flexibility, creativity, and a willingness to experiment.

We have now discussed the fuel (4Cs) and the structure of the Lantern to explore the starting points of our blueprint for transformation. We will now turn to the light inside the lantern—agency that is generated through building leadership qualities and cultural conditions.

Courageous leadership

Courageous leadership refers to the personal capacities required to take the bold actions necessary to transform schools. These are inherent in individuals such as those we describe in the Leadership Wheel. Courageous leaders are those who believe deeply in the agentic potential of their staff, students and community. They are guided by values and context to ensure consistent progress can be made to make beneficial change in schools.

Crucially, courageous leadership engages with the 4Cs to create and communicate a vision, collaborate to make it happen and facilitate critical reflection. Courageous leaders have agency when they have a shared vision, are aware of their influence and can navigate structures to make change happen. They boldly take action to develop the agency and leadership of others through leadership-as-practice.

To nurture courageous leadership, consider the following actions:

- Cultivate critical hope and courage: Actively foster a mindset of critical hope and courage within yourself and among staff. For instance, encourage and model resilience and determination in the face of challenges.
- Develop personal 4C capabilities: Make time to develop your own capacity for creativity, critical reflection, communication and collaboration, recognizing that they need continuous exercise. For instance, leader's could build critical reflection through coaching or professional supervision.
- Reflect on influence and power: Engage in critical reflection to understand how power structures operate and your own position within them, enabling effective navigation and advocacy for change. Use exercises like the Power Switch (see chapter 3) to explore how power is exercised.
- Build belief in capacity: As a courageous leader, build people's beliefs in their capacity for agency and provide the environment, resources, and supports they need to take action. For instance, a courageous leader might recognize a team member's unique strengths during a meeting and/or assign them a lead role on a project to build their confidence and skills.

Courageous leadership is not sufficient by itself. It must be situated within a culture of leadership to ensure transformation is achievable. Leadership-as-practice can support cultural change.

Leadership-as-practice

Leadership-as-practice is a way of understanding leadership that looks to the culture of the school. It sees leadership everywhere, in anyone, at any time. It focuses on what can be accomplished together rather than solely on the actions of one person. Leadership-as-practice is developed in a school culture through embedded social practices – the 'sayings, doings and relatings'[4] of the community. Changing practices means shifting these embedded sayings, doings, and relatings. However, simply changing practices is not enough; the underlying 'practice architectures' or arrangements that hold these practices in place must also be revealed, interrogated, and new arrangements created.

Leadership-as-practice is intrinsically linked with developing collective agency. It requires the development of a culture where leadership is practiced by everyone. Leadership-as-practice enables and develops agency in people through continued support, reflection, stimulated challenge, experience and determined focus. A school's organizational culture and capacity for evolution and transformation are influenced by collaborations, especially when connected by positive communication feedback loops and a shared vision.

To build leadership-as-practice:

- Analyse existing practices: Leaders could use frameworks, such as the 'sayings, doings and relatings' approach, to analyse the school's current leadership practices and identify areas for change.
- Develop the 4Cs culturally: Embed the 4Cs as foundational capabilities and processes within the school culture. Ensure they become the 'way we do things around here'. This could be achieved by mapping where the 4Cs are already evident in a school and where the opportunities might be for further development.
- Empower collective action: Foster leadership-as-practice to empower collective action, enabling everyone to develop agency in their own situation. Support people to collaborate and achieve shared goals, building collective efficacy.
- Embed deep and continuing professional learning: Make professional learning a critical part of the school's culture, rather than the exception, requiring persistence from leadership.

The aim of all these initiatives is ultimately to build a school where the whole school community can exercise and enact agency. An agentic school in this way is a product of courageous leadership and leadership-as-practice.

Agency

Just as a lantern radiates light to illuminate the surroundings, agency represents the power of acting and leading in the world, enabling transformation. Agency is at the core of transformative leadership. Agency is an inseparable relationship with an individual's capacity for courageous leadership and developing a culture of leadership-as-practice.

Agency becomes practice in a school's culture when leaders and teachers collaborate and learn together, exploring effective approaches. It is when all voices are heard and enabled towards actions that transform practices and processes in a school. Agency is crucial for leadership-as-practice as it encourages action; it is energizing and gives people the motivation to act, intervene and enable others. People sharing moments of joy together also deeply connects them. Developing understanding and belief in agency are vital first steps towards leading transformation in people and environments.

The following actions can encourage agency:

- Conduct an 'agency audit': Use reflective processes to explore people's understandings and misunderstandings of agency, their beliefs in the concept, their perception of agency in the school.
- Foster belief in possibilities: Create an environment where people believe change is possible and necessary, providing opportunities for collaboration towards a shared vision. Courageous leadership builds this belief in capacity.
- Develop autonomy, competence and relatedness: Cultivate the conditions where people experience these core psychological needs, drawing on insights from Self-Determination Theory. The Leadership Wheel can be used as a tool to explore how these are cultivated.
- Support collective efficacy: Support people to collaborate and achieve shared goals, recognizing that leading transformation needs collective efficacy driven by agentic leadership. Work with others and influence those with resources to affect change beyond individual control.

The Lantern in action: a dynamic blueprint

The Leadership Lantern is not a static model but a dynamic interplay of its elements. The 4Cs fuel the process, guided by values and context, manifested through the combined efforts of individual and cultural capabilities, ultimately radiating agency that illuminate the path for transformation.

Transformation in schools is often incremental, with fits and starts, cascading effects, feedback loops and tipping points. It takes many small actions and connections between people to build agency and transform aspects of schooling. The blueprint derived from the Leadership Lantern embraces this complexity, advocating for persistent, connected actions.

Concluding reflections

In our postnormal world, marked by rapid, often disorienting, change from intensifying climate crises and enduring inequalities to the rise of AI and democratic backsliding – the call for transformation in education is not merely a theoretical aspiration, but an urgent necessity. Our schools are hamstrung by system status quo policy and multiple competing demands. Leadership for transformation matters profoundly for the future of our schools and, critically, for the future of our communities as it provides a way of generating agency and re-invigorating our educational institutions through critical hope.

As we discussed in the opening chapters, UNESCO's 'Reimagining Our Futures Together: A New Social Contract for Education',[5] makes a compelling case: educational transformation is the key to societal transformation. Education organizes the intergenerational exchange of knowledge generation and co-creation, connecting us to the world and to others, exposing our students to new possibilities, and strengthening our capacities for communication, collaboration, creativity and critical reflection. To shape the futures we need, education must be transformed. This transformation would address systemic inequities, seeking to make high quality, relevant learning a right for all students. It is about fundamentally reimagining schools' values and context, that then drive all aspects of school life including pedagogy, curriculum and wellbeing.

This vital, perhaps daunting, task falls to educational leaders. But how do we move beyond acknowledging the gravity, immediacy and urgency of this need to make transformation a tangible reality? This is the central question this book, and our exploration through the Leadership Lantern framework, takes on the 'how'. Leadership for transformation provides the pathway. It is not about quick fixes, silver bullets or simply improving what already exists; it is about reimagining and reshaping values, practices and policies so educators can effectively respond to the challenges and opportunities they face in their contexts. This requires next-level leadership, moving beyond simplistic dichotomies and embracing the richness and complexity of the challenges and opportunities.

At the core of this transformative process, illuminated by the Leadership Lantern, sits agency. Agency is the capacity and opportunity to produce and shape our experiences by exercising judgement in the interest of others and of ourselves. It is the power of acting and leading in the world because we have the skills and supports to do so. Agentic individuals and cultures are not passive but actively engage with their environments. Leadership for transformation is inherently linked to developing both individual courageous leadership and a culture of leadership-as-practice, and agency is necessary for both and generates both. Courageous leaders are those who believe deeply in the agentic potential of their staff, students and community. They use their influence and navigate structures to make change happen. Leadership-as-practice sees leadership embedded in the everyday activities of everyone in the school community.

The fuel for this agentic transformation is the 4Cs: Creativity, Critical Reflection, Communication and Collaboration. These are not mere skills but foundational capacities that underpin human thriving and are critical for leadership for transformation. They enable the 'heavy lifting' that transformation requires.

- Creativity allows us to imagine and drive what is possible, moving beyond the status quo to innovate and find new responses to challenges. Agency drives creativity by fostering empowerment and challenging the status quo.
- Critical reflection is the rigorous process of questioning assumptions, analysing experiences and reforming ideas to inform wise action, helping us understand power dynamics and navigate complex systems. It is crucial for agency, enabling examination of assumptions that shape actions.
- Communication is about organizing and interpreting experiences, purpose, and aspirations as shared understandings, empowering voices and generating action and agency through authentic dialogue.
- Collaboration is the process of co-constructing and connecting to change strategies and practices, fostering collective agency and shared purpose. Transformation needs the collective efficacy generated by collaboration.

Ultimately, the future of our schools and communities depends on developing the capacity for agency for all. Developing agency is vital for fostering critically reflective, socially engaged, and responsible citizens equipped to address global challenges.

This is not a quick process; it takes time and many small, connected and persistent actions. It requires leaders to cultivate belief in possibilities, develop autonomy, competence, and relatedness, and support collective efficacy.

The Leadership Lantern, with its values and context structural supports, 4Cs fuel, and the light of agency born from courageous leadership and leadership-as-practice, offers a dynamic blueprint for this essential work. Leading transformation means steadily, purposefully cultivating agency in ourselves and others, enabling our schools to become vibrant, responsive ecosystems capable of meeting the complex needs of a changing world and shaping a better future for all.

Glossary

4C transformation The building of capabilities in creativity, critical reflection, communication and collaboration to reimagine culture, practice, approach and structures that strengthen human agency in organizations.

4Cs The shorthand for developing the capabilities of creativity, critical reflection, communication and collaboration. The potential and capacity to transform from 'what is' to 'what could be' are developed through processes in the 4Cs.

Agency The capacity for individuals or groups to act with intent and autonomy within their contexts. Agency enables educators and learners to make meaningful choices, exercise influence, and participate actively in transformation.
See also: Creativity, Noticing, Transformation

Assumptions (Paradigmatic, Prescriptive, Causal) Fundamental beliefs shaping decisions and actions.

Autonomy The condition of self-directedness and capacity to make choices aligned with one's values and goals. A core element of motivation and agency.
See also: Motivation, Agency

Capability Having the freedom, opportunity and power to develop an ability to do something that achieves wellbeing.

Coherence makers The schemas that organize knowledge that bring meaning and structure to critical concepts in education.

Collaboration Circles A coherence maker describing cyclical interactions – offering, yielding, challenging, evaluating and extending – building coherence in collaborative efforts.
See also: Collaboration, Yielding, Offering

Collaboration Working collectively across differences to generate synergy and innovative outcomes. Requires trust and psychological safety.
See also: Collaboration Circles, Voice, Psychological safety

Communication Leadership skill involving awareness of messaging, enabling voice, conveying meaning and purpose, and supporting action through feedback loops.
See also: Voice, Feedback Loops, Collaboration

Connectedness A sense of belonging and relational depth contributing to engagement and wellbeing.
See also: Culture, Collaboration

Context The complex web of settings – historical, social, cultural – in which schools and leadership practices operate.
See also: Noticing, Transformation

Courageous leadership The personal capacities and capabilities required to take the bold actions necessary to transform schools. These leaders believe deeply in the agentic potential of their staff, students, and communities.

Critical reflection Deliberate examination of assumptions, values and actions to deepen insight and ethical practice. Often represented by the Crucible metaphor.
See also: Assumptions, Crucible, Reflection

Crucible (Metaphor) Symbolizes the refining process of leadership through challenging reflection and practice under pressure.
See also: Critical reflection

Culture Shared norms, values and practices shaping school life and leadership.
See also: Connectedness, Leadership-as-practice

Doings The actions and behaviours constituting everyday professional practice.
See also: Sayings, Relatings, Leadership-as-practice

Emotion/Emotional Climate The affective atmosphere influencing learning, motivation and leadership dynamics.
See also: Joy, Motivation

Empowerment Increasing capacity, autonomy and confidence to shape decisions and action. *See also: Agency, Motivation*

Horizon thinking Reflective framework for envisioning current realities and future possibilities across layered spatial metaphors.
See also: Noticing, Agency

Inquiry Inquiry engages with focused question to be posed, solved, challenged and re-solved by the learners.

Intrinsic motivation Self-driven engagement fuelled by interest and values rather than external reward.
See also: Motivation, Autonomy

Joy Positive, energizing emotion that supports motivation, creativity and well-being.
See also: Celebration, Motivation

Leadership A socially enacted influence process involving shaping purpose, culture, and outcomes.
See also: Leadership-as-practice, Agency, Critical reflection

Leadership Wheel Divides leadership into autonomy, competency and relatedness domains, and identifies the capacities for leadership that can be developed.

Leadership-as-practice Viewing leadership as distributed and embedded in everyday interactions – sayings, doings and relatings.
See also: Sayings, Doings, Relatings

Liebig's Law Principle that growth is limited by the scarcest resource; applied to leadership by focusing development on key 'threshold' capabilities.
See also: Leadership development, Reflection

Mapping Visual or representational tool to analyse relationships, practices, or ideas in context.
See also: Network, Collaboration

Motivation The driving force behind actions, ranging along a continuum from amotivation to intrinsic motivation as explained by Self-determination Theory.
See also: Autonomy, Joy, Self-determination Theory

Narrative/Storytelling Using stories to communicate, shape identity and influence culture within organizations.
See also: Culture, Collaboration

Network Interconnected relationships and collaborations sustaining community and information flow.
See also: Mapping, Collaboration

Noticing Focused attention on phenomena and dynamics in context, foundational to insight and creative leadership.
See also: Critical reflection, Why? Really Why? Agency

Offering The initial proposal of an idea, perspective, or resource within a collaborative process.
See also: Yielding, Gift of Offering and Yielding

Paradigmatic Beliefs about how things work.

Pedagogy The knowledge and skills base that connects teaching to the theories and practice of learning.

Play/Playing Engaging in experimentation or improvisation to unlock creativity and new possibilities.
See also: Playfulness, Creativity

Playfulness Engaging attitudes promoting creativity, experimentation, and joy.
See also: Joy, Creative Practice

Practices Repeated patterns of actions, behaviour, talk and relationships constituting culture.
See also: Leadership-as-practice, Doings

Praxis The marriage of theory and praxis in context.

Prescriptive assumptions Beliefs about socially accepted norms or ways of doing things.
See also: Assumptions

Psychological safety An environment where team members feel safe to take interpersonal risks without fear of negative consequences.
See also: Collaboration, Voice

Reflection Ongoing, purposeful review of experience and assumptions to inform adaptive action.
See also: Critical reflection, Leadership Development

Relatedness The need to have a sense of belonging, connection and care from others.

Resilience The capacity to sustain effort and well-being amidst setbacks during transformation.
See also: Joy, Agency

Sayings The verbal or written expressions shared among practitioners shaping culture.
See also: Doings, Relatings, Leadership-as-practice

Self-determination Theory (SDT) Psychological theory explaining how autonomy, competence, and relatedness support motivation and well-being.
See also: Motivation, Autonomy

Story Narrative used to convey meaning, values, or identity within a community.
See also: Narrative/Storytelling

Transformation A deliberate process that moves people and organizations beyond their current realities to new practices and approaches. It involves the changing of mindsets, habits of mind and organizational culture.
See also: Agency, 4Cs, Critical reflection

Transformative learning Being critically reflective of our assumptions and the assumptions of others, and to take action on that transformed perspective.

Transformative values A set of values that guide and anchor transformative action through individual and collaborative action to create transformation.

Values A set of acceptable and expected norms for the individual members of an organization.

Voice The ability and opportunity of all members to express ideas and be heard in decision-making and everyday practice.
See also: Communication, Psychological safety, Collaboration

Why? Really Why? Reflective inquiry process tracing surface issues to root causes and complex relationships to generate insight and action.
See also: Noticing, Critical reflection

Yielding Acceptance and creative development of others' contributions in collaborative process.
See also: Offering, Gift of Offering and Yielding

Notes

Introduction

1 Hargreaves, A. and Fullan, M. (2020). 'Professional capital after the pandemic: Revisiting and revising classic understandings of teachers' work'. *Journal of Professional Capital and Community, 5*(3/4): 327–36; Lingard, B. (2010). 'Policy borrowing, policy learning: Testing times in Australian schooling'. *Critical Studies in Education, 51*(2): 129–47.

2 Datnow, A. (2020). 'The role of teachers in educational reform: A 20-year perspective'. *Journal of Educational Change, 21*(3): 431–41; Spillane, J. P. and Healey, K. (2010). 'Conceptualizing school leadership and management from a distributed perspective: An exploration of some study operations and measures'. *The Elementary School Journal, 111*(2): 253–81.

3 Au, W. (2007). 'High-stakes testing and curricular control: A qualitative metasynthesis'. *Educational Researcher, 36*(5): 258–67.

4 By 'our work' we are referring to the partnerships 4C Transformative learning has initiated and sustained. We have been involved in many of these partnerships. More information can be found at www.4ctransformativelearning.org

5 Kemmis, S. (2019). *A Practice Sensibility: An Invitation to the Theory of Practice Architectures.* Singapore: Springer.

1 Leadership for transformation

1 Yousafzai, M. (2013). 'The day I woke up in the hospital'. *TIME.* Retrieved from https://time.com/3490769/malala-yousafzai-the-day-i-woke-up-in-the-hospital/

2 Yousafzai, M. (2014). Nobel Lecture (PDF). Retrieved from NobelPrize.org. https://www.nobelprize.org/uploads/2018/06/yousafzai-lecture_en.pdf

3 Freire, P. (1998). *Pedagogy of Freedom: Ethics, Democracy, and Civic Courage.* Lanham, MD: Rowman & Littlefield.

4 Grain, K. (2022). *Critical Hope: How to Grapple with Complexity, Lead with Purpose, and Cultivate Transformative Social Change*, 39. Berkeley, CA: North Atlantic Books.

5 International Commission on the Futures of Education. (2021). 'Reimagining our futures together: A new social contract for education'. UNESCO. Retrieved from https://unesdoc.unesco.org/ark:/48223/pf0000379707/PDF/379707eng.pdf.multi

6 International Commission on the Futures of Education. (2021). 'Reimagining our futures together: A new social contract for education'. UNESCO. Retrieved from https://unesdoc.unesco.org/ark:/48223/pf0000379707/PDF/379707eng.pdf.multi

7 Mincu, M. (2022). 'Why is school leadership key to transforming education? Structural and cultural assumptions for quality education in diverse contexts'. *Prospects, 52* (3–4): 231–42. https://doi.org/10.1007/s11125-022-09625-6

8 Mandela, N. (1990). Speech at Madison Park High School, Boston. As reported regarding education: 'Education is the most powerful weapon which you can use to change the world'.

9 United Nations Development Programme. (2022). *Human Development Report 2021/2022: Uncertain Times, Unsettled Lives – Shaping our Future in a Transforming World*. United Nations. https://hdr.undp.org/content/human-development-report-2021-22

10 Kruse, K. (2020). 'Top 6 reasons your leadership development program is failing'. *Forbes*. https://www.forbes.com/sites/kevinkruse/2020/01/07/top-6-reasons-your-leadership-development-program-is-failing/ For an up-to-date breakdown go to https://trainingindustry.com/wiki/learning-services-and-outsourcing/size-of-training-industry/

11 Ly, D. B., Dudovitz, R. N., Rünger, D., Jackson, N. J. and Wong, M. D. (2021). 'Chaos in schools and its relationship to adolescent risk behaviors'. *Academic Pediatrics, 21*(2): 329–35.

12 Fullan, M. (2023). 'Why we can't escape the status quo in education: 200 years of doing the same thing just won't cut it'. Opinion. *Education Week*. Retrieved from https://www.edweek.org/leadership/opinion-why-we-cant-escape-the-status-quo-in-education/2023/01

13 Fullan, M. (2023). 'Why we can't escape the status quo in education: 200 years of doing the same thing just won't cut it'. Opinion. *Education Week*. Retrieved from https://www.edweek.org/leadership/opinion-why-we-cant-escape-the-status-quo-in-education/2023/01

14 Csikszentmihalyi, M. (1990). *Flow: The Psychology of Optimal Experience*. New York: Harper & Row.

15 Mincu, M. (2022). 'Why is school leadership key to transforming education? Structural and cultural assumptions for quality education in diverse contexts'. *Prospects, 52*(3–4): 231–42, https://doi.org/10.1007/s11125-022-09625-6

16 Glăveanu, V. P. (2015). 'From individual agency to co-agency'. In *Constraints of Agency: Explorations of Theory in Everyday Life*, 249. Cham: Springer.

17 Glăveneau calls dichotomies antimonies. The Oxford Dictionary explains that an antinomy is a 'contradiction between two beliefs or conclusions that are in themselves reasonable; a paradox. There are not many short novels capable of accommodating bewildering antinomies.'

18 Jefferson, M. and Anderson, M. (2021). *Transforming Education: Reimagining Learning, Pedagogy and Curriculum*. London: Bloomsbury

19 Beerel, A. (2021). *Rethinking Leadership: A Critique of Contemporary Theories*, 25. Abingdon: Routledge.

20 Beerel, A. (2021). *Rethinking Leadership: A Critique of Contemporary Theories*, 25. Abingdon: Routledge.

21 Raelin, J. A. (2017). 'Leadership-as-practice: Theory and application – An editor's reflection'. *Leadership, 13*(2): 215–21.

22 Beerel, A. (2021). *Rethinking Leadership: A Critique of Contemporary Theories*, 25. Abingdon: Routledge.

23 Avolio, B. J., and Gardner, W. L. (2005). 'Authentic leadership development: Getting to the root of positive forms of leadership'. *The Leadership Quarterly, 16*(3), 315–38.

24 Avolio, B. J. and Gardner, W. L. (2005). 'Authentic leadership development: Getting to the root of positive forms of leadership'. *The Leadership Quarterly, 16*(3): 315–38; Matshoba-Ramuedzisi, T., De Jongh, D. and Fourie, W. (2022). 'Followership: A review of current and emerging research'. *Leadership & Organization Development Journal, 43*(4): 653–68.

25 For a full discussion of leading learning through curation see Jefferson, M. and Anderson, M. (2021). *Transforming Education: Reimagining Learning, Pedagogy and Curriculum*. London: Bloomsbury.

2 Leadership: lighting for the path of transformation

1 Raelin, J. A. (2017). 'Leadership-as-practice: Theory and application – An editor's reflection'. *Leadership, 13*(2): 215–21.

2 Another term used for our current situation is VUCA. VUCA is an acronym to describe the volatility, uncertainty, complexity and ambiguity of general conditions and situations. Warren Bennis and Burt Nanus first published the term in Bennis, W. and Nanus, B. (1985). *Leaders: The Strategies for Taking Charge*. New York: Harper. Row, 41.

3 Sardar, Z. (2002). 'Welcome to postnormal times'. *Futures, 34*(3–4): 289–99.

4 Nussbaum, M. C. (2011). *Creating Capabilities: The Human Development Approach.* Cambridge, MA: The Belknap Press of Harvard University Press.

5 Jefferson, M. and Anderson, M. (2017). *Transforming Schools: Creativity, Critical Reflection, Communication, Collaboration*. London: Bloomsbury.

6 Craft, A. (2005). *Creativity in Schools: Everyday Creativity*. Abingdon: Routledge.

7 Alexander, R. (2014). Anna Craft. *Cambridge Primary Review Trust*. Retrieved from https://cprtrust.org.uk/cprt-blog/anna-craft/

8 Rodgers, C. (2002). 'Defining reflection: Another look at John Dewey and reflective thinking'. *Teachers College Record, 104*(4): 842–66 (864).

9 Raelin, J. A. (2016). 'Imagine there are no leaders: Reframing leadership as collaborative agency'. *Leadership, 12*(2): 131–58.

10 Purdue Pharma L. P. (n.d.). 'Purpose statement and values'. Purdue Pharma. Retrieved 18 August 2025 from https://www.purduepharma.com/about/ethics-and-compliance/purpose-statement-values/

11 For a detailed discussion on values in education see Jefferson and Anderson (2021) *Transforming Education,* chapter 3. Originally agency was a transformative value but to avoid repetition we are discussing this as an element in our leadership for transformation coherence maker, the leadership lantern.

12 Jefferson, M. and Anderson, M. (2021). *Transforming Education: Reimagining Learning, Pedagogy and Curriculum*. London: Bloomsbury. 229.

13 Beerel, A. (2021). *Rethinking Leadership: A Critique of Contemporary Theories*, 25. Abingdon: Routledge.

14 Deci, E. L. and Ryan, R. M. (1985). *Intrinsic Motivation and Self-determination in Human Behavior*. New York: Plenum Press.

15 Deal, T. E. and Kennedy, A. A. (1982). *Corporate Cultures: The Rites and Rituals of Corporate Life*. Reading, MA: Addison-Wesley.

16 Schein, E. H. (2010). *Organizational Culture and Leadership* (4th ed.). Hoboken, NJ: Jossey-Bass.

17 Deci, E. L. and Ryan, R. M. (1985). *Intrinsic Motivation and Self-determination in Human Behavior*. New York: Plenum Press.

18 Jefferson, M. and Anderson, M. (2017). *Transforming Schools: Creativity, Critical Reflection, Communication, Collaboration*. London: Bloomsbury.

19 Glăveanu, V. (2015). 'From individual agency to co-agency'. In C. Gruber, M. Clark, S. Klempe and J. Valsiner (eds.), *Constraints of Agency* (Annals of Theoretical Psychology, vol. 12), 241–54. Cham: Springer.

20 Deci, E. L. and Ryan, R. M. (2000). 'The "what" and "why" of goal pursuits: Human needs and the self-determination of behavior'. *Psychological Inquiry, 11*(4): 227–68.

21 George, B. (2015). *Courage: The Defining Characteristic of Great Leaders.* Boston, MA: Harvard Business School Working Knowledge.

22 Wilkinson, J. (2020). 'Educational leadership as practice'. In G. W. Noblit (ed.), *Oxford Research Encyclopedia of Education*, 1. Oxford: Oxford University Press.

23 These definitions are paraphrases of Stephen Kemmis outlined in Kemmis, S. (2019). *A Practice Sensibility: An Invitation to the Theory of Practice Architectures*. Singapore: Springer.

24 Wilkinson, J. (2020). 'Educational leadership as practice'. *Oxford Research Encyclopedia of Education*. Retrieved 5 February 2026, from https://oxfordre.com/education/view/10.1093/acrefore/9780190264093.001.0001/acrefore-9780190264093-e-613.yep

3 Leading through critical reflection

1 Sourced from https://pixabay.com/photos/crucible-foundry-molten-bronze-2109202/

2 Anderson, M. and Jefferson, M. (2019). *Transforming Organizations: Engaging the 4Cs for Powerful Organizational Learning and Change*. London: Bloomsbury.

3 Jefferson, M. and Anderson, M. (2017). *Transforming Schools: Creativity, Critical Reflection, Communication, Collaboration*. London: Bloomsbury.

4 Foucault, M. (1980). *Power/Knowledge: Selected Interviews and Other Writings, 1972–1977*. New York: Pantheon Books.

5 Jefferson, M. and Anderson, M. (2021). *Transforming Education: Reimagining Learning, Pedagogy and Curriculum*. London: Bloomsbury.

6 Fook, J. and Gardner, F. (2007). *Practising Critical Reflection: A Resource Handbook* (1st ed.). Maidenhead: Open University Press.

7 Dewey, J. (1933). *How We Think: A Restatement of the Relation of reflective thinking in the Educative Process*, 9. Boston, MA: Heath and Company.

8 Fook, J., Psoinos, M. and Sartori, D. (2015). 'Evaluation studies of critical reflection'. In Jan Fook, Val Collington, Fiona Ross, Gillian Ruch and Linden West (eds), 90–106. *Researching Critical Reflection*. Abingdon: Routledge.

9 Fook, J., Royes, J. and White, A. (2017). 'Critical reflection'. In *Psychiatric and Mental Health Nursing*, 117–24. Abingdon: Routledge.

10 Jefferson, M. and Anderson, M. (2024) (eds). *How Schools Transform: Practices, Research and Actions That Change Schools*. London: Bloomsbury.

11 Adams, D. and Carwardine, M. (1990). *Last Chance to See*, 81. New York: Harmony Books.

12 Brookfield, S. D. (2017). *Becoming a Critically Reflective Teacher*. Hoboken, NJ: John Wiley & Sons. https://ebookcentral.proquest.com/lib/usyd/detail.action?docID=4790372

13 De Houwer, J., Richetin, J., Hughes, S. and Perugini, M. (2019). 'On the assumptions that we make about the world around us: A conceptual framework for feature transformation effects'. *Collabra: Psychology*, *5*(1).

14 Kahneman, D. (2011). *Thinking, Fast and Slow*. New York: Farrar, Straus and Giroux.

15 Suveren, Y. (2022). 'Unconscious bias: Definition and significance'. *Psikiyatride Guncel Yaklasimlar*, *14*(3): 414–26.

16 Beachum, F. D. and Gullo, G. L. (2020). 'School leadership: Implicit bias and social justice'. In R. Papa (ed.), *Handbook on Promoting Social Justice in Education*. Cham: Springer.

17 Image from https://www.dreamstime.com/stock-photo-wild-landscape-australian-mangroves-daintree-national-park-tropical-north-queensland-australia-image71296109

18 The Yolgnu are an Aboriginal Australian nation living in Northeastern Arnhem Land in the Northern Territory of Australia.

29 Yunkaporta, T. (2019). *Sand Talk: How Indigenous Thinking Can Save the World*. 229. Melbourne: Text Publishing.

20 Chesner, A., Ryan, S., Read, J., Owen, D., Hewson, J., Wilmot, J., Wilmot, J., Zografou, L., Encke, J. and Hawkin, P. 2007. *Passionate Supervision*. London: Jessica Kingsley Publishers.

21 Mezirow, J. (n.d.). 'How critical reflection triggers transformative learning'. Retrieved 18 August 2025, from https://www.colorado.edu/plc/sites/default/files/attached-files/how_critical_reflection_triggers_transfo.pdf

4 Leading through collaboration

1 Jefferson, M. and Anderson, M. (2017). *Transforming Schools: Creativity, Critical Reflection, Communication, Collaboration.* London, UK: Bloomsbury.
2 Aristotle. (350 bce). *Metaphysics* (trans. W. D. Ross). Retrieved 18 August 2025, from http://classics.mit.edu/Aristotle/metaphysics.8.viii.html
3 Heifetz, R. A., Grashow, A. and Linsky, M. (2009). *The Practice of Adaptive Leadership: Tools and Tactics for Changing Your Organization and the World.* Brighton, MA: Harvard Business Review Press.
4 Snyder, S. (2013). *The Simple, the Complicated, and the Complex: Educational Reform Through the Lens of Complexity Theory* (OECD Education Working Papers No. 96). OECD Publishing. https://doi.org/10.1787/5k3txnpt1lnr-en
5 Snyder, S. (2013). *The Simple, the Complicated, and the Complex: Educational Reform Through the Lens of Complexity Theory* (OECD Education Working Papers No. 96). OECD Publishing. https://doi.org/10.1787/5k3txnpt1lnr-en
6 The London Underground tube map was designed to resemble an electrical circuit.
7 Moran, S. and John-Steiner, V. (2004). 'How collaboration in creative work impacts identity and motivation'. In D. Miell and K. Littleton (eds), *Collaborative Creativity: Contemporary Perspectives*, 11–25. London: Free Association Books.
8 Cheruvelil, K. S., Soranno, P. A., Weathers, K. C., Hanson, P. C., Goring, S. J., Filstrup, C. T. and Read, E. K. (2014). 'Creating and maintaining high-performing collaborative research teams: The importance of diversity and interpersonal skills'. *Frontiers in Ecology and the Environment, 12*(1): 31–8. https://doi.org/10.1890/130001
9 Glveanu, V.P. (2011). 'How are we creative together?: comparing sociocognitive and sociocultural answers'. *Theory & Psychology, 21*(4): 473–92.
10 Glveanu, V.P. (2011) How are we creative together? Comparing sociocognitive and sociocultural answers. *Theory and Psychology, 21*(4): 473–92.
11 Raelin, J. A. (2011). 'From leadership-as-practice to leaderful practice'. *Leadership, 7*(2): 195–211.
12 Sawyer, K. (2007). *Group Genius: The Creative Power of Collaboration.* New York: Basic Books.
13 John-Steiner, V. (2000). *Creative Collaboration.* Oxford: Oxford University Press.
14 Gardner, H. K. (2016). *Smart Collaborations: How Professionals and their Firms Succeed in Breaking Down Silos.* Brighton, MA: Harvard Business Review Press. Cheruvelil, K. S., Soranno, P. A., Weathers, K. C., Hanson, P. C., Goring, S. J., Filstrup, C. T. and Read, E. K. (2014). 'Creating and maintaining high-performing collaborative research teams: The importance of diversity and interpersonal skills'. *Frontiers in Ecology and the Environment, 12*(1): 31–8.
15 Duhigg, C. (2016). 'What Google Learned from its Quest to Build the Perfect Team'. *The New York Times.* Retrieved 18 August 2025, from https://www.nytimes.com/2016/02/28/magazine/what-google-learned-from-its-quest-to-build-the-perfect-team.html
16 Moran, S. and John-Steiner, V. (2004). 'How collaboration in creative work impacts identity and motivation'. In D. Miell and K. Littleton (eds), *Collaborative Creativity: Contemporary Perspectives*, 11–25. London: Free Association Books; Bandura, A. (2006). 'Toward a psychology of human agency'. *Perspectives on Psychological Science, 1*(2): 164–80.

17 Moran, S. and John-Steiner, V. (2004). 'How collaboration in creative work impacts identity and motivation'. In D. Miell and K. Littleton (eds), *Collaborative Creativity: Contemporary Perspectives*, 1–25. London: Free Association Books.

18 Lencioni, P. M. (2002). *The Five Dysfunctions of a Team*. San Francisco: Jossey-Bass; Paulus, P. B. (2000). 'Groups, teams and creativity: The creative potential of idea-generating groups'. *Applied Psychology, 49*(2): 237–62.

Paulus, P. B. and Nijstad, B. A. (2003). *Group creativity: Innovation Through Collaboration*. Oxford: Oxford University Press.

19 Merrington, N. (n.d.). 'The five dynamics of an effective team'. Think with Google. Retrieved 18 August 2025, from https://www.thinkwithgoogle.com/intl/en-emea/consumer-insights/consumer-trends/five-dynamics-effective-team/; Friedman, Z. (2019). 'Google says the best teams have these 5 things'. *Forbes*. Retrieved 18 August 2025, from https://www.forbes.com/sites/zackfriedman/2019/01/28/google-says-the-best-teams-have-these-5-things/

20 Jefferson, M. and Anderson, M. (2017). *Transforming Schools: Creativity, Critical Reflection, Communication, Collaboration*. London: Bloomsbury.

21 Follett, M. P. (1996). *Prophet of Management: A Celebration of Writings from the 1920s*. Brighton, MA: Harvard Business School Press.

22 Follett, M. P. (1996). *Prophet of Management: A Celebration of Writings from the 1920s*, 119. Brighton, MA: Harvard Business School Press.

5 Leading through communication

1 The Sydney Opera House was transformed into an animated canvas of Australian Indigenous art featuring contemporary works from Karla Dickens, Djon Mundine, Gabriella Possum Nungurrayi, Reko Rennie, Donny Woolagoodja and the late Gulumbu Yunupingu.

2 Michael and Miranda are non-Indigenous Australians who recognize and value the ancient wisdom of First Nations peoples.

3 Neale, M. and Kelly, L. (2020). *First Knowledges Songlines: The Power and Promise*, 9. Melbourne: Thames & Hudson Australia.

4 Gay'Wu Group of Women: Burarrwanga, L., Ganambarr, B., Ganambarr, R., Ganambarr-Stubbs, M., Lloyd, K., Maymuru, D., Suchet-Pearson, S. and Wright, S. (2019). *Song Spirals: Sharing Women's Wisdom of Country Through Songlines*, xvi. Crows Nest, NSW: Allen & Unwin.

5 Campos, M. N. (2009). 'Critical constructivism'. In S. Littlejohn and K. Foss (eds), *Encyclopedia of Communication Theory*, 216–19. London: Sage.

Campos, M. N. (2007). 'Ecology of meanings: A critical constructivist communication model'. *Communication Theory, 17*(4): 386–410.

6 Campos, M. N. (2009). 'Critical Constructivism'. In Littlejohn, S. and Foss, K. (eds), 216–19 in Encyclopedia of Communication Theory. London: Sage.

7 Mary Catherine Bateson quoted in Flickinger, M. (19 July 2021). 'Storytelling as part of effective leadership'. *Forbes*. https://www.forbes.com/sites/markflickinger/2021/07/19/storytelling-as-part-of-effective-leadership/?ctpv=searchpage

8 Gardner, H. and Laskin, E. (2011). Preface/Conclusion. In *Leading Minds: An Anatomy of Leadership*. New York: Basic Books.

9 Espedal, G. and Synnes, O. (2022). 'A narrative approach to exploring values in organisations'. In Espedal, G., Jelstad Løvaas, B., Sirris, S. and Wæraas, A. (eds), *Researching Values: Methodological Approaches for Understanding Values Work in Organisations and Leadership*, 201. Cham: Palgrave Macmillan. https://doi.org/10.1007/978-3-030-90769-3_11

10 Gardner, H. and Laskin, E. (2011). Preface/Conclusion. In *Leading minds: An Anatomy of Leadership*. New York: Basic Books.
11 Révai, N. and Guerriero, S. (2017). 'Knowledge dynamics in the teaching profession'. In Guerriero, S. (ed.), *Pedagogical Knowledge and the Changing Nature of the Teaching Profession*, 37–71. Paris: OECD Publishing; Davis, B. and Sumara, D. (2009). 'Complexity as a theory of education'. *Transnational Curriculum Inquiry, 5*(2): 33–44; Snyder, S. (2013). 'The Simple, the Complicated, and the Complex: Educational Reform Through the Lens of Complexity Theory' (OECD Education Working Paper No. 96). Paris: OECD Publishing.
12 Wheatley, M. J. (2006). *Leadership and the New Science: Discovering Order in a Chaotic World* (3rd ed.), 104. Oakland, CA: Berrett-Koehler Publishers.
13 Best, A. and Holmes, B. J. (2010). 'Systems thinking, knowledge and action: Towards better models and methods'. *Evidence & Policy, 6*(2): 145–59.
14 Sternberg, R. J. (2003). *Wisdom, Intelligence, and Creativity Synthesized*. Cambridge: Cambridge University Press.
15 Fiorella, L. and Mayer, R. E. (2015). *Learning as a Generative Activity: Eight Learning Strategies That Promote Understanding*. Cambridge: Cambridge University Press.
16 Shapiro, L. and Spaulding, S. (2024). 'Embodied cognition'. In E. N. Zalta and U. Nodelman (eds.), *The Stanford Encyclopedia of Philosophy* (Summer 2024 edition).
17 Other 4C schemas include Collaboration Circles, Creativity Cascade and the Critical Reflection Crucible (see chapter 2).
18 Salazar, A. J. (2002). 'Self-organizing and complexity perspectives of group creativity: Implications for group communication'. In L. R. Frey (ed.), *New Directions in Group Communication*, 179–99. London: Sage.
19 Salazar, A. J. (2009). 'Creativity in groups'. In S. Littlejohn and K. Foss (eds), *Encyclopedia of Communication Theory*, 210–13. London: Sage.
20 Hecht, M. L. and Phillips, K. E. (2021). 'Communication theory of identity: Understanding the multilayered nature of identity'. In *Engaging Theories in Interpersonal Communication*. Abingdon: Routledge; Yingling, J. (2014). *A Lifetime of Communication: Transformations Through Relational Dialogues*. Abingdon: Routledge.
21 Freire, P. (2006). *Pedagogy of the Oppressed* (30th anniversary ed.), 88. London: Continuum.
22 Gay'Wu Group of Women: Burarrwanga, L., Ganambarr, B., Ganambarr, R., Ganambarr-Stubbs, M., Lloyd, K., Maymuru, D., Suchet-Pearson, S. and Wright, S. (2019). *Song Spirals: Sharing Women's Wisdom of Country Through Songlines*. xvi, xxii. Crows Nest, NSW: Allen & Unwin.

6 Leading through creativity

1 Drucker, P. F. (1985). *Innovation and Entrepreneurship*, 33. New York: Harper & Row.
2 Perkins, M. (2018). *21 questions from Aussie startups: Highs, lows & lessons learned during Canva's journey so far* (Part 1).*Medium*. https://medium.com/canva/21-questions-from-aussie-startups-highs-lows-lessons-learned-during-canvas-journey-so-far-da07723ff545
3 Sardar, Z. (2010). 'Welcome to postnormal times'. *Futures, 42*(5): 435–44.
4 We are arguing that this definition is the most used across the research community in education. For further discussions on definitions see Puryear, J. S. and Lamb, K. N. (2020). 'Defining creativity: How far have we come since Plucker, Beghetto, and Dow? *Creativity Research Journal, 32*(3): 206–14.

5 Plucker, J., Beghetto, R. and Dow, G. (2004). 'Why isn't creativity more important to educational psychologists? Potentials, pitfalls, and future directions in creativity research'. *Educational Psychologist*: *39*(2).
6 Puryear, J. S. and Lamb, K. N. 'Defining creativity: How far have we come since Plucker, Beghetto, and Dow? *Creativity Research Journal*, *32*(3): 206–14.
7 Glăveanu, V. P. (2020) *The Possible: A Sociocultural Theory*, 173. Oxford: Oxford University Press.
8 Glăveanu, V. P. (2023). 'Possibility studies: A manifesto'. *Possibility Studies & Society*, *1*(1–2): 3–8.
9 Glăveanu, V. P. (2023). 'Possibility studies: A manifesto'. *Possibility Studies & Society*, *1*(1–2): 3–8.
10 Glăveanu, A. (2020). *Creativity: A Very Short Introduction*, 112. Oxford: Oxford University Press.
11 Glăveanu, A. (2020). *Creativity: A Very Short Introduction*, 112. Oxford: Oxford University Press.
12 Amabile, T. M. and Pratt, M. G. (2016). 'The dynamic componential model of creativity and innovation in organizations: Making progress, making meaning'. *Research in Organizational Behavior*, *36*: 157–83.
13 Ryan, R. M. and Deci, E. L. (2000). 'Self-determination theory and the facilitation of intrinsic motivation, social development, and well-being'. *American Psychologist*, *55*(1): 68–78.
14 Avolio, B. J. and Mhatre, K. H. (2012). 'Advances in theory and research on authentic leadership'. In K. S. Cameron and G. M. Spreitzer (eds), *The Oxford Handbook of Positive Organizational Scholarship*, 773–83. Oxford: Oxford University Press.
15 Bass, B. M., and Riggio, R. E. (2006). *Transformational Leadership* (2nd ed.). Mahwah, LJ: Lawrence Erlbaum Associates.
16 Harris, A. (2013). 'Distributed leadership: Friend or foe?' *Educational Management Administration & Leadership*, *41*(5): 545–54.
17 Amabile, T. M. and Khaire, M. (2008). 'Creativity and the role of the leader'. *Harvard Business Review*, *86*(10): 100–9, 142.
18 Sardar, Z. (2010). 'Welcome to postnormal times'. *Futures*, *42*(5): 435–44.
19 Glăveanu, V. P. (2023). 'Possibility studies: A manifesto'. *Possibility Studies & Society*, *1*(1–2): 3–8.
20 Davenport, T. and Beck, J. (2001). *The Attention Economy: Understanding the New Currency of Business*. Boston, MA: Harvard Business School Press.
21 Hari, J. (2023). *Stolen Focus: Why You Can't Pay Attention – and How to Think Deeply Again*. New York: Crown.
22 While Hari's approach may be hyperbolic the experienced teachers, we work with have observed a deterioration in student's ability to focus and notice. This is backed by psychologist and neuroscientists Adam Gazzaley and Glenn Rosen. They reported in 2016 that students in a three-hour study session 'spent more than an hour listening to music and experienced thirty-five interruptions of six seconds or longer, totalling twenty-six disrupted minutes in just three hours'.
23 Johnson, J. F., Uline, C. L. and Perez, L. G. (2011). 'Expert noticing and principals of high-performing urban schools. *Journal of Education for Students Placed at Risk (JESPAR)*, *16*(2): 122–36.
24 This list contains edited direct quotations form the research report cited above.
25 Colour reproductions of this artwork are readily available on the Internet and from the Prado Museum website if you would like to project a larger image of this work.
26 Rourke, A. and Freebody, K. (2024). 'Transforming teacher education: The power of praxis and inquiry'. In M. Jefferson and M. Anderson (eds), *How Schools Transform: Practices, Research and Actions That Change Schools*, 165–80. London: Bloomsbury.

27 Rourke, A. and Freebody, K. (2024). 'Transforming teacher education: The power of praxis and inquiry'. In M. Jefferson and M. Anderson (eds), *How Schools Transform: Practices, Research and Actions That Change Schools*, 176. London: Bloomsbury.
28 Raelin, J. A. (2016). 'Imagine there are no leaders: Reframing leadership as collaborative agency'. *Leadership, 12*(2): 131–58.
29 Biddulph, J. and Gibrid, N. (2025). 'Playful school leadership: being serious about leadership playfully'. In A. Durning, S. Baker, P. Ramchandani (eds), *Empowering Play in Primary Education*, 147–66. Abingdon: Routledge.
30 Craft, A., Wegerif, R., Li, L. and Kaufman, J. C. (eds) (2015). 'Possibility thinking'. In *The Routledge International Handbook of Research on Teaching Thinking*, 346–75. Abingdon: Routledge.
31 Mainemelis, C. (2001). 'The power of play: A leadership perspective'. *Academy of Management Review, 26*(4): 606–22.
32 Jefferson, M. and Anderson, M. (2021). *Transforming Education: Reimagining Learning, Pedagogy and Curriculum*, 229. London: Bloomsbury.
33 Biddulph, J. and Gibrid, N. (2024). 'Playful school leadership: being serious about leadership playfully'. In A. Durning, S. Baker and P. Ramchandani (eds), *Empowering Play in Primary Education*, 147–67. Abingdon: Routledge.
34 Woodman, R. W., Sawyer, J. E. and Griffin, R. W. (1993). 'Toward a theory of organizational creativity'. *Academy of Management Review*, 18(2): 293–321.
35 Carmeli, A., Reiter-Palmon, R. and Ziv, E. (2010). 'Inclusive leadership and employee involvement in creative tasks in the workplace: The mediating role of psychological safety'. *Creativity Research Journal, 22*(3): 250–60.
36 Carr, W. and Kemmis, S. (1986). *Becoming Critical: Education, Knowledge, and Action Research*. London: Falmer Press.

7 Leading through joy and motivation

1 The 30 plus videos made by Belgium artist Francis Alÿs can be accessed freely on his website, http://francisalys.com/category/childrens-games/

2 Raelin, J. A. (2016). 'Introduction to leadership-as-practice: Theory and application'. In J. A. Raelin (ed.), *Leadership-as-practice: Theory and Application*, 1–17. Abingdon: Routledge.
3 Ryan, R. M., Reeve, J., Kaplan, H., Matos, L., and Cheon, S. H. (2023). 'Education as flourishing: Self-determination theory in schools as they are and as they might be'. In R. M. Ryan (ed.), *The Oxford Handbook of Self-determination Theory*, 591–618. Oxford: Oxford University Press; Eyal, O. and Roth, G. (2011). 'Principals' leadership and teachers' motivation: Self-determination theory analysis'. *Journal of Educational Administration, 49*(3): 269–88; Alfayez, A. A., Noman, M., Alqahtani, A. S., Altuwaijri, A. I. and Kaur, A. (2021). 'Principal's learning-centred leadership practices and teacher's wellbeing: A self-determination theory perspective'. *Educational Studies*: 1–19.
4 Hargreaves, A. (2021). 'The future of learning lies in engagement'. ASCD, *79*(4). https://www.ascd.org/el/articles/the-future-of-learning-lies-in-engagement
5 Ryan, R. M., Reeve, J., Kaplan, H., Matos, L. and Cheon, S. H. (2023). 'Education as flourishing: Self-determination theory in schools as they are and as they might be'. In R. M. Ryan (ed.), *The Oxford Handbook of Self-determination Theory*, 591–618. Oxford: Oxford University Press.
6 Prochazkova, E. and Kret, M. E. (2017). 'Connecting minds and sharing emotions through mimicry: A neurocognitive model of emotional contagion'. *Neuroscience & Biobehavioral Reviews, 80*: 99–114.

7 Csikszentmihalyi, M. (1996). *Creativity: Flow and the Psychology of Discovery and Invention*, 110. New York: HarperCollins.

8 Ryan, R. M. and Deci, E. L. (2019). 'Brick by brick: The origins, development, and future of self-determination theory'. *Advances in Motivation Science*, *6*: 111–56.

9 Raelin, J. A. (2011). 'From leadership-as-practice to leaderful practice'. *Leadership*, *7*(2): 195–211

10 Li, L., Gow, A. D. I. and Zhou, J. (2020). 'The role of positive emotions in education: A neuroscience perspective'. *Mind, Brain, and Education 14*(3): 220–34.

11 Li, L., Gow, A. D. I. and Zhou, J. (2020). 'The role of positive emotions in education: A neuroscience perspective'. *Mind, Brain, and Education*: 222.

12 Li, L., Gow, A. D. I and Zhou, J. (2020). 'The role of positive emotions in education: A neuroscience perspective'. *Mind, Brain, and Education.*

13 Hargreaves, A. (2021). 'The future of learning lies in engagement'. ASCD, *79*(4). https://www.ascd.org/el/articles/the-future-of-learning-lies-in-engagement

14 Shirley, D., Hargreaves, A. and Washington-Wangia, S. (2020). 'The sustainability and unsustainability of teachers' and leaders' well-being'. *Teaching and Teacher Education*, *92*: 103001.

15 Shirley, D., Hargreaves, A. and Washington-Wangia, S. (2020). 'The sustainability and unsustainability of teachers' and leaders' well-being'. *Teaching and Teacher Education*, *92*: 103001. 10.

16 Lui, A. (2019). 'Making joy a priority at work'. *Harvard Business Review.* https://hbr.org/2019/07/making-joy-a-priority-at-work

17 Emmons, R. A. (2020). 'Joy: An introduction to this special issue'. *The Journal of Positive Psychology*, *15*(1): 1–4.

18 Meadows, C. M. (2014) *A Psychological Perspective on Joy and Emotional Fulfillment.* New York: Routledge.

19 Fredrickson, B. L. (2001). 'The role of positive emotions in positive psychology: The broaden-and-build theory of positive emotions'. *American Psychologist, 56*(3): 218–26; Tugade, M. M., Devlin, H. C. and Fredrickson, B. L. (2020). 'Positive emotions'. In C. R. Snyder, S. J. Lopez, L. M. Edwards and S. C. Marques (eds), *The Oxford Handbook of Positive Psychology* (3rd ed.), 18–32. Oxford: Oxford University Press.

20 Meadows, C. M. (2014). *A Psychological Perspective on Joy and Emotional Fulfillment.* New York: Routledge.

21 Johnson, M. K. (2020). 'Joy: A review of the literature and suggestions for future directions'. *The Journal of Positive Psychology*, *15*(1): 5–24.

22 Johnson, M. K. (2020). 'Joy: A review of the literature and suggestions for future directions'. *The Journal of Positive Psychology*, *15*(1): 5–24.

23 Yale Center for Faith and Culture. (n.d.). *Theology of Joy and the Good Life*. Yale University. Retrieved 20 August 2025, from https://faith.yale.edu/legacy-projects/theology-of-joy

24 'Joy and Positive Psychology'. *The Journal of Positive Psychology* (2020), *15*(1): 1–154; *The Oxford Handbook of Positive Psychology* (3rd edn). C. R. Snyder, Shane J. Lopez, Lisa M. Edwards, Susana C. Marques (eds) (2016). New York: Oxford University Press USA.

25 Yogman, M., Garner, A., Hutchison, J., Hirsh-Pasek, K. and Golinkoff, R. M. (2018). 'The power of play: A pediatric role in enhancing development in young children'. *Pediatrics*, *142*(3); Nijhof, S. L., Vinkers, C. H., van Geelen, S. M., Duijff, S. N., Achterberg, E. J. M., van der Net, J., Veltkamp, R. C., Grootenhuis, M. A., van de Putte, E. M., Hillegers, M. H. J., van der Brug, A. W. and Lesscher, H. M. B. (2018). 'Healthy play, better coping: The importance of play for the development of children in health and disease'. *Neuroscience & Biobehavioral Reviews*, *95*: 421–9.

26 Nijhof, S. L., Vinkers, C. H., van Geelen, S. M., Duijff, S. N., Achterberg, E. J. M., van der Net, J., Veltkamp, R. C., Grootenhuis, M. A., van de Putte, E. M., Hillegers, M. H. J., van der Brug, A. W. and Lesscher, H. M. B. (2018). 'Healthy play, better coping: The importance of play for the development of children in health and disease'. *Neuroscience & Biobehavioral Reviews, 95*: 421–9.

27 Yogman, M., Garner, A., Hutchison, J., Hirsh-Pasek, K. and Golinkoff, R. M. (2018). 'The power of play: A pediatric role in enhancing development in young children'. *Pediatrics, 142*(3).

28 Jefferson, M and Anderson, M. *Transforming Schools* (2017); *Transforming Organizations* (2019); *Transforming Education* (2021); Mainemelis, C. and Ronson, S. (2006). 'Ideas are born in fields of play: Towards a theory of play and creativity in organizational settings'. Research in *Organizational Behavior, 27*, 81–131; Biddulph, J. and Gibrid, N. (2024). 'Playful school leadership: Being serious about leadership playfully'. In A. Durning, S. Baker and P. Ramchandani (eds). *Empowering Play in Primary Education*, 147–67. Abingdon: Routledge.

29 Biddulph, J. and Gibrid, N. (2024). 'Playful school leadership: Being serious about leadership playfully'. In A. Durning, S. Baker and P. Ramchandani (eds). *Empowering Play in Primary Education*, 147–67. Abingdon: Routledge.

30 Porter, E. H. (2017 [1913]). *Pollyanna* (ProQuest Ebook Central edn). Minneapolis: Lerner Publishing Group.

31 Johnson, M. K. (2020). 'Joy: A review of the literature and suggestions for future directions'. *The Journal of Positive Psychology*, *15*(1), 5–24.

32 Jefferson, M. and Anderson, M. *Transforming Schools* (2017); *Transforming Organizations* (2019); *Transforming Education* (2021); Jefferson, M. and Anderson, M. (2024) (eds). *How Schools Transform: Practices, Research and Actions That Change Schools.* London: Bloomsbury.

33 Johnson, M. K. (2020). 'Joy: A review of the literature and suggestions for future directions'. *The Journal of Positive Psychology*, *15*(1): 5–24.

34 Johnson, M. K. (2020). 'Joy: A review of the literature and suggestions for future directions'. *The Journal of Positive Psychology*, *15*(1): 5–24.

35 Van den Broeck, A. and Slemp, G. R. (2023). 'Leadership: A self-determination theory perspective'. In R. M. Ryan (ed.), *The Oxford Handbook of Self-determination Theory*, 920–38. Oxford: Oxford University Press.

36 Johnson, M. K. (2020). 'Joy: A review of the literature and suggestions for future directions'. *The Journal of Positive Psychology*, *15*(1): 5–24.

37 Lumpkin, A. and Achen, R. M. (2018). 'Explicating the synergies of self-determination theory, ethical leadership, servant leadership, and emotional intelligence'. *Journal of Leadership Studies, 12*(1): 6–20.

38 Fredrickson, B. L. (2001). 'The role of positive emotions in positive psychology: The broaden-and-build theory of positive emotions'. *American Psychologist, 56*(3): 218–26.

39 Gilbert, S. L. and Kelloway, E. K. (2014). 'Leadership'. In M. Gagné (ed.), *The Oxford Handbook of Work Engagement, Motivation, and Self-determination Theory*, 181–98. Oxford: Oxford University Press.

40 Jefferson, M. and Anderson, M. (2017). *Transforming Schools: Creativity, Critical Reflection, Communication, Collaboration*. London: Bloomsbury.

41 Jefferson, M. and Anderson, M. (2017). *Transforming Schools: Creativity, Critical Reflection, Communication, Collaboration*. London: Bloomsbury.

42 Louie, D., Brook, K., Frates, E. (2016). 'The Laughter Prescription: A tool for lifestyle medicine'. *Am J Lifestyle Med. 10*(4): 262–7

43 Diefendorff, J. M. and Chandler, M. M. (2011). 'Motivating employees'. In S. Zedeck (ed.), *APA Handbook of Industrial and Organizational Psychology: Maintaining, Expanding, and Contracting the Organization*. Vol. 3. American Psychological Association: 65–135.

44 Forner, V. W., Jones, M., Berry, Y. and Eidenfalk, J. (2021). 'Motivating workers: How leaders apply self-determination theory in organizations'. *Organization Management Journal*, 18(2): 76–94.
45 Diefendorff, J. M. and Chandler, M. M. (2011). 'Motivating employees'. In S. Zedeck (ed.), *APA Handbook of Industrial and Organizational Psychology: Maintaining, Expanding, and Contracting the Organization*. Vol. 3. American Psychological Association: 183–240).
46 Ryan, R. M. and Deci, E. L. (2019). 'Brick by brick: The origins, development, and future of self-determination theory'. *Advances in Motivation Science, 6*: 111–56.
47 Ryan, R. M. and Deci, E. L. (2019). 'Brick by brick: The origins, development, and future of self-determination theory'. *Advances in Motivation Science, 6*: 111–56.
48 Ryan, R. M. and Deci, E. L. (2000) 'Self-determination Theory and the facilitation of intrinsic motivation, social development, and well-being'. *American Psychologist, 55*(1): 68–78.
49 Ryan, R. M. and Brown, K. W. (2005). 'Legislating competence: High-stakes testing policies and their relations with psychological theories and research'. In A. J. Elliot and C. S. Dweck (eds), *Handbook of Competence and Motivation*, 354–72). New Yrok: The Guilford Press.
50 Ryan, R. M. and Deci, E. L. (2019). 'Brick by brick: The origins, development, and future of self-determination theory'. *Advances in Motivation Science, 6*: 111–56.
51 Ryan, R. M. and Deci, E. L. (2019). 'Brick by brick: The origins, development, and future of self-determination theory'. *Advances in Motivation Science, 6*: 111–56.
52 Ryan, R. M. and Deci, E. L. (2000). 'Self-determination Theory and the facilitation of intrinsic motivation, social development, and well-being'. *American Psychologist 55*(1): 68–78.
53 Gilbert, S. L. and Kelloway, E. K. (2014). 'Leadership'. In M. Gagné (ed.), *The Oxford Handbook of Work Engagement, Motivation, and Self-determination Theory*, 181–98. Oxford: Oxford University Press.
54 Ryan, R. M., Reeve, J., Kaplan, H., Matos, L. and Cheon, S. H. (2023). 'Education as flourishing: Self-determination theory in schools as they are and as they might be'. In R. M. Ryan (ed.), *The Oxford Handbook of Self-determination Theory*, 591–618. Oxford: Oxford University Press.
55 Ryan, R. M., Reeve, J., Kaplan, H., Matos, L. and Cheon, S. H. (2023). 'Education as flourishing: Self-determination theory in schools as they are and as they might be'. In R. M. Ryan (ed.), *The Oxford Handbook of Self-determination Theory*, 591–618. Oxford: Oxford University Press.
56 Ryan, R. M., Reeve, J., Kaplan, H., Matos, L. and Cheon, S. H. (2023). 'Education as flourishing: Self-determination theory in schools as they are and as they might be'. In R. M. Ryan (ed.), *The Oxford Handbook of Self-determination Theory*, 591–618. Oxford: Oxford University Press.
57 Ryan, R. M., Reeve, J., Kaplan, H., Matos, L. and Cheon, S. H. (2023). 'Education as flourishing: Self-determination theory in schools as they are and as they might be'. In R. M. Ryan (ed.), *The Oxford Handbook of Self-determination Theory*, 591–618. Oxford: Oxford University Press.
58 Ryan, R. M., Reeve, J., Kaplan, H., Matos, L. and Cheon, S. H. (2023). 'Education as flourishing: Self-determination theory in schools as they are and as they might be'. In R. M. Ryan (ed.), *The Oxford Handbook of Self-determination Theory*, 591–618. Oxford: Oxford University Press.
59 Eyal, O. and Roth, G. (2011). 'Principals' leadership and teachers' motivation: Self-determination Theory analysis'. *Journal of Educational Administration, 49*(3): 269–88.
60 Eyal, O. and Roth, G. (2011). 'Principals' leadership and teachers' motivation: Self-determination Theory analysis'. *Journal of Educational Administration, 49*(3): 269–88.

8 Leading transformation through agency

1 Tromly, C. E. (2014). 'Schools and complexity'. *Complicity: An International Journal of Complexity and Education, 11*(2): 40–58; Mason, M. (2008). 'What is complexity theory and what are its implications for educational change?' *Educational Philosophy and Theory, 40*(1): 35–49.

2 Carmichael, T. and Hadžikadić, M. (2019). 'The fundamentals of complex adaptive systems'. In T. Carmichael, A. J. Collins and M. Hadžikadić (eds), *Complex Adaptive Systems: Views from the Physical, Natural, and Social Sciences*, 1–16. Cham: Springer.

3 Bandura, A. (2018). 'Toward a psychology of human agency: Pathways and reflections'. *Perspectives on Psychological Science, 13*(2): 130–6; Frost, D. (2006). 'The concept of agency in leadership for learning'. *Leading and Managing, 12*(2): 19–28; Goller, M. and Harteis, C. (2017). 'Human agency at work: towards a clarification and operationalization of the concept'. In M. Goller and S. Paloniemi (eds), *Agency at Work: An Agentic Perspective on Professional Learning and Development*, 85–103. Cham: Springer.

4 Montuori, A. and Donnelly, G. (2018). 'Transformative leadership'. In J. Neal (ed.), *Handbook of Personal and Organizational Transformation*, 319–50. Cham: Springer.

5 Biesta, G. and Tedder, M. (2007). 'Agency and learning in the lifecourse: Towards an ecological perspective'. *Studies in the Education of Adults, 39*(2): 132–49.

6 Raelin, J. A. (2011). 'From leadership-as-practice to leaderful practice'. *Leadership, 7*(2): 195–211.

7 Darling-Hammond, L., Flook, L., Cook-Harvey, C., Barron, B. and Osher, D. (2020). 'Implications for educational practice of the science of learning and development'. *Applied Developmental Science, 24*(2): 97–140; Jefferson, M. and Anderson, M. (2021). *Transforming Education: Reimagining Learning, Pedagogy and Curriculum*. London: Bloomsbury.

8 Organisation for Economic Co-operation and Development. (2018). *Student Agency for 2030: Concept note*. OECD. Retrieved from https://www.oecd.org/content/dam/oecd/en/about/projects/edu/education-2040/concept-notes/Student_Agency_for_2030_concept_note.pdf

9 Hannon, V. (2011). *Learning Futures*. OECD/CERI. Retrieved from https://web-archive.oecd.org/2013-01-06/221573-valerie%20hannon.learning%20futures.pdf

10 Bandura, A. (2006). 'Toward a psychology of human agency'. *Perspectives on Psychological Science, 1*(2): 164–80.

11 Ryan, R. M. and Deci, E. L. (2019). 'Brick by brick: The origins, development, and future of self-determination theory'. *Advances in Motivation Science, 6*: 111–56.

12 Deci, E.L. (with Richard Flaste) (1995). *Why Do We So What We Do: The Dynamics of Personal Autonomy*, 98.New York: Grosset/Putnam.

13 Ryan, R. M. and Deci, E. L. (2019). 'Brick by brick: The origins, development, and future of self-determination theory'. *Advances in Motivation Science, 6*: 111–56.

14 Priestley, M., Biesta, G. and Robinson, S. (2015). *Teacher Agency: An Ecological Approach*. London: Bloomsbury.

15 Priestley, M., Biesta, G. and Robinson, S. (2015). *Teacher Agency: An Ecological Approach*. London: Bloomsbury.

16 Priestley, M., Biesta, G. and Robinson, S. (2015). *Teacher Agency: An Ecological Approach*, 128. London: Bloomsbury.

17 Priestley, M., Biesta, G. and Robinson, S. (2015). *Teacher Agency: An Ecological Approach*. London: Bloomsbury.

18 UNESCO 2021 Report, 'Reimagining Our Future Together: A new social contract for education'. https://unesdoc.unesco.org/ark:/48223/pf0000379707.locale=en; Organisation for Economic Co-operation and Development (OECD), Future of Education and

Skills 2030 https://www.oecd.org/content/dam/oecd/en/about/projects/edu/education-2040/concept-notes/Student_Agency_for_2030_concept_note.pdf

19 Biesta, G. and Tedder, M. (2007). 'Agency and learning in the lifecourse: Towards an ecological perspective'. *Studies in the Education of Adults, 39*(2): 132–49.

20 Priestley, M., Biesta, G. and Robinson, S. (2015). *Teacher Agency: An Ecological Approach*. London: Bloomsbury.

21 Priestley, M., Biesta, G. and Robinson, S. (2015). *Teacher Agency: An Ecological Approach*. London: Bloomsbury.

22 Bandura, A. (2006). 'Toward a psychology of human agency'. *Perspectives on Psychological Science*, *1*(2): 164–80.

23 Glăveanu, V. P. (2015). 'From individual agency to co-agency'. In C. W. Gruber, et al. (eds), *Constraints of Agency*, 245–65. Annals of Theoretical Psychology. Cham: Springer.

24 Glăveanu, V. P. (2015). 'From individual agency to co-agency'. In C. W. Gruber, et al. (eds.), *Constraints of Agency*, 245–65. Annals of Theoretical Psychology. Cham: Springer.

25 Organisation for Economic Co-operation and Development (2018). *Student Agency for 2030: Concept note*. OECD. Retrieved from https://www.oecd.org/content/dam/oecd/en/about/projects/edu/education-2040/concept-notes/Student_Agency_for_2030_concept_note.pdf

26 Biesta, G. and Tedder, M. (2007). 'Agency and learning in the lifecourse: Towards an ecological perspective'. *Studies in the Education of Adults*, *39*(2): 132–49.

27 Emirbayer, M. and Mische, A. (1998). 'What is agency?' *American Journal of Sociology*, *103*(4): 962–1023.

28 Biesta, G. and Tedder, M. (2007). 'Agency and learning in the lifecourse: Towards an ecological perspective'. *Studies in the Education of Adults, 39*(2): 132–49.

29 Biesta, G. and Tedder, M. (2007). 'Agency and learning in the lifecourse: Towards an ecological perspective'. *Studies in the Education of Adults*, *39*(2): 132–49.

30 Emirbayer, M. and Mische, A. (1998). 'What is agency?' *American Journal of Sociology*, *103*(4): 962–1023.

31 Bandura, A. (2000). 'Exercise of human agency through collective efficacy'. *Current Directions in Psychological Science*, *9*(3): 75–8.

32 Carney, S. (2022). *Reimagining Our Futures Together: A New Social Contract for Education by UNESCO, Paris, UNESCO, 2021. Comparative Education*, *58*(4): 568–9.

33 Organisation for Economic Co-operation and Development. (2019). *Student Agency for 2030.* Concept note (Education 2030 concept notes). OECD. 77. Retrieved from https://www.oecd.org/content/dam/oecd/en/about/projects/edu/education-2040/concept-notes/Student_Agency_for_2030_concept_note.pdf

34 Chen-Levi, T., Buskila, Y. and Schechter, C. (2024). 'Leadership as agency'. *International Journal of Educational Reform, 33*(2): 127–41.

9 The Leadership Wheel: Cultivating the conditions for transformative leadership in context

1 Biesta, G. and Tedder, M. (2007). 'Agency and learning in the lifecourse: Towards an ecological perspective'. *Studies in the Education of Adults*, *39*(2): 137.

2 Ryan, R. M. and Deci, E. L. (2019). 'Brick by brick: The origins, development, and future of self-determination theory'. *Advances in Motivation Science*, *6*: 111–156.

3 Pelligrino, J. and Hilton, M. (2012). *Education for Life and Work: Developing Transferable Knowledge and Skills in the 21st Century.* Washington, DC: The National Academies Press.
4 Pelligrino, J. and Hilton, M. (2012). 'A Preliminary Classification of Skills and Abilities' In *Education for Life and Work: Developing Transferable Knowledge and Skills in the 21st Century.* Washington, DC: The National Academies Press.
5 Kotter, J.P (2012). *Leading Change*, 28. Boston, MA: Harvard Business Review Press.
6 Shields, C. M. (2020). *Becoming a Transformative Leader: A Guide to Creating Equitable Schools*. Abingdon: Routledge.
7 Sinek, S. (2011). *The Infinite Game*. New York: Simon & Schuster.
8 Pisano, G. P. (2019). *Creative Construction: The DNA of Sustained Innovation.* New York: PublicAffairs; Kotter, J. P. (2012). *Leading Change*, 28. Boston, MA: Harvard Business Review Press.
9 Kotter, J. P. (2014). *Accelerate: Building Strategic Agility for a Faster-Moving World.* Boston, MA: Harvard Business Review Press.
10 Ryan, R. M. and Deci, E. L. (2002). 'Overview of self-determination theory: An organismic dialectical perspective'. In E. L. Deci and R. M Ryan (eds). *Handbook of Self-determination Research*, 3–33. Rochester, NY: University of Rochester Press.
11 Feedback loops are explained by Complexity Theory and can be applied to education systems and schools. Snyder, S. (2013), 'The Simple, the Complicated, and the Complex: Educational Reform Through the Lens of Complexity Theory', *OECD Education Working Papers*, No. 96. Paris: OECD Publishing.
12 Heifetz, R., Grashow, A. and Linksy, M. (2009), *The Practice of Adaptive Leadership: Tools and Tactics for Changing Your Organization and the World.* Boston, MA: Harvard Business Press.
13 Dweck, C. S. (2016). *Mindset: The New Psychology of Success*. New York: Ballantine Books.
14 Fook, J., Gardner, F. and White, S. (2006). 'Critical reflection: A review of contemporary literature and understandings'. In *Critical Reflection in Health and Social Care*, 3–20. Maidenhead: Open University Press; Michael Anderson and Miranda Jefferson *Transforming Schools* (2017); *Transforming Organizations* (2019); *Transforming Education* (2021); Jefferson, M. and Anderson, M. (2017). *Transforming Schools: Creativity, Critical Reflection, Communication, Collaboration.* London: Bloomsbury; Anderson, M. and Jefferson, M. (2019). *Transforming Organizations: Engaging the 4Cs for Powerful Organizational Learning and Change*. London: Bloomsbury.
15 Hitchcock, D. (2018). 'Critical thinking'. In E. N. Zalta (ed.), *The Stanford Encyclopedia of Philosophy* (Fall 2018 Edition). Retrieved from https://plato.stanford.edu/entries/critical-thinking/
16 Beres, L. and Fook, J. (2020). 'Learning critical reflection'. In L. Beres and J. Fook (eds), *Learning Critical Reflection: Experiences of the Transformative Learning Process*, 1–20. Abingdon: Routledge.
17 Beres, L. and Fook, J. (2020). 'Learning critical reflection'. In L. Beres and J. Fook (eds), *Learning Critical Reflection: Experiences of the Transformative Learning Process*, 1–20. Abingdon: Routledge.
18 Sternberg, R. J. (2003). *Wisdom, Intelligence, and Creativity Synthesized.* Cambridge: Cambridge University Press.
19 Gilbert, S. L. and Kelloway, E. K. (2014). 'Leadership'. In M. Gagné (ed.), *The Oxford Handbook of Work Engagement, Motivation, and Self-determination Theory*, 181–98. Oxford: Oxford University Press; Lumpkin, A. and Achen, R. M. (2018). 'Explicating the synergies of self-determination theory, ethical leadership, servant leadership, and emotional leadership'. *Journal of Leadership Studies, 12*(1).

20 Jefferson, M. and Anderson, M. *Transforming Schools* (2017), *Transforming Organizations* (2019); *Transforming Education* (2021). London: Bloomsbury.
21 Gilbert, S. L. and Kelloway, E. K. (2014). 'Leadership'. In M. Gagné (ed.), *The Oxford Handbook of Work Engagement, Motivation, and Self-determination Theory*, 181–98). Oxford: Oxford University Press.
22 Jefferson, M. and Anderson, M. (2017). *Transforming Schools: Creativity, Critical Reflection, Communication, Collaboration*. London: Bloomsbury.
23 Gilbert, S. L. and Kelloway, E. K. (2014). 'Leadership'. In M. Gagné (ed.), *The Oxford Handbook of Work Engagement, Motivation, and Self-determination Theory*, 181–98). Oxford: Oxford University Press.
24 Gilbert, S. L. and Kelloway, E. K. (2014). 'Leadership'. In M. Gagné (ed.), *The Oxford Handbook of Work Engagement, Motivation, and Self-determination Theory*, 181–98). Oxford: Oxford University Press.
25 Kotter, J. P. (2012). *Leading Change*, 28. Boston, MA: Harvard Business Review Press.
26 Jefferson, M. and Anderson, M. (2017). *Transforming Schools: Creativity, Critical Reflection, Communication, Collaboration*. London: Bloomsbury; Anderson, M. and Jefferson, M. (2019). *Transforming Organizations: Engaging the 4Cs for Powerful Organizational Learning and Change*. London: Bloomsbury.
27 Jefferson, M. and Anderson, M. (2017). *Transforming Schools: Creativity, Critical Reflection, Communication, Collaboration*. London: Bloomsbury; Anderson, M. and Jefferson, M. (2019). *Transforming Organizations: Engaging the 4Cs for Powerful Organizational Learning and Change*. London: Bloomsbury.
28 Pisano, G. P. (2019). *Creative Construction: The DNA of Sustained Innovation*. New York: PublicAffairs.
29 Jefferson, M. and Anderson, M. (2017). *Transforming Schools: Creativity, Critical Reflection, Communication, Collaboration*. London: Bloomsbury.
30 Pisano, G. P. (2019). *Creative Construction: The DNA of Sustained Innovation*. New York: PublicAffairs.
31 Daly, A. (2015). 'Refocusing the lens: educational research in an era of relationships'. *Journal of Educational Administration, 53*(1). https://doi.org/10.1108/JEA-11-2014-0135
32 See also 'Education and Leadership', researcher Alan Daly's work on human pyramids on https://www.youtube.com/watch?v=p6rAmAn9hrQ
33 Accredited to John Quincy Adams, sixth president of the US, quoted in Lumpkin, A. and Achen, R. M. (2018). 'Explicating the synergies of self-determination theory, ethical leadership, servant leadership, and emotional leadership'. *Journal of Leadership Studies, 12*(1); Anderson, M. and Jefferson, M. (2019). *Transforming Organizations: Engaging the 4Cs for Powerful Organizational Learning and Change*. London: Bloomsbury.
34 Gilbert, S. L. and Kelloway, E. K. (2014). 'Leadership'. In M. Gagné (ed.), *The Oxford Handbook of Work Engagement, Motivation, and Self-determination Theory*, 181–98. Oxford: Oxford University Press.
35 Gilbert, S. L. and Kelloway, E. K. (2014). 'Leadership'. In M. Gagné (ed.), *The Oxford Handbook of Work Engagement, Motivation, and Self-determination Theory*, 181–98. Oxford: Oxford University Press.
36 Frost, D., et al. (2008). 'The legacy of the Carpe Vitam Leadership for Learning project'. *inFORM, 8*: 1–8. Retrieved from https://www.educ.cam.ac.uk/networks/lfl/about/inform/PDFs/InForm_8.pdf
37 Frost, D. (2006). 'The concept of "agency" in leadership and learning'. *Leading and Managing, 12*(2): 19–28.
38 Lumpkin, A. and Achen, R. M. (2018). 'Explicating the synergies of self-determination theory, ethical leadership, servant leadership, and emotional leadership'. *Journal of Leadership Studies, 12*(1).